Living the Wiccan Life

· · · ·

About the Author

Debbe Tompkins is a high priestess in the Correllian Tradition and legally ordained clergy. She also holds the position of president of Witch School International, Inc. She was the founder of a Correllian temple that went on to become one of the largest in the Tradition. Currently she is the head of a contemplative order within the Tradition.

Born into a Christian family, she learned the importance of having a spiritual life. As an adult, her religious affiliation changed to the Catholic Church, which gave her a love for ritual. Later she was introduced to the Rosicrucians, Theosophy, and metaphysical ideas, leading her to Wicca. Keeping with her belief that all religions are valid, her diverse religious background facilitates her tolerance and acceptance of all religious paths.

Debbe holds a master's degree in education. Originally a native of Oregon, she makes her home in Rossville, Illinois, and has raised two children.

The Correllium, above, is the symbol of the Highcorrell family and the Correllian Tradition as a whole. The Correllium represents the oneness of being and is usually explained in this way: at the top, the Vault of Heaven is indicated by (usually) a double line representing the elements of air and fire (light). At the center, a cross represents the element of earth and the four directions. At the bottom, a wave represents the element of water. The circle encompassing all is Spirit. The Correllium has its origin as a personal vision symbol and was later used in the manner of a familial crest.

Debbe Tompkins

witch school

Living the Wiccan Life

Llewellyn Publications
Woodbury, Minnesota

Second Printing, 2010
SECOND EDITION
(first edition ©2005 Witchschool.com)

Book design by Rebecca Zins
Cover design by Kevin R. Brown
Interior priest and priestess
illustrations from Dover Publications;
other interior artwork by
Llewellyn Art Department

**Library of Congress
Cataloging-in-Publication Data**
Tompkins, Debbe, 1954-
  Witch School : living the Wiccan life /
Debbe Tompkins.—2nd ed.
      p. cm.—(Witch School series; #5)
  Includes index.
  ISBN 978-0-7387-1495-0
  1. Wicca—Textbooks. I. Title.
  BP605.W53T66 2009
  299'.94—dc22
                        2008042293

Llewellyn Publications
A Division of Llewellyn Worldwide, Ltd.
2143 Wooddale Drive,
Dept. 978-0-7387-1495-0
Woodbury, MN 55125-2989
www.llewellyn.com

Printed in the United States of America

• • • •

Other Books in
the Witch School Series

Witch School First Degree

Witch School Second Degree

Witch School Third Degree

Witch School Ritual, Theory & Practice

Contents

Welcome to *Living the Wiccan Life*. This course was conceived and created with the idea of helping the student who is completely new to Wicca learn what the religion and movement are about from the point of view of the practitioner who does not wish to pursue the path of the Priesthood.

The Living the Wiccan Life course has evolved through several versions. The course began from an idea by Witch School founder Ed Hubbard. Ed hired Rev. Krystel High-Correll to write the first version of the course. When it was decided that a new course was needed, Ed called upon me to write it. Along the way, the course has grown and developed, shaping itself to the expressed needs of the students.

The course is presented in forty-nine lessons, intended to be done at a rate of one per week so as to carry a person through an extended period of growth and learning as a Wiccan. It can, of course, be read through at any pace you choose, but it

Introduction

is wise to allow ample time for lessons and exercises to sink in.

From its inception, the course has been organized in a highly patterned manner—that is, the way the course is laid out is itself used as a teaching tool. The lessons will contain a core lesson, exercises, and rituals. Throughout these lessons, you will also find topics that will be introduced in one lesson and be expanded on in subsequent lessons—the purpose being to give the student enough time to digest the information for topics that may be more complex.

Once you have finished these lessons, you should have at least a rudimentary understanding of Wiccan principles and practices. You will also be given information that may not be found in a traditional beginning Wiccan course, such as pathworking. Finally, at the end of the course, you will be given a self-dedication ritual, which is a spiritual commitment to the Wiccan path.

Part I

Lesson 1:
Connecting with Deity

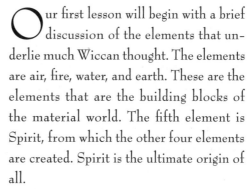

Our first lesson will begin with a brief discussion of the elements that underlie much Wiccan thought. The elements are air, fire, water, and earth. These are the elements that are the building blocks of the material world. The fifth element is Spirit, from which the other four elements are created. Spirit is the ultimate origin of all.

These elements are considered to be the fundamentals of creation, which are present in all things and can be used to help us understand all things.

Of course, you must understand that it is not the physical substances that are meant here. The elements are merely represented by them to better define them. Rather, it is the dynamic qualities represented by these physical substances to which we are actually referring when we speak of the elements. Thus, when we speak of earth as an element inherent in all of creation, we are not referring to soil but to the qualities earth represents. These dynamic qualities may be briefly described as follows:

The element of earth is the element of the physical world—what you can see, feel, taste, touch, and smell. It is the element of manifestation. This part of the lesson will deal with the physical aspects of experience and learning.

The element of air is the element of the mind, intellect, beginnings, choice, and discrimination. This part of the lesson will present things for you to think about and present choices that you may or may not choose to make. It will help you develop your mind and your skills of discernment.

The element of fire is the element of inspiration, creativity, will, desire, and psychic experience. This part of the lesson will help you learn to focus and to develop your will, and present ways to strengthen your psychic ability.

The element of water is the element of cycles, change, endings, and releasing. This part of the lesson will teach you about cycles, show you how to place yourself into the flow of events, and suggest ways to direct that flow to achieve your goals.

The fifth element is Spirit. Spirit is Deity, which Wiccans perceive as both Goddess and God, Mother and Father.

Spirit is the source and center of all that exists. This part of the lesson will deepen your understanding of the Lady and the Lord and enable you to experience them personally in your life.

To the Wiccan, all that exists is alive and is conscious of itself as itself. It does not have the same kind of consciousness as ourselves, perhaps, but it does have a self-awareness at a spiritual level. Everything—including the chair you sit in, the pictures on your wall, the sidewalk outside your house—*everything*, literally, that exists is alive and aware. In turn, everything that exists also has the ability to be aware of you and can respond to you. This relationship is present because everything that exists is made from Spirit, as you are too. Regardless of the apparent qualities of the physical form, its spiritual aspect is always alive and aware.

Everything—every object, plant, flower, microbe, and star—seeks value fulfillment. Everything, whether natural or created, has a purpose for being and wants to express that purpose. Brooms want to sweep, beds want to be slept in, houses want to shelter and protect.

In this week's lesson, we will discuss the consciousness of all that exists. The following exercises will aid you in attuning to this consciousness.

Connecting with Your Surroundings

For this first exercise, take some time every day and really *see* the objects that surround you, both at home and at work.

Do you have belongings that you rarely use? Do you have things that you have forgotten about? This does not honor those objects. Consider using them more often, or, if they are no longer needed, give them to a charity store like Goodwill or to someone who may have a use for them.

Notice the plants, flowers, and trees around you. Be aware of any animals, whether domesticated or wild, and any birds. Pay attention to the buildings you see. All of these are conscious and aware of you in their own way.

Try to identify the trees, plants, flowers, animals, and birds. As they feel your attention, they may respond to you, especially the trees. You may suddenly be aware of the odor of the tree or feel a wave of energy flowing from them to you. If this does not happen right away, know that it will eventually as you practice.

• • • •

For the second exercise, take a few moments to consider the importance of the things in your life and the role they play in your day-to-day existence. Consider the seemingly inanimate things around you; choose one. Imagine yourself as the object you have chosen. What is its existence like? How does its existence feel? While understanding that its spiritual being is different from your own, try to imagine what that spiritual being is like and how it experiences creation. What was this item created for? Are these purposes being fulfilled? When using this object in the future, reflect on these questions and try to view the object with a new awareness: a knowledge that it has a purpose for being and a desire that that purpose be fulfilled. Follow this process with several objects, and you may find yourself looking at the world around you very differently.

• • • •

For the third exercise, you will be using your inner senses (part of your psychic ability) to connect with the energy of your surroundings.

Sit in a room, close your eyes, and relax. Be aware of your breathing—do not try to control it, just be aware of it. Now be aware of the way your body feels; mentally feel each part of your body, then all of it at once. Be aware that you have an energy body that fills and surrounds you. Feel this energy body as a bubble of energy around you, and if you cannot feel it, imagine it as being there. Now feel your energy body growing larger, expanding further and further out from your body, until it fills the room.

Now imagine small openings in your energy body, and know that these are opening your intuitive abilities. Feel the energy of the room. Is it an alert energy or an inward energy? Is it welcoming or indifferent? Does the room have a desire to shelter, nurture, and comfort, or does it feel neglected, or possibly some other feeling? Take some time with this, then ask the room if there is anything you can do for it. Thank the room for what it does for you. If you feel it wants or needs something, make sure you fulfill its needs.

Now consciously close the openings in your energy body, then feel your energy body returning to its normal size, about two to twelve inches around your body. After you do this, open your eyes, stretch, and move around to come completely back into your body. These actions are grounding, which means being fully present in your body. Grounding may also be achieved by eating something or putting a pinch of salt under your tongue.

• • • •

The Cycle of Water

No doubt you learned about the cycle of water during your secular schooling. The heat of the sun causes water to evaporate. This vapor rises and become clouds. The vapor condenses and becomes precipitation in the form of rain or snow, which returns to the earth. Melted snow and rain is carried back to the oceans by the streams and rivers and also absorbed by the earth, becoming the water table. Eventually, this water becomes the water that flows from your faucet.

But have you considered that this water is the same water that has existed from the beginning of time? Since the human body is about 75 percent water, this water has been a part of every person that has ever lived. Water, like everything, is conscious. At the cellular level, it has a memory of everything it has ever experienced, and your body has these same memories.

Once a day this week, turn on your faucet and cup the water in your hands. Think about the connectedness of water. Be awed by the wonder of this. The water in your hands has been part of every ocean and every river and every person and every time period in the world. Does this change the way you experience water?

During the week, sit and imagine that you are a drop of water in the ocean, remembering that all water is one water. Even though you are only one drop, you are also the whole ocean. How does this feel? Then visualize yourself evaporating and rising to become a cloud. Experience "being" a cloud. How does it feel to be so light, so high above the earth? Now become a drop of rain falling to the earth or into a river, and imagine yourself becoming the water that is the drinking water for a city. Follow your journey to a faucet, then experience being the water someone drinks, and become the fluid part of a cell. How is this experience? Compose your own journey from here, letting your imagination have free rein. At the end of your journey, you are once more a drop of water in the ocean.

Relax, and have fun with this exercise. There is no wrong way to do it.

• • • •

How Wiccans View Deity

One of the most common misperceptions about Wiccans is that we do not believe in God. Actually, we believe very much in God, but we see God as both Mother and Father, as both Female and Male, as both Goddess and God.

So Wiccans have *two* deities? Not exactly. Goddess and God are both aspects of the same universal power, which previously we have spoken of as Spirit. Wiccans often think of Goddess and God in very specific, human-like terms, but we know that these are ways of looking at cosmic forces. Goddess and God are not a human couple living in the clouds somewhere with superhuman powers, they are forces whose totality is beyond human comprehension. We use symbolic forms to help us understand and emotionally interact with what we know is, in reality, beyond full understanding.

The concept of Goddess and God is very similar to the eastern idea of yin and

yang. The Goddess is yin, associated with internal qualities like spirit, emotion, and integration. She is often represented by the night and the moon. The God is yang, associated with external qualities like action, manifestation, and the physical world. He is often represented by the day and the sun. Both Goddess and God are aspects of Spirit, as are all things.

In addition to this very existential way of looking at Deity, Wiccans also use very personal ways to interact with Goddess and God. Wiccans regard all of humanity's many gods as being real and able to be interacted with. All are equal aspects of Spirit—as are we ourselves. You can think of God as a diamond, a single stone with many facets. The many gods are the facets, each of which can be worked with separately or as part of the larger whole. Many Wiccans will have one or more of these many gods as a patron deity, who acts as their special deity and guide in life. Each of these many gods can be associated with one (and sometimes more) of seven archetypes of Goddess and God. The Goddess has three archetypes: Maiden, Mother, and Crone. The God has four archetypes: Hero, Lover, King, and Sorcerer.

Each of these archetypes is a way of interacting, understanding, and connecting with Deity on a personal level. Some examples of these personal gods include Diana, Isis, Yemaya, Thor, Cernunnos, and

Shiva, to name only a very few, for there are millions. While the forms of these goddesses and gods are archetypes, they also represent very real energies that we can interact with.

It is very important to remember that your connection to Deity is inside yourself, not outside. This is true for Spirit, for Goddess and God, for all the millions of personal gods and goddesses. You call upon Deity from your heart, which is the true altar. However, external elements can be comforting to people and can help them to access their internal connections; therefore, an external altar is often used. The altar serves as a focal point for worship.

The following is a very simple ritual to help you connect with Goddess and God.

For this ritual, you will need an altar. It can be very simple or as elaborate as you would like to make it. The altar should include two candles: a white candle for Goddess and a red candle for God. White and red are one of many color combinations that are commonly used to represent Goddess and God.

Once a day, preferably at the same time each day, you should use this altar to consciously connect to Goddess and God. Begin by focusing on Goddess. Imagine her as clearly as possible. Speak to her, either aloud or in your heart: ask her to help you to connect with her, to build a closer relationship with her, to better feel her influence in

your life. Now light the white candle. Next, focus on God. Imagine him as clearly as you can, and ask him to help you to connect with him and build a closer relationship. Then light the red candle. Now let the candles burn for a short time, preferably at least five minutes, and think about all of the good things in your life and the many ways in which you interact with Goddess and God every day. You can also take this time to ask them for help or guidance.

When you are finished, thank them for this time together and snuff out the candles.

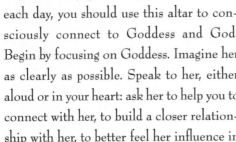

Lesson 2:
The Wiccan Liturgical Year

We have spoken about how, for Wiccans, all things that exist are alive and aware. As Wiccans, we try to be mindful of this and to remember it in our daily interactions with the world. Because of this, we have great respect for Earth and her cycles: the daily cycle of night and day, the monthly cycle of the moon, the yearly cycle of the seasons. The observance of these cycles forms the Wiccan Wheel of the Year, the liturgical calendar of the Wiccan faith (we will discuss this more later on in this lesson). We interact with Goddess and God at these times, just as we do each day at the altar. By doing these things, we experience the energies of these cycles and of Goddess and God within us. Wiccans know these energies are real because they live them, and they see the effects of these interactions within their lives.

• • • •

Wheel of the Year

The Wheel of the Year, the Wiccan liturgical calendar, is the observance of the earth's natural cycles and has two types of ceremonies: the esbat and the sabbat. An esbat is a lunar ceremony held at the new and full moons. Ideally, the esbat is held on the day when the new or full moon is

considered to be exact, but in practice it is often held on a convenient day close to the actual date. A sabbat is a ceremony celebrating the changing seasons. Sabbats also have specific dates but may, in practice, be held on a convenient day close to the actual date.

There are eight sabbats in total, and they are further divided into the lesser and the greater sabbats. The lesser sabbats fall on the solstices and the equinoxes. These are Yule (December/Winter Solstice), Ostara (March/Spring Equinox), Midsummer (June/Summer Solstice), and Mabon (September/Fall Equinox). The greater sabbats are Samhain (November 1), Imbolc (February 1), Beltane (May 1), and Lammas (August 1). Because the solstices and equinoxes are determined by the position of the sun, they do not fall on the same date each year but usually will be between the nineteenth and twenty-second of their given month. As the wider world regards the solstices and equinoxes as the formal start date for each season, they are noted in most calendars.

Samhain: Samhain is the festival of the dead, when we honor the spirits of our ancestors and our beloved departed. This holiday is especially connected with ideas of divination and magic. Samhain is also the beginning of the Wiccan liturgical year. Samhain is associated with the Goddess in her Crone aspect, which is the archetype of the Halloween Witch.

Yule: Yule is the longest night of the year but also the rebirth of the sun. From this point on, the days grow longer again. Yule is a time of celebration and gift giving. Yule is associated with the God in his Sorcerer aspect, which is the archetype of the Santa Claus figure.

Imbolc: Imbolc is the dawn of the year and celebrates the return of light and life to the world. It is a time for new beginnings and fresh starts. Imbolc is associated with the Goddess in her aspect as Maiden.

Ostara: Ostara is the spring festival, when we celebrate the greening of the earth. Ostara is associated with the God in his archetype of Hero, especially in the form of the Green Man.

Beltane: Beltane is the festival of life. Beltane is associated with light, flowers, and Maypole dances. Beltane is often thought of as the time of union between Goddess and God.

Midsummer: Midsummer is the longest day of the year and the celebration of summer. Midsummer is associated with the God in his form as Lover and consort of the Goddess.

Lammas: Lammas is the first harvest, when we give thanks for the bounty of the earth and when we thank the grain for sacrificing itself for us. Lammas is associated with the Goddess in her archetype as Mother.

Mabon: Mabon is the second harvest. Like Lammas, Mabon is also a time of thanksgiving, but it is also often used as a time to reflect upon our lives and the effects of our actions during the past year. This is a time to take stock of our lives and to consider issues of personal responsibility. Mabon is associated with the God in his archetype as King.

• • • •

Study the list of sabbats above and consider the given associations. How might you represent these qualities on an altar or in artwork? How might you celebrate these holidays? Do you see similar celebrations in the wider community? Consider what each of these times of year means to you.

Much of the Wheel of the Year revolves around the planting and harvest seasons. What seeds do you wish to plant in your life for the coming year? What do you hope to harvest? What do you wish to release? Make two lists: one for the things you want to accomplish and one for the things you want to release.

····
Releasing and Manifestation

For your first exercise in this lesson, you will be doing a ritual of releasing your past and bringing things into your life that you want. This is best done outside at night, sitting in front of a fire. If this is not possible, you may do it indoors with a candle. Do this alone, and allow at least an hour.

If you are outside, you will need to gather twigs, placing them within easy reach. Have your two lists beside you. Consider all the things that have ended in your life and all the things, situations, habits, and negative ways of thinking you need to release. Now pick up a twig, and choose one thing you want to release. Hold the twig while you think about it—what it has meant to you, the good and/or bad it has brought to you. Then put the twig into the fire. As the twig burns, you are releasing it from your life. Continue this until you have nothing more to release.

When you have released everything, take the list of the things you wanted to release and put it in the fire, saying:

> *As these things burn,*
> *so are they released.*

Watch the flames burn. Now imagine the heat of the flame inside yourself. Know that this inner flame is consuming all the residue of these things within you.

Now take the list of the things you want to accomplish, and read them over. When you have done this, put the list into the fire, saying:

> *As these things burn, so are they*
> *accomplished, and they come to me*
> *in perfect timing and in harmony,*
> *with harm to none. So mote it be.*

You will still need to do the necessary work in the mundane world to accomplish them, but you have manifested them in the astral world, where the energies of our desires accumulate and take form.

If you are doing this indoors, use a red, orange, or yellow candle. Take strips of paper and hold them one at a time while you think about each thing you are releasing. Then light them with the candle and put them in a flame-proof container. Continue with this as you would with the fire.

You have just done a spell. It is important in spellwork never to manipulate or control anyone else. In a love spell, you would work for the perfect love for you at this time, not for a specific person to fall in love with you. If you want a better job, you would work for the best job for yourself at this time, not someone else's job specifically. You do this because it is moral, and it is important to remember that whatever you do to someone else comes back to you.

Spells will be discussed in depth in a later lesson.

Ritual Baths

In this next exercise, you will be introduced to the concept of taking a ritual bath. To be most effective, take a cleansing ritual bath three times this week. A ritual bath removes negativity on all levels. It can energize you as well as increase your psychic awareness and ability. (This can also be adapted if you only have a shower.)

Gather a muslin bag or a small, square cloth. Choose one purifying herb and one or more of the other herbs from the following list:

Burdock: for purification

Cinnamon: raises spiritual vibrations

Dandelion leaf: for purification

Jasmine flowers: promotes psychic ability

Lavender flowers: purification

Peppermint leaf: increases psychic ability

Raspberry leaf: promotes visions

Red rose petals: clairvoyance, happiness, and joy, sacred to the Goddess

Most of these herbs can be found in health-food stores, often as teas. You should be able to find all of them at a metaphysical bookstore, or they can be ordered online. You can choose to use oils instead of the herbs if you have them, or you can use a mixture of herbs and oils.

Place your choice of herbs in the muslin bag or cloth, and tie it so no particles escape. Place it in the bathroom. You can also light a candle and burn your favorite incense for this occasion.

Take the phone off of the hook, and arrange not to be disturbed. Start running the bath water, to a temperature comfortable to you, and place the herbs under the running water. If using a candle, let that be your only source of light. Take a moment to relax, and with your hands by your sides, release all tension and worry, seeing it as dark-colored light or as sand running from your hands into Mother Earth.

Get in the tub, close your eyes, and relax. Pour water over your body, but be sure to keep it out of your eyes and nose. Some herbs, such as cinnamon and peppermint, can burn mucus membranes. Small particles from the herbs can get into your eyes and burn or scratch them. Some oils can also burn the eyes.

Feel the purifying energy move through your body as light or as a wave of energy. Feel your energy become pure and clear.

When you are relaxed and feel purified and clear, get out of the tub and dry off. Go to your altar, and if it is morning, spend your daily devotional time with the Goddess and the God. If it is evening or night, spend time with the Goddess and the God, and thank them for the blessings of the day. You can also discuss any plans or concerns about tomorrow with them.

If you are using a shower, wet the bag of herbs thoroughly and rub it over your body. Be sure to keep it out of your eyes and off of any mucus membranes. See/imagine the purifying energy move through you, as described above. When you are relaxed and feel purified and clear, get out, dry off, go to your altar, and proceed as above.

When you have finished your time at the altar, check to see how you feel. Did the ritual bath affect the way you feel? If not, continue to do the ritual bath two more times this week, and stay in tune with your feelings.

• • • •

Altar Preparation

You began a simple altar last week with the Goddess and God candles and whatever else you chose to put there. Now we will talk about altars in greater depth.

Your altar is the outer expression of your inner self and your spirituality. It is a tool that deepens your connection to Deity. It is your spiritual battery. It is important that your altar be beautiful to you, and everything on your altar should have meaning to you.

Your altar can be used for many different purposes. So far, we have only discussed the altar as a personal or devotional

place. In this lesson and future lessons, we will talk about adding items to your altar for specific purposes.

Your altar can contain Goddess and God images, statues, and/or candles. It can be as simple or elaborate as you want it to be. You can put flowers on it, and ribbons, shells, and incense. You can have stones or candles to represent the four directions and the elements. You can have pictures of departed family members and other ancestors. Many Wiccans keep their athame, wand, chalice, and pentacle on this altar.

Some items are used for specific rituals and will vary depending on the intent. When certain items are not in use, acquiring a storage container would be beneficial to keep them in. For those who are especially organized, separate containers could be used for each type of ritual you perform that contains the appropriately colored altar cloths, candles, and decorations specific to the ritual.

Below is a beginning list of some of the items you may want to acquire for your altar:

An altar surface: Ideally, this altar should to be at least two feet in length. It can be circular, oval, square, or rectangular.

Altar cloth: Make sure it is large enough to cover the altar.

An athame: This is a knife with a double blade.

A wand: The wand can be handmade or storebought. Directions to make your own will be provided in lesson 3.

A chalice: This is a footed glass or goblet, like a wine glass, that can be obtained through metaphysical stores, catalogs, or online.

A quartz crystal or crystal cluster.

A pentacle: This is often round, with a pentagram drawn or inscribed on it. This can be wood, ceramic, or a found stone that can be painted. A recommended size for the pentacle is four to seven inches across.

Lesson 3:
Energy

The subject of this week's lesson is energy. Energy is called many things, including prana, chi, or Spirit. Energy is the substance of which existence is composed. All things are made from it as well as by it. A Wiccan would say that Deity (often simply called Spirit) is the source of the energy from which the world is made, but we would also say that Deity *is* that energy from which the world is made. Deity uses its own substance—energy—to create the physical world as we know it.

This energy is not static but dynamic and expansive. All the things that are made from energy also create more energy of their own. When we work magic, which is simply the direction of energy, we use the energy of Deity that we find inside ourselves, as well as energy from outside ourselves, such as the energy of the earth, moon, or sun. Objects such as stones, crystals, and plants also all have their own distinctive energies that can be drawn upon in magic, but all of this energy is ultimately from the same divine source.

Our bodies also produce energy, but in working magic, we try not to draw directly upon it, as this can have a depleting effect on the body. Rather, we channel the divine energy *through* ourselves, from our internal connection to it.

We protect our own energy by shielding ourselves daily. This prevents others from siphoning our energy away from us. It also prevents others from influencing, controlling, and manipulating us. You will learn how to shield later in this lesson.

Wiccans celebrate the lunar phases of the moon, called esbats. In these rituals, we draw the energy of the moon inside ourselves, for healing, to energize our spells, and to increase our psychic skills. Doing this also deepens our relationship to the Lady and the Lord. You will learn about the new moon esbat later in this lesson.

· · · ·

Grounding and Shielding

We will now discuss the idea of grounding and shielding. Grounding is the idea of releasing excess energy. This is very important, because excess energy can cause us to feel unbalanced in various ways. It can make us feel unexpectedly giddy, manic, or even sleepy. Excess energy can also clog up our energetic system. For all of these reasons, you should ground your energy frequently, especially when doing any kind of spiritual work.

Shielding, on the other hand, is a technique we use to keep out unwanted energy that we might otherwise pick up from other

people or from the ambient energy around us. Shielding should be done once a day, in connection with grounding and also anytime you feel the need for it.

To ground, or release, excess energy, you should begin by putting yourself into a comfortable position. This can be either sitting or standing. If you are standing, keep your arms at your sides and place your hands parallel to the ground with palms down. If you are sitting, raise your hands a few inches above your lap with palms down. Now imagine all of the excess energy running out of you like water, flowing down your body and out through the palms of your hands and the soles of your feet. Let this excess energy flow out of you and take with it all tension, stress, or anxiety you may be holding. Let it flow out of your body and return to the universe to be recycled for other purposes.

Next, imagine the energy of the earth as a golden light, entering through the bottoms of your feet and filling your body. When your body is filled with this energy, see the flow of the energy stop.

Now imagine a bubble of blue-white light surrounding you in all directions. This is your aura. The aura is composed of the energy of your body, emotions, mind, and spirit. The aura surrounds you, rather like a bubble of energy, extending above, around, and below your physical body.

Imagine the bubble of blue-white light as clearly as you can, and see it extending three to six feet beyond the surface of your body. Set your intent that the boundaries of your aura shall act as a barrier to all unwanted energy, a protection that shields you from all negative energy, from all harm, and from the attempts of anyone to control or manipulate you. Focus on the idea that this barrier will admit positive energy but repel negative energy, and imagine it as having a mirrored surface, smooth as glass, that unwanted energy will be unable to penetrate.

When this is clear in your mind, you may let the image fade, but know that the protection remains.

Again, you should release any excess energy, just as you did when you began. This should be done after any magical working. Techniques such as this may not be what you initially think of as being magic, but they are very much a magical working.

• • • •

Book of Shadows

Many Wiccans keep a special journal, called a Book of Shadows. The Book of Shadows is usually thought of as a spell book, and it does have that aspect, but it is also much more than this. A Book of Shadows is a personal record of a Witch's growth in spirit as well as knowledge. In the

Book of Shadows, we record techniques we learn, and also our experiences in working with these techniques. The Book of Shadows can also be used to record dreams, visions, and oracles you may receive. You can record anything you feel is relevant to your spiritual growth and magical practice in your Book of Shadows. You do not have to keep a Book of Shadows, and not everyone does, but it can be very useful to have one.

The Book of Shadows is also a creative project for many people. They use the Book of Shadows as an artistic means to express themselves, as well as to express their expanding relationship to Spirit through symbols and artwork. Many Books of Shadows are very beautiful, having highly decorative covers and much artwork in the pages. In recent years, scrapbooking techniques often have been used to embellish the Book of Shadows. However you choose to decorate your Book of Shadows, if in fact you keep one, it is important that it reflects your taste and personality. It is personal to you, and its appearance should evoke a positive feeling in you.

The Book of Shadows is an external record of your growth in spirit, but that growth actually occurs internally, of course. How do we open ourselves to this growth? Perhaps the best first step is to still your mind. This is harder than it sounds, as you shall see. The Zen Buddhists say that you cannot fill a bowl which is already full. Similarly, you cannot hear the voice of Spirit when your head is full of your own thoughts.

To still your mind, first still your body. Sit or lie in a comfortable position. Now try not to think. What does this mean? Does it mean that there must be nothing in your mind, that your brain should be immobile? That is not possible. No, rather, it means that you should not actively think. Ideas or images will come into your head, but you must not "grab onto" them. Just let the ideas float across and out of your mind like clouds floating across a summer sky, and do not interact with them. This may be very hard at first, but keep trying; soon it will be easy. Try to stay in this state for about ten minutes each day, and it is best if you can do this exercise at a regular time each day. This "non-thinking" will bring you to a point of inner stillness. Granted, this may not happen the first time you try the exercise. You may have to practice it for a while. But it will come. When you reach this inner stillness, allow yourself to float within it. In this state, you should feel at peace. You will also find that it increases your energy afterward.

· · · ·
New Moon Esbat

An esbat is a lunar ceremony celebrated by Wiccans at the new moon, full moon, and sometimes the waning moon. This ceremony is, as stated, for the new moon.

The new moon represents the Maiden aspect of the Goddess. The Maiden is the goddess of new beginnings, dawn, spring, and youth. She is the goddess of creativity, arts, beauty, and passion. The Maiden is often spoken of as the Virgin, but she is a "virgin" in the older sense of the word, meaning that she is an independent, single woman as opposed to a wife or mother. The Maiden is the goddess of the waxing moon, and her color is red—the color of menstrual blood, which separates a maiden from a child.

You will first need to create sacred space. You create sacred space by visualizing/imagining a bubble of protective energy around you. You use the energy of the earth, the sky, or the stars to do this. Here, we will be using the energy of the stars for sacred space.

Sit or stand in a comfortable position. See/imagine the energy of the stars flowing as a pale blue-white light far above you. See it flow in a stream of light to a position two feet above your head, where it collects in a sphere of concentrated blue-white light. The light of all the stars is condensed into this sphere, which acts as a transformer to release a safe amount of this light into you. Now feel the top of your head opening to receive this light, and feel it enter you and flow from your head down into your heart. Now see/imagine the light expanding out in all directions around you so that it completely surrounds you and the room. Now close the top of your head, and say:

I am in sacred space, surrounded and protected by the light of the stars. Only good can be here. Only good can enter in here.

When you have finished this exercise, see/imagine the light re-entering your body through your heart, then feel your head open, and feel the light flowing up through your head, up into the sphere above your head, and then flowing back to the stars. Be sure to close the opening in your head when you are done.

Practice this exercise two or three times before the night of the new moon so that you are familiar with it. You draw down the energy of the sky in the same way. To draw energy from the earth for this purpose, imagine a golden-yellow light from the center of the earth flowing to a sphere two feet below the surface of the earth, where the energy collects. Then see the light flowing upward from the sphere into your feet, and up into your heart, and proceed as above. Release the energy of the earth downward into your feet and into the sphere, to be returned to the center of the earth.

Try all three ways of creating sacred space so you know which one works best. They are all equally effective.

Some Wiccans perform rituals in robes or other clothing used specifically for that purpose. This can aid entering into a ritual state of mind. Some Wiccans perform rituals nude, termed "skyclad," or wear regular clothing. Try all three ways, and see which way you prefer.

You will need the following items for the new moon ritual:

- A white or silver candle to represent the Goddess
- A yellow or gold candle to represent the God
- A purple candle for the ancestors (either your physical ancestors or your philosophical ancestors)
- Two white working candles
- Red flowers for the altar (red is the color of the Maiden)
- An altar cloth, something that feels special to you
- A candlesnuffer
- A lighter or matches
- A black candle and a white candle (these can be mini candles)

- A flame-proof container for burning paper
- A knife to use in burning paper
- A list of goals and desires you want to accomplish
- A list of any obstacles or blockages to these you are aware of, such as lack of confidence, fear, or procrastination
- Candleholders
- Anointing oil

New Moon Ritual

You will want to have everything set up ahead of time. Try to decorate the altar in a way that is pleasing to you and that helps you to feel connected to it. The altar is a sacred place and should also be a place of beauty. In addition to the specified materials, you should also include items that are special to you or that just make you feel magical—stones, altar statues, pictures, etc.—anything that will help to put you in the proper mindset. You may stand during the entire ritual, or you may sit during parts of it. Take your time with each step of this ritual. Give yourself time to experience and enjoy it.

Begin by clearing and releasing all excess energy. Imagine the excess energy pouring out of you like water, down through your body, through your legs, and out through

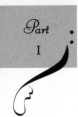

your feet, returning to the earth, where it can be reused in other ways.

Light the working candles. The flame of a candle creates energy and acts like a small psychic battery. These working candles will help to provide energy for your ritual. They also provide light.

Turn out any other lights in the room.

Create sacred space, as you have practiced.

Light the incense.

Create your inner stillness.

State your purpose for this ritual. To state the purpose, you might say something along these lines:

Behold, I have come to celebrate the Maiden Goddess at this time of the new moon. From now until the full moon, the moon's energy waxes and grows strong, carrying my wishes and my desires forward to be manifested.

Take up the lighter or matches, and approach the Goddess candle. Invoke the Maiden Goddess. You might say something like this:

O holy Maiden Goddess, Red Lady of the Dawn and of Spring, Mistress of the Waxing Moon, I call upon you and ask you to be with me in this, my ritual.

Inspire me, I pray, with your creativity and joy, that my heart may be light and my life a delight. Bless me with your passion and enthusiasm! Holy Maiden, I bid you hail and welcome!

Now light the Goddess candle. Open your heart to the presence of the Goddess. Know that she is there with you. You may be able to feel a shift in the energy because of her presence. You may almost feel you can see her, or you may just have a quiet knowing that she is there. Every person will perceive her in a different way, the way that is best for them. You may even perceive her differently at different times.

Still holding the lighter or matches, turn to the God candle and say something along the lines of:

O holy God, Lord of Light and Beauty, Lord of the Dance of Life, Master of the Seasons of the Year, I call upon you and ask you to be here with me in this, my ritual. Share with me, I pray, your gifts of courage and determination! Help me to bring my goals and desires into manifestation, even as you manifest the physical world and its cycles! Holy God, I bid you hail and welcome!

Now light the God candle. Open your heart to the God, just as you did to the Goddess. Know that he is there with you.

Now turn to the ancestor candle. Say something like:

Beloved ancestors, you who have gone before and prepared the way, I call upon you and ask you to be here with me in this, my ritual. I honor you, whose lives have shaped my ideas and beliefs, and prepared my foundations, and I ask you to guide me as I go forward. O beloved ancestors, may you blessed be!

Light the ancestor candle, and open yourself to the presence of your ancestors. Again, these may be your physical ancestors, but they don't need to be—anyone who has helped to shape your life or whose example you follow may be thought of as being among your ancestors.

Now you will draw energy from the moon. Imagine the crescent moon high above you. Picture it in your mind as clearly as possible. See its beautiful, silvery arc in the night sky. Now imagine a beam of clear white light coming down from the moon, a beam of clear, beautiful white light. Imagine that beam of light descending upon you from above and entering your body through the top of your head. Let the light enter your body and fill your heart, forming a large ball of white light around your heart.

As the light continues to pour into you from the moon, imagine it expanding from your heart to fill your entire body. Allow the light to fill your chest, your abdomen, your arms and legs; allow the light to fill every part of you. When your body is completely filled with light, imagine the light expanding around you—just a little at first, an inch or two around your body, then increase it further. Let the light form a ball around your body, so that you are in the center of a ball of white light. Let that ball of white light continue to fill with energy from the moon and continue to expand until it is about six feet in diameter.

Feel the strength and peace of this energy. Allow it to heal you of anything that needs healing. Allow it to suffuse and rejuvenate your entire being.

Now let the image of the beam of light fade, but continue to hold the extra energy it has brought you. You do not need to continue visualizing the ball of energy around you, but know that it is still there. You will release whatever part of that energy you don't need, the excess, after the end of the ceremony.

Now you will do a self-blessing. Pick up the oil, put some on your fingers, and touch the top of your head. Say:

*Bless me, Mother, for
I am your child.*

Touch the area between your eyebrows, your third eye (your psychic eye), and say:

*Bless my mind's eye, that I
may see your beauty and power,
both within me and without.*

Anoint your throat with oil, saying:

*Bless my throat, that I may
know and speak my truth.*

Anoint your heart, and say:

*Bless my heart, that it may
be filled with your love.*

Anoint yourself just above the pelvic bone, and say:

*Bless my creativity
and my sexuality.*

Anoint your feet, and say:

*Bless my feet, that I may
walk in your ways. Bless me,
Mother, for I am your child.*

Prepare to do the candle burning. Place the burning dish in front of you and have handy the matches or the lighter and the knife to aid in the burning, and pick up the list of the blockages you want to release.

Light the black candle. Read over the list of these things you will release, and think about each of them. When you are ready, read the list out loud, and say:

*As this paper burns, so are these
things released from me to bother
me no more. All of these things,
and anything I may not be aware
of that blocks or limits me, I now
release to bother me no more.*

Loosely fold the paper lengthwise, and light one end of it from the black candle. Place it in or on the burning dish. Use the knife to lift the paper so that the paper is completely consumed.

Now light the white candle, and pick up the list of your goals and desires. Read it over, thinking about each thing, then fold it as you did the other list. Light it from the white candle, and say:

*As this paper burns, these things
I desire are manifested into my
life. I ask for these, I accept these,
I receive these, and I give thanks
for these. By my will, this is so.*

Now take time to simply enjoy the beauty of the altar and the soft light of the candles. Notice how well they light the room, now that your eyes have adjusted to them. Enjoy the energy within the circle and within yourself.

To close the ritual, release and give thanks to all those you have invoked. Begin with the ancestors, who were the last to be called. You might say something like:

Beloved ancestors, I thank you for your presence and your aid in this, my ritual. Know that I love you always, and I am always grateful for the role you play in my life—as much now that you are in spirit as when you were in life. With love and with respect, I thank you, and may you blessed be!

Now extinguish the ancestor candle. Now thank the God. You might say:

O holy God, Lord of Light and Beauty, Brother, Consort, and Son of the Goddess, I thank you for your presence and your aid in this, my ritual. I pray that we shall go forward together always, hand in hand, and I know that you are always with me. Holy One, may you blessed be!

Extinguish the God candle, and now thank the Goddess. You might say:

O Maiden Goddess of the Waxing Moon, Lady of Beauty, Joy, and Growth, I thank you for your presence and your aid in this, my ritual. I pray that we

shall go forward together always, hand in hand, and I know that you are always with me. Holy One, may you blessed be!

Now clear and release all excess energy, imagining it running out through the soles of your feet like water and draining into the earth to be recycled for other purposes.

. . . .

Making and Consecrating Your Wand

A wand is one of the fundamental tools used by Wiccans. Many Wiccans feel that their wand should be handmade because it will contain more personal energy. My personal belief is that a store-bought wand can be just as effective. However, if you wish to make your own, traditionally a wand is the length of your forearm, from the bend in your elbow to your fingertips.

The easiest material to work with is wood. If you take the wood from a live shrub or tree, be sure to ask permission of the shrub or tree before you do so. You will experience that answer as a feeling of yes or no within yourself. Be sure to give thanks, and leave an offering of some kind, such as a coin, a hair from your head, or possibly a crystal.

If you harvested the wand, strip the bark from it, and let it dry completely. Sand it until it is smooth. If the wand is already

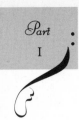

dry, you need only to strip off the bark and sand it. When it is thoroughly dry, you can carve symbols into it, if you choose. You should coat your wand with a protective finish to prevent decay.

What you do with your wand from this point is up to you. You can make it as elaborate or as simple as you wish. You can put a crystal on the tip of it, or an acorn. You can hang bells or shells from it. You can decorate it with paint. You can decorate it with leather, feathers, or ribbons. It is important that every detail of the wand has a specific meaning to you.

It is recommended that you decorate your wand slowly, over time. Give yourself time to connect with the wand and to know which symbols or decorations, if any, are right for you. You may decide you want to keep it as it is, and that is fine.

Your wand is ready to be used in ritual from the moment it is consecrated and charged. That can be done at any time, and you can continue to work on your wand at leisure.

How to Consecrate and Charge Your Wand

Although this ceremony could be done anywhere you wish, it is customary to do it at your altar. Begin by clearing and releasing all excess energy. Let all excess energy run out of you like water, pouring down through your body and your legs, out through your feet, to be returned to the earth so it can reused for other things. Have your wand on the altar. Begin by cleansing it, just the same way we discussed for cleansing the ashes left over from a burning spell. Hold your hands over the wand, palms down, and imagine a yellow-white light coming from your hands and flooding over the wand, filling it with yellow-white energy, which will absorb and transform negativity. You might say something like:

*Behold, I cleanse this wand,
casting out of it any negativity
that may lie within.*

Now change the yellow-white light to a blue-white light, and focus on the wand's vibration, attuning it for magical work. You might say something like:

*Behold, I do bless and consecrate
this wand to my use, that it
may be a tool of magic to be
used for the highest good,
with harm toward none.*

Now allow the image of the light to fade, and know that your wand has been consecrated. You may place the wand with your other ritual tools, or display it on the altar itself.

This same simple technique can be used to consecrate any item for ritual use.

Add the following items to the list of things you need for your altar.

- Candles and candleholders
- Containers for water and salt
- A dish to use for offerings
- An incense holder

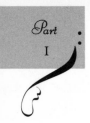
Lesson 4:
Elemental Attributes

In lesson 1, we spoke briefly about the elements and some of their qualities. In this lesson, we will discuss this further and how they are the spiritual essence, or higher vibration, of the actual physical elements. For example, earth is dense and stable. Water flows and is shaped by the container that holds it (our thoughts and beliefs create our emotions). Air is light and mutable, and fire is hot and feeds on air. In other words, our thoughts fuel our passions. Therefore, our thoughts and beliefs are the containers that shape, or create, our emotions and fuel our passions. Air is the element that is invoked first, because everything comes from thought. Our thoughts create the reality we experience.

When casting a circle, earth provides a structure for the goals we choose to manifest—a form for the energies to manifest as. It grounds us in the present moment between the worlds, outside of time and space.

Air provides clarity about our choices, calls us to be responsible for our actions, and asks us to be clear about our true desires, to be sure that they are ours and are not influenced by others or by what we think we should want.

Fire gives focus to the passion that fuels our desires, the energy that collects and builds until it has enough density to manifest in our lives. Fire is our True Will, that portion of the Lady and the Lord that is expressed in ourselves. Our True Will is what we came into this lifetime to learn, to do, and to be. It can take a great deal of time and inner work to uncover that level of our being.

Water is emotion, or need, and also fuels our desires and helps manifest them in our lives. Elemental water is the astral sea, the energy of the astral plane that is given shape by our thoughts, fueled by our will and our emotions, and in the physical world, it manifests as our desires.

Below is a list of attributes, qualities, and correspondences for the elements and the directions they are associated with. Becoming familiar with these helps us to connect with them easily. When we invoke earth while thinking about winter, the frozen cold of midnight, and the mystery represented by the direction of the north, the earth element becomes real to us. We are calling a real energy to be present with us in the circle.

Take the time to learn these attributes, qualities, and correspondences. Think about each direction, and begin to build the inner correspondences that will connect you to each element and direction. If you wish to, make a drawing of the symbols for each direction. A scene at night with snow can represent earth and the north, or a picture of a mountain, or a scene with a bear, or buffalo, whatever connects you to the element of earth and the direction of the north. When you have done this, put the drawing on the wall in the appropriate direction. As you go through your day, glance at these drawings, and they will become part of your inner correspondences. When you cast a circle in later lessons, you won't have to think about the qualities you need for the elements; they will be a part of you.

Earth

Earth is associated with the direction of north, nighttime, the season of winter, and the dark of the moon in the lunar cycle. The qualities of earth are integration, understanding, and stability. On the altar, earth is often represented by a stone or a quartz crystal. Within ourselves, earth corresponds to the physical body and the qualities of persistence, patience, and the ability to be silent.

Air

Air is associated with the direction of east, the dawn of the day, the season of spring, and the waxing moon in the lunar cycle. The qualities of air are thought, inspiration, and imagination. On the altar, air is represented by the athame. Within ourselves, air corresponds to the conscious mind.

Fire

Fire is associated with the direction of south, noontime, the season of summer, and the full moon in the lunar cycle. The qualities of fire are passion, enthusiasm, and courage. On the altar, fire is represented by the wand. Within ourselves, fire corresponds to our True Will and our Higher Self.

Water

Water is associated with the direction of west, the dusk of the day, the season of autumn, and the waning moon in the lunar cycle. The qualities of water are emotion, compassion, and receptivity. On the altar, water is represented by the chalice. Within ourselves, water corresponds to emotion, intuition, and the ability to dare.

Spirit

Spirit is the element of the center. It is the doorway between the worlds. It is all time and all possibilities. It is represented in the circle by the pentacle.

We ourselves correspond to Spirit. We, like everything in the universe, are the union of Goddess and God. Within us the Goddess is the life force, expressed as our soul, and the God is our physical body. Each of us is the sacred marriage of the Goddess and the God.

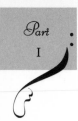

• • • •

Throughout these lessons, there will be topics that are not specific to any one lesson but are necessary to include. Two of these topics follow.

• • • •

Disposing of Ashes from Candle-Burning Rituals

Many of the spells and rituals we will discuss involve burning a piece of paper, which will, of course, leave ashes behind. Before you dispose of the ashes, you will want to remove any negativity lingering within them. This is very important, since the negativity being released is very real. It must be kept in mind that negativity, in this context, does not necessarily mean intentionally destructive; it can simply mean unfocused energy or energy carrying a negative emotional charge that can impede the flow of positive energy. At any rate, this is easily cleared. To do this, hold your hands over the ashes, palms down. Imagine a yellow-white light coming from your hands and permeating the ashes. Focus on the idea that this yellow-white light will absorb and transform any negativity that might be present. When you feel it has been absorbed, dispose of the ashes outside, on the ground or in a stream or river. You can also use this simple technique to clear negativity from any object.

• • • •

Meditation

It is important to meditate every day. Meditation is easy to do and can be done in ten or fifteen minutes. Meditation aligns you on every level, increases your energy, opens up and increases your psychic ability, relieves stress, and helps make your life flow smoothly.

To meditate, take the phone off of the hook, and make sure you will not be disturbed. Sit in a comfortable position. Close your eyes, and be aware of your breathing. Do not try to control or change your breathing, just be aware of it. Now relax your body, starting with your feet. Tell yourself that your feet are relaxed, and do not wait to feel the relaxation—know that it has happened. Relax your ankles next, and so on, all the way up your body. Be sure to relax your scalp as the last step.

Now check your body for tension. If you find any, let it go. Next, put your awareness in your heart area, and just breathe there for a minute or two. Finally, focus your attention on the area between your eyebrows, your third eye, and hold your attention there. Let this be easy; do not strain to do it. If thoughts intrude, let them float gently on by. If your mind wanders, gently bring it back. Do this for ten or fifteen minutes to start with. You can increase the time you spend in meditation later if you choose.

When you have finished, release any excess energy into Mother Earth, then ground and shield, even though you have already done it once today. You need to release excess energy, because meditation can give you too much energy and leave you unbalanced. Signs of this are clumsiness, irritation, and being spacey.

Lesson 5:
Casting a Circle

In this lesson, we will discuss the art of casting a magic circle. A magic circle is created from energy and is visualized as a ring, or sphere, of energy surrounding the ritual space. It is basically an externalized version of the exercise you have already learned for creating sacred space. The purpose of the magic circle is to create sacred space for ritual and to intensify the energy that is raised and directed in ritual.

Before you cast your circle, you must first cleanse and charge your space, as you have learned to do in previous lessons. Then take a moment to center yourself.

Now extend the index and middle fingers of your dominant hand (the hand you write with). See/imagine blue fire coming from them. Start at the east, and walk clockwise in a circle, pointing the blue fire you see/imagine from your fingers at the edge of the circle you want to create. See/imagine the blue fire defining the boundary as you cut it. Say:

Behold, I do cut apart a boundary
between the worlds, apart from
time and space, that shall focus and
contain any energy I raise herein.

Now see/imagine the circle of blue flame extending above and below the ritual space, becoming a sphere of blue flaming light. Let the blue flame dissolve, but know that the circle/sphere is there. Say:

Behold, this circle is now cast.

You will now call the quarters. Calling the quarters consists of bringing in the energy of the element associated with each given direction and invoking the spiritual energies of that element. Calling the quarters does three things in a ritual: (1) it emphasizes our connection to all that exists and the underlying unity of all being; (2) it is a symbolic representation of the act of creation by which the world was and continually is created by Spirit; and (3) it is used to create an energetic construct that acts as a kind of battery to add extra energy to the working.

Begin in the east. East is associated with air, as you will recall, and with new beginnings—dawn, spring, youth, etc.—as well as with the mind, thought, and inspiration. Focus on the concept of the east quarter and all of the associations it represents. Imagine a pillar of white light rising up before you in the east—a pillar of pure, beautiful white light. Invoke the quarter now, calling it forth and requesting its aid. You might say something like:

*O powers of east, element of
air, I do invoke you and ask you
to be with me and guide me in
this, my working. Share with
me your qualities of inspiration,
I pray! Powers of the east, I
bid you hail and welcome!*

There will be a definite change in energy once the element is invoked. Take the time you need to actually feel this change. If you do not feel anything the first few times, be patient. You will eventually be able to feel the energy.

Now turn to the south and invoke the southern quarter in the same way, using the correspondences you have learned for the south. Then you will do the same for the west, and finally the north.

At least three times this week, practice invoking and devoking (releasing) the quarters. Do this by first releasing, grounding, and shielding. Create sacred space, and enter your stillness.

To devoke the quarter, you will begin by thanking it and then imagining the pillar of white light sinking back down into the earth. Begin with the last quarter that was invoked. This will be north. You might say something like:

*O powers of north, element
of earth, I thank you for your
presence and your aid in this,*

*my working! May there be peace
between us now and always!
I bid you hail and farewell!*

Now imagine the pillar of light shrinking down and disappearing back into the earth. Turn to the west and thank it in the same way, taking down its pillar of light. Then devoke the south, and finally the east, where you began.

You decast the circle in much the same way, in the reverse order from how you cast it. Walk around the boundary of the circle, this time counterclockwise, with the index and middle fingers of your dominant hand extended, and imagine the energy of the circle, the blue flame, returning through your fingers as you release the circle. Say something like:

This circle is now open.

Release all excess energy.

· · · ·

Review of Exercises

Below is a review of the daily exercises that have been recommended to build your skills and develop your magical muscles.

Once a day, you spend time with Goddess and God at your altar.

You have done various kinds of paperburning/candle magic, beginning with releasing your past (lesson 2), and you

released blockages and manifested goals in your sacred space (as part of the new moon ritual in lesson 3).

You have taken a ritual bath at least three times and are now familiar with it.

You know how to release, ground, and shield, and you do this daily, once in the morning and once before bedtime.

You have your Book of Shadows and you use it.

You work daily to develop your stillness (lesson 3).

You know how to create sacred space.

You have performed a new moon ritual.

You practice connecting to the elements and their directions, to build an inner connection to them. Possibly you have drawn pictures of each element and its direction and hung them on the wall to better connect with them (lesson 4).

You know how to release negative energy from the ashes of paper-burning magic.

You know how to cleanse, consecrate, and charge your ritual tools.

You meditate every day, for at least ten to fifteen minutes.

Three times this week, you will practice invoking and devoking the elements.

If you have skipped any of these exercises, or need more practice to do them with ease, now is the time to catch up. Your magic will only be as powerful as your skills.

· · · ·

Full Moon Ritual

Below is a full moon ritual. It is recommended that you read it over for familiarity before you actually perform it.

You will need the following items for the full moon ritual:

- A white or silver candle to represent the Goddess
- A yellow or gold candle to represent the God
- Two white working candles
- Candleholders
- White flowers for the altar (white is the color of the Mother)
- An altar cloth, preferably white
- A candlesnuffer
- A lighter or matches
- Incense
- An incense burner
- A black and a white candle
- A flame-proof container for burning paper
- A list of goals and desires you want to accomplish
- A list of any obstacles to these you are aware of
- A robe or special outfit, if you desire one
- A copy of this ritual

Have your altar set up with everything you will need. The white working candles go toward the back of your altar, one on each side. The Goddess candle goes on the left side, more towards the front of the altar, and the God candle goes on the right side. The black and the white candles should be to the side until they are needed. Arrange everything else in a way that pleases you.

Your altar should be a visual feast for you.

Double-check your list to be sure you have everything you need. Read the ritual over once, then take your ritual bath.

You may stand during the entire ritual, or you may sit during parts of it. Take your time with each step of this ritual. Give yourself time to experience and enjoy it.

Release, ground, and shield.

Light the working candles.

Turn out any other lights in the room.

Light the incense.

Create sacred space.

Create your inner stillness.

State your purpose for this ritual:

*I am here tonight to celebrate
the Goddess in her form as
the Mother of All Living and
Queen of the Wise. I seek to
experience her mystery and her
love, her compassion, and her
joy, for I am her child, and I
would rejoice in her presence.*

Pick up the lighter or matches, and say something to the effect of:

*Divine Mother Goddess, you who
are the source and sustenance of all
that is, I invoke you on this night
of the full moon, when your radiant
light bathes all in beauty. May your
love be within my heart, now and
always. I do say hail and welcome.*

Light the Goddess candle. Take a few minutes to feel her presence, for she will be there with you. You will probably feel her energetically in some way, however subtle. Don't have any preconceptions of what this should be.

Still holding the lighter or matches, turn to the God candle, and say something like:

*Divine Father God, Son, Brother
and Consort of the Goddess, I
invoke you on this night of the full
moon, for where the Goddess is,
you are also. You are the Lord of
Time and Space, and you are the
manifestation of the Goddess's
desire. You, who turn the wheel
of time and dance the dance of
life, be here with me now, and
I do say hail and welcome!*

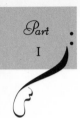

Light the God candle. Take a few minutes to feel the presence of the God, as you did with the Goddess.

Now you will draw the energy of the moon inside yourself. If you are able to see the moon, look up at her while doing this ritual. Otherwise, imagine the fullness of the moon above you and her radiant light upon all things.

Feel/imagine the light of the actual moon above you, falling upon you, surrounding you, and filling you. Breathe this light into you and feel its energy charging you, making you glow. Enjoy this feeling as long as you want, then, still filled with the light of the moon, read the Charge of the Goddess, written below. Read this a few times before the ritual, and think about what you are saying.

Charge of the Goddess

*Hear now the words of the Great
   Mother
Who was of old called many names by
   the hearts of humankind—
Selv, Diana, Brighid, Laksmi, Yema-
   ya, Kuan Yin, and many others
Both known and unknown:*
Whenever you have need of
   anything
Once in a month and better it be
   when the Moon is full

Then you shall assemble in some
   sacred place
And adore Me, Who am the spirit
   of the Moon.
And you shall sing and dance, make
   music and make love
All in My name, Who am the
   Queen of all the Wise
And you shall be free from slavery
And as a sign that you are truly
   free, you shall be open in your
   rites.
For Mine is the ecstasy of spirit,
   and Mine too the joys of the
   senses
And My law is love unto all beings
Nor do I demand ought of sacrifice
For I am the Mother of All Living,
   and My love is poured out upon
   creation.
Keep pure this highest ideal, strive
   ever toward it
Let nothing turn you aside
For Mine is the cup of the wine of
   life
The sacred cauldron which is the
   grail of immortality.
On Earth I give knowledge of the
   Spirit Eternal
And beyond Death I give peace and
   freedom

And reunion with those who have
gone before
For I am the Gracious Goddess,
Who gives joy unto the human
heart.
*Hear now the words of the Star
Goddess*
*In the dust of Whose feet are the
Hosts of Heaven*
*And Whose body encircles the
universe:*
I am the beauty of the Green Earth
and the White Moon among the
stars
And the Mystery of the Waters
I call unto your soul: "Arise and
come unto Me."
For I am the Soul of Nature, Who
gives life to the universe.
From Me all things proceed, and
unto Me all must return
Before My face—O beloved of
Gods and humankind—
Let your Highest Self rejoice
And be enfolded in the rapture of
the Infinite.
For My worship is in the Heart that
rejoices
And behold—All acts of love and
pleasure are my rituals.
Therefore let there be beauty and
strength, power and compassion,

Honor and humility, mirth and
reverence within you.
And you who seek to find Me
In the depths of the sea or the
shining stars
Know that your seeking will avail
you not
Unless you know the Mystery;
For if that which you seek you find
not within yourself
You will never find it
For behold—I have been with you
since the beginning
And I am that Which is attained at
the end of desire.

[There are many versions of the Charge
of the Goddess. This is the Correllian
Recension of the Charge of the Goddess,
from *Witch School: First Degree*, published
by Llewellyn.]

• • • •

When you are ready, release the image of
the moon's light falling upon you. The
moon's energy stays within your body.

Prepare to do the candle burning. Place
the burning dish in front of you. Have the
matches or lighter and the knife readily
available, then pick up the list of blockages
you want to release.

Light the black candle. Read over the
list of these things you want to release, and

think about each of them. When you are ready, read the list out loud, and say:

As this paper burns, so are these things released from me, to bother me no more. All of these things, and anything I may not be aware of that blocks or limits me, I now release, to bother me no more.

Loosely fold the paper lengthwise, and light one end of it from the black candle. Place it in the burning dish. Use the knife to lift the paper so it is completely consumed.

Now light the white candle, and pick up the list of your goals and desires. Read it over, thinking about each item, then fold it as you did the other list, and light it from the white candle. Say:

As this paper burns, these things I desire are manifested into my life. I ask for these, I accept these, I receive these, and I give thanks for these. By my will, this is so.

Now take time to simply enjoy the beauty of the altar and the soft light of the candles. Enjoy the energy within the circle and within yourself.

To close the ritual, release and give thanks in reverse, thanking and releasing the God first. Say:

Divine Father God, Son, Brother, and Consort of the Goddess, thank you for your presence with me here tonight. With love and with respect, I do say hail and farewell.

Take a moment to feel his energy leave. Then extinguish the God candle.

Now say:

O Divine Mother Goddess, source and sustenance of all that is, radiant one of the full moon, I thank you for your presence here with me tonight. With love and with respect, I do say hail and farewell.

Take a moment to feel her energy leave. Then extinguish the Goddess candle.

Pull the energy of your sacred space back inside of yourself, and see it returning to the source from where it came.

Release excess energy the same way you release tension and stress. Then ground and shield.

Extinguish all candles except the white working candles. Turn on the lights, and extinguish the working candles. Save the candles for future use. Be sure to dispose of the ashes properly.

Write what you have done tonight into your Book of Shadows. Be sure to put down the date and the goals/desires you worked for. Save space to list the dates that your desires manifest. Be aware of your energy

for the next few days, and see if you notice any changes in yourself.

• • • •

List of Ritual Tools

By now, you should have most, if not all, of your tools, and all of the items needed for your altar. They are reviewed below.

- Athame
- Wand
- Chalice
- Stone or crystal
- Pentacle
- Black altar cloth
- Candles—black and white
- Candleholders
- A candlesnuffer
- Containers for water and salt
- A dish to use for offerings
- Incense
- An incense holder
- Salt
- A statue of the Goddess and of the God—you don't need these immediately, but find the statues that pull at your heart.

Cleanse, consecrate, and charge your tools at your altar in sacred space.

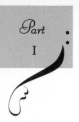

Lesson 6:
Magical Tools

What is the difference between a pentagram and a pentacle? First and most importantly, you must understand that different people will give you different answers to that question. The reason is that terms are defined differently by different groups. Consequently, the definition we are about to give, while among the most common, is far from the only definition you will find.

A pentagram is a five-pointed star. This five-pointed star may be drawn separately or inside a circle. Both forms are pentagrams, and both are widely used as such. The five-pointed star represents Spirit and magic, and has for millennia. The pentagram has its origins in ancient Egypt, where the five-pointed star was called *Tua* and carried the hieroglyphic meaning of "spirit" or "magic," while the five-pointed star within a circle was called *Tuat* and represented the Otherworld, the land of the spirits. The five-pointed star, both with and without the circle, was also used by a number of Greek and Roman groups, notably the Pythagoreans, as a symbol for spirit and magic. It has remained popular in this context right up to the present day.

A pentacle is something else altogether. While the term *pentagram* refers to a specific symbol no matter what context it is being used in, the term *pentacle* always refers to a physical object, usually made of metal, ceramic, or paper and paint. This object is used to focus energy in ritual or magic. The pentacle can be made with any metaphysical symbol, but it is originally and most commonly a pentagram. For some groups, a pentacle is always and only a pentagram, leading to the two words often being used interchangeably. Most people make little or no distinction between the two.

The pentagram is the ultimate symbol of Wicca as a religion. Its meaning as a symbol is very important to Wiccans. The five points of the star symbolize the five elements. The top point of the star is the element of Spirit, symbolizing that Spirit rules the other elements—earth (body), air (mind), water (emotions), and fire (will). The pentagram also symbolizes humanity (the star being taken as a kind of stick-figure representation of a person) being one with the universe (the circle).

The magical tools you will use are the athame, the wand, the chalice, the stone or crystal, and the pentacle. These first four tools are physical keys to qualities within yourself. The magic you seek is inside of you, and these tools, once cleansed, consecrated, charged, and worked within ritual, connect you to that magic.

The pentacle is the physical key to Spirit, Goddess and God, and the doorway between the worlds.

By using these tools in ritual, you build energy into the tools themselves and within your mind, which will alter consciousness every time you cast a magic circle.

The athame is the tool representing air and your mind. A knife cuts, thereby separating or discriminating between one thing and another. This is choice.

The athame also represents the God in some of its ritual uses.

The wand represents fire and your will. This can be your personal will, directed and focused to a specific goal, or your True Will.

The chalice represents water and emotions. To "emote" is to draw from or out of. You draw power to manifest magic from your emotions and feelings.

The chalice also represents the Goddess. The chalice and the athame are used to enact the Great Rite, or Sacred Marriage, of the Goddess and the God.

The stone or quartz crystal represents earth, manifestation, and structure. Magic draws power from the astral plane, and the physical world provides a structure for your desires to manifest.

· · · ·
Making Sacred Space

In this part of the lesson, you will learn to cleanse and consecrate ritual space and cut a boundary between the worlds. You will do this at your altar.

When you see/imagine the blue light in the exercise below, know that this energy is real. You may not be able to see or feel it at first, but know when you are doing it that you are working with actual energy. This is the same blue light you use to form the invoking/devoking pentagrams.

You will need:

- Two white working candles
- Candleholders
- An altar cloth
- A lighter or matches
- A candlesnuffer
- A container of salt
- A container of water
- Incense
- An incense burner
- Anything else you enjoy on your altar

Have your altar set up with everything you will need.

Read this exercise over once, then take your ritual bath.

Dress as you usually do for ritual.

Release, ground, and shield.

Light the working candles.

Turn out any other light in the room.

Create your inner stillness.

Take the container of salt in one hand, and with the other hand, make pulling motions from the salt. Say:

*Behold, I remove all negativity
from you, O creature of salt.*

Flick this energy toward the floor (earth), and know that it will be absorbed and transmuted by Mother Earth. Pull and flick the energy until the salt feels clean to you.

Now, still holding the container of salt, hold your hand over it, with the palm down, and imagine blue flames coming from your palm and surrounding and permeating the salt. Say:

*And I do consecrate
thee to this work.*

Set the container of salt back on the altar.

Put the container of water in one hand, and with the other, make pulling and flicking motions while saying:

*Behold, I remove all negativity
from you, O creature of water.*

Pull and flick the energy until the water feels clean to you.

Now, still holding the container of water, hold your hand over it, with the palm down, and imagine blue flames coming from your palm and surrounding and permeating the water. Say:

*And I do consecrate
thee to this work.*

Set the container of water back on the altar. Say:

*Behold, the salt is pure;
behold, the water is pure.*

Put three pinches of salt into the water, and stir with your finger. Say:

*Purity into purity, then,
and purity be blessed.*

Walk in a counterclockwise circle around your ritual space, and flick the salt water as you go, to cleanse the ritual area.

See/imagine the energy become bright and clear, with any negativity leaving the space, or dissolving.

Place the container of salt water back on the altar.

Place the incense in the incense holder and the lighter or matches on the altar. Hold the incense in one hand, and with the other, remove negativity from it with the pulling/flicking motions, and say:

*Behold, I remove all negativity
from you, O creature of air.*

Pull and flick until the energy of the incense feels clear to you.

Now, still holding the incense in your hand, place the other hand over it, palm down, and imagine blue flames coming from your palm and surrounding and permeating the incense, and say:

*And I do consecrate
thee to this work.*

Place the incense back on the altar.

Hold the lighter or matches in one hand, and with the other, remove negativity from it with the pulling, flicking motions. Say:

*Behold, I remove all negativity
from you, O creature of Fire.*

Pull and flick until the energy of the lighter or matches feels clear to you.

Now, still holding the lighter or matches in your hand, place the other hand over it, palm down, and imagine blue flames coming from your palm and surrounding and permeating the lighter or matches, and say:

*And I do consecrate
thee to this work.*

Now light the lighter or matches, pick up the incense, and say:

*Behold, the air is pure;
behold, the fire is pure.*

Light the incense, saying:

*Purity into purity, then,
and purity be blessed.*

Take the incense in a clockwise circle around the ritual area, and say:

*With this incense, I charge
and consecrate this area to
this work I do tonight.*

See/imagine the energy of the ritual area become even more bright and clear and pure.

Return to the altar, and place the incense on it. Say:

*Behold, this space is cleansed
and consecrated.*

Stand quietly at the altar for a minute. Now extend the index and middle fingers of your dominant hand. See/imagine blue fire coming from them. Start at the east, and walk clockwise in a circle, pointing the blue fire you see/imagine from your fingers at the edge of the circle you want to create. See/imagine the blue fire defining the boundary as you cut it. Say:

*Behold, I do cut apart a boundary
between the worlds, apart from
time and space, that shall focus and
contain any energy I raise herein.*

Now see/imagine the circle of blue flame extending above and below the ritual space, becoming a sphere of blue, flaming light. Let the blue flame dissolve, but know that the circle/sphere is there. Say:

Behold, this circle is now cast.

Take some time now to feel the energy of the cast circle. When you are finished, walk around the boundary of the circle counter-clockwise, with the index and middle fingers of your dominant hand extended, and feel/imagine the energy of the circle, the blue flame, returning through your fingers as you release the circle. Say:

This circle is now open.

Release excess energy.

Ground and shield.

Turn on the lights, and extinguish the working candles.

Pour the saltwater combination down the drain, thanking it for its help.

Do this exercise two more times this week. This procedure may look involved and time consuming as you read it from this lesson. Once you become familiar with it, it will be easy for you and will only take minutes.

• • • •

Psychic Communication

Psychic communication is a way of talking to people who are not physically present. Mindwalking is a kind of psychic communication, a way of talking to people who are not physically present. It is not like having an ordinary conversation with the person. You are talking to their higher self, not their conscious mind. They will not, as a rule, have any conscious knowledge of this

ever having happened, but their higher self, their soul, will have received your message. People actually do this all the time without knowing it, but here we will learn how to do it consciously.

Obviously, this technique should only be used for positive purposes. Remember that all you do comes back to you, so do only good things.

This is a good way to communicate with someone when you are not on speaking terms with them but still need to say something to them. You also can use it to heal a disagreement.

Simply sit in a comfortable position, and imagine the person sitting in front of you. Then tell them whatever it is you want to say to them. Be relaxed when you do this. Then sit for a few minutes. You will probably have a feeling of the person getting the message. The person probably won't get the exact words that you used and may not be consciously aware of receiving the message. They will receive it on an inner level, though, and it can affect the way they feel about you.

You may have been on the receiving end of this. If you have found yourself doing something you didn't want to do or had decided not to do, and wondered why, this may be the reason. Or perhaps you felt that you should call someone, only to find they were thinking of you.

On a similar note, if you find that everyone you see on a particular day reminds you of a certain person, that person may be thinking of you.

Experiment with this exercise, in a positive way only, and you will have a valuable tool for communication.

Lesson 7:
Altered States
of Consciousness

In this lesson, we will discuss how to alter your consciousness and why you would want to do so. You have altered your consciousness many times in these lessons, but now you will learn to do it deliberately.

Our consciousness is a gateway; through it, we can access many different aspects of reality, many different worlds and dimensions. Altering one's consciousness is often termed "trance," and there are many levels of trance, from light to deep. A light trance state, which people often experience when they are particularly engrossed in such activities as reading, watching television, or daydreaming, is the level that is most useful and the easiest one to work with. It is the level you use during meditation and ritual. It is the level used during divination, such as scrying, and to do pathworkings, which are guided visualizations into other dimensions.

The word "trance" sometimes scares people. They have seen "trances" in movies and know that it means a drastically altered state where your consciousness leaves your body and all sorts of weird things happen. But, of course, as with most things magical, Hollywood is not a reliable source of

realistic information. In reality, trance is a deep level of focus that shifts our consciousness. The guided visualization in the air section of this lesson is an example of this. As your skill in visualization and pathworking increases, you may find yourself in deeper levels of trance, which will allow you to achieve a deeper connection and a stronger effect from your working.

What practical value do visualizations and pathworkings have? These things work with the higher levels of your being through symbolism and deep focus of consciousness, and they can effect deep changes in your life. By using these techniques wisely and with sensible self-knowledge, you can transform your life in many positive ways.

• • • •

The Wiccan Rede

We will now take a moment to discuss morality. Wiccan ideas of right and wrong revolve around the Wiccan Rede: "And it harm none, do as you will." The Wiccan Rede is a corollary to Rabelais' famous Law of Thelema ("Do as you will"), which has been popular in ceremonial magic.

The actual sentiment of what we accept today as the Wiccan Rede has its roots in many writings throughout the centuries, including St. Augustine from the fourth century and John Stuart Mill from the nineteenth century. There is little agreement as to its true origin, and no one really knows when the Wiccan Rede was created as such. However, it is the subject of a famous poem called "The Wiccan Rede" by Adriana Porter, which was written around 1910. The Wiccan Rede is based upon the ideas of fate, or karma—meaning whatever we do, whether it be good or bad, will come back to us.

Some people believe that fate, or karma, brings our actions back to us a certain number of times—for many, the belief is that an action returns three times. However, the Correllian Tradition holds that karma brings our actions back to us as many (or as few) times as we need to learn the lessons offered by those actions. Whenever you are considering any action, you should ask yourself how you will feel when this action comes back to you; if you wouldn't feel good to be on the receiving end, you shouldn't do it.

Mindful of the Wiccan Rede, many Wiccans will include in every spell the words "with harm to none." This is a very good practice. However, you must remember that when we say "harm," we mean it in the ordinary sense of the word, as it would be used by any ordinary person, not in any exaggerated sense. "Harm" as meant by the Wiccan Rede might be summed up as "unprovoked or egregious damage."

• • • •
Guided Visualization

We will now do a guided visualization, which is a form of pathworking. To begin, be sure you will not be disturbed, then ground, center, shield, and enter your stillness.

From this relaxed, focused state, close your eyes, and imagine a spiral staircase going down. Let this staircase be wooden, stone, or whatever you like, but see/imagine it in detail. Feel the smoothness of the wood or the coolness of the stone. See what color the walls are around you. Be aware of any smells. Feel your feet on each step as you go down. As you descend, count from one to ten. Say:

One—I am going down;
Two—deeper and deeper;
Three—I am relaxed;
Four—deeper still;
Five—here I am safe
and protected;
Six—I am focused;
Seven—deeper and deeper;
Eight—I am relaxed and aware;
I will remember all that I
experience;
Nine—deeper still;
Ten—I am in my personal
Hall of Consciousness.

Your personal Hall of Consciousness is an entryway to many dimensions and levels of consciousness. See it as a long hallway with many doors on either side. These doors may all look alike or they may each be different. Each person's experience is unique to them. Each of these many doors leads somewhere, and in future visits we shall open some of them. But for now we will stay in the hallway.

What does your Hall of Consciousness look like? Is it large and spacious? Long and narrow? Are there chairs or benches between the doors? Artwork? Is the hallway bright with light or dim? All of these things are keys to the state of your consciousness. Observe all the details you can, and tell yourself that you will remember them.

When you are ready to return, start up the spiral staircase, counting down from ten to one. Again, be aware of the details. Feel your feet on the stair steps. Feel your hands on the railings, if there are any. If not, be sure to touch the walls as you go. Make this experience as clear as you can. Say:

Ten—I am going up;
Nine—I will remember all I have
experienced;
Eight—higher and higher;
Seven—I am returning to my
normal state of consciousness;

Six—higher still;
Five—and yet higher;
Four—coming back to myself;
Three—almost there;
Two—when I reach the count
of one, I will be fully awake
and present;
One—I am back in my normal
state of consciousness.

Ground, center, and shield. Stretch, then have something to eat or drink.

Write your experience in your Book of Shadows.

What you have just experienced is a real journey to a real place. It isn't in the physical world, but it is equally as real. When it is said to "imagine something," it means that you should experience it in whatever way you can. Some people never visually "see" during their journey. Many people "sense" rather than see, but their astral experiences are just as real.

Do this visualization once a day this week. Always stay in your Hall of Consciousness, but become familiar with the process. The more you do it, the easier it becomes and the more you will experience the visualization as real.

As you become familiar with the counting, it isn't necessary to say it exactly as written. It is important to feel yourself going deeper, to know that you are safe, to become more focused, and to tell yourself you will remember all that you experience. When returning, emphasize the feeling of going up and that you are returning to your normal consciousness.

• • • •

Beginning Candle Magic

We will experiment with affecting a candle flame. Ground, center, and shield. Enter your stillness. Sit facing a lit candle, and gaze at the flame in a relaxed way. Be careful to have the candle where drafts will not affect the flame. Be aware of the beauty of the candlelight, and notice if the glow around the candle increases as your attention continues. Check to see if your breathing is causing any changes. If so, move the candle as needed or be more careful with your breath. Try consciously to make the flame taller or move in a certain direction. Relax, and have fun with this. Write any results in your Book of Shadows.

• • • •

Making a Scrying Mirror

Now we will discuss how to make a magic mirror for scrying (divination), which will be used in the waning moon ritual covered in next week's lesson. You will need the following items:

- A picture frame of any shape that has a stand
- Glossy black enamel

Remove the glass from the frame, and spray paint the glass with the glossy black enamel. When it dries, put it back in the frame, with the painted side as the back side of the glass. You have now made a magic mirror. Cleanse, consecrate, and charge it, as you have done with your other tools.

• • • •

Soul Retrieval

Soul retrieval is a method of spiritual healing that can be used to clear blockages, heal unresolved issues or fears, and release pain or trauma. Soul retrieval is a very powerful technique that can be extremely transformative for a person.

The idea behind soul retrieval is that when a traumatic event occurs, it creates an energetic blockage. A small portion of the soul is caught in this blockage, bound up in the energy of this traumatic event. In addition to traumatic events, limiting belief systems, fears, and even the simple unwillingness to let go of something also can cause this kind of blockage to occur, binding part of the soul.

This is the same idea Buddhists call attachment. Soul retrieval releases the blockage and "retrieves" the part or parts of the soul that were bound by the blockage. The importance of this technique cannot be emphasized too much.

Begin by sitting in a comfortable position. Be certain you will not be disturbed.

Clear and release all excess energy.

Breathe quietly for a few minutes.

Ask Deity (Goddess and/or God) to be there with you.

Tell Deity what you want to be healed, describing this in detail. You can do this out loud or silently.

Ask Deity to heal this issue. See/imagine the healing as a shower of golden light flowing through you. Take a few minutes to experience this. See/imagine the light entering from above you and flowing through every part of your body.

Ask Deity to help you accept the healing. Imagine this as a wave of warm energy moving through you. Say:

I accept, I accept, I accept.

Continue to say this until you have the feeling of acceptance.

Ask Deity to help you integrate this healing into your being. Imagine the integration as a wave of energy flowing into your heart. Say:

I integrate the healing, I integrate the healing, I integrate the healing.

As above, continue saying this until you have the feeling of integration.

Give Deity all of the burdens and pain associated with the issue that has been healed. See them as packages, or stones, or whatever image has this meaning for you. Hold your hands out in front of you as though you were holding these packages, and physically put them into Deity's hands.

See/imagine them consumed or absorbed by purple light as Deity takes them.

Forgive every person, place, and situation that is involved with this issue that has been healed, and release all attachment to these. Forgive yourself as well for anything you blame yourself for, then forgive Deity as well. Say:

I forgive, I forgive, I forgive.

Ask Deity to help you reclaim the lost parts of your being that have been caught in the issue that has been healed. Imagine these returning to you as bits of colored light.

Now ask Deity to heal the lost parts of yourself that have been returned to you. Visualize the healing as a shower of golden light. Say:

I am healed, I am healed, I am healed.

Now ask Deity to help you accept the healing of these lost parts of yourself. Imagine this as a wave of warm energy moving through you. Say:

I accept, I accept, I accept.

Ask Deity to help you integrate the healing of the lost parts of yourself into your being. Imagine the integration as a wave of energy pouring into your heart. Say:

I integrate, I integrate, I integrate.

Finally, give thanks to Deity for the healing you have received. Then ground and shield.

Do not do this more often than twice a week. The effects can be more powerful if you have someone read this exercise for you. You do not need to know exactly what needs healing. If bringing money into your life is difficult or you have problems with relationships, for instance, ask to be healed of whatever is blocking you from the things you want.

Most issues can be healed by doing this once. However, some issues that may be especially deep-rooted may need two or more soul retrievals. In these cases, the healing is working with one layer at a time.

Lesson 8:
Waning Moon Ritual

In this lesson, you will cast a magic circle, consecrate the altar, do a waning moon ritual, scry with your magic mirror, and begin learning to communicate with the so-called dead.

The earth, air, fire, water, and spirit sections are combined for this lesson.

The waning moon ritual should be done within three or four days of the new moon, but definitely before it. Once the new moon has occurred, the waning phase is over and the waxing has begun.

By now, you should have all of your tools, and they are cleansed, consecrated, and charged. These tools are the athame, the wand, the chalice, the stone or crystal, and the pentacle. It is helpful to have a small table or other surface within reach of your altar to hold your tools and other required items until you place them onto the altar. You will erect your altar a step at a time, and each step builds important energy and focus.

You will erect your altar the same way every time. On this altar, you will use a black candle to represent the Goddess and a white candle to represent the God. You may also have statues of the Goddess and the God, but the candles are used as you invoke and devoke them.

Have the following items ready for the waning moon ritual:

- Table for altar, set in the center of the ritual space
- Athame
- Wand
- Chalice
- Stone or crystal
- Pentacle
- Black altar cloth
- A black candle for the Goddess
- A white candle for the God
- Two black candles and one white votive candle for scrying
- Two white working candles
- Candleholders
- A candlesnuffer
- Containers for water and salt
- Incense
- An incense holder
- Salt
- Water
- Statues of the Goddess and the God, if you have them
- The waning moon ritual
- A chair to sit in while filling yourself with the energy of the waning moon and while you scry with your magic mirror

Have the table for the altar set up, with everything you will need within reach.

· · · ·

Altar Consecration

Read this exercise over once, then take your ritual bath.

Dress as you usually do for ritual.

Release, ground, and shield.

Create your inner stillness.

Place the altar cloth on the altar.

Place the two white working candles on the altar, light them, and turn out all other lights.

Place the dish of salt and the container of water on the altar. Take the container of salt in one hand, and with the other hand, make pulling motions from the salt, and say:

Behold, I remove all negativity
from you, O creature of salt.

Flick this energy toward the floor (earth), and know that it will be absorbed and transmuted by Mother Earth. Pull and flick the energy until the salt feels clean to you.

Now, still holding the container of salt, hold your hand over it, with the palm down, and imagine blue flames coming from your palm and surrounding and permeating the salt. Say:

And I do consecrate
thee to this work.

Set the container of salt back on the altar.

Put the container of water in one hand, and with the other hand, make pulling and flicking motions while saying:

Behold, I remove all negativity
from you, O creature of water.

Pull and flick the energy until the water feels clean to you.

Now, still holding the container of water, hold your hand over it, with the palm down, and imagine blue flames coming from your palm and surrounding and permeating the water. Say:

And I do consecrate
thee to this work.

Set the container of water back on the altar. Say:

Behold, the salt is pure;
behold, the water is pure.

Put three pinches of salt into the water, and stir with your finger. Say:

Purity into purity, then,
and purity be blessed.

Walk in a counterclockwise circle around your ritual space, and flick the salt water as you go, to cleanse the ritual area. Say:

With earth and water, I
cleanse and remove all
negativity from this space.

See/imagine the energy become bright and clear, with any negativity leaving the space, or dissolving.

Place the container of salt water back on the altar.

Place the incense, the incense burner, and the matches or lighter on the altar.

Place the incense in the incense holder. Hold the incense in one hand, and with the other, remove negativity from it with the pulling, flicking motions, and say:

> *Behold, I remove all negativity*
> *from you, O creature of air.*

Pull and flick until the energy of the incense feels clear to you.

Now, still holding the incense in your hand, place the other hand over it, palm down, and imagine blue flames coming from your palm and surrounding and permeating the incense, and say:

> *And I do consecrate*
> *thee to this work.*

Place the incense back on the altar.

Hold the lighter or matches in one hand, and with the other, remove negativity from it with the pulling, flicking motions. Say:

> *Behold, I remove all negativity*
> *from you, O creature of fire.*

Pull and flick until the energy of the lighter or matches feels clear to you.

Now, still holding the lighter or matches in your hand, place the other hand over it, palm down, and imagine blue flames coming from your palm and surrounding and permeating the lighter or matches, and say:

> *And I do consecrate*
> *thee to this work.*

Now light the lighter or matches, pick up the incense, and say:

> *Behold, the air is pure;*
> *behold, the fire is pure.*

Light the incense, saying:

> *Purity into purity, then,*
> *and purity be blessed.*

Take the incense in a clockwise circle around the ritual area, and say:

> *With fire and air, I charge*
> *and consecrate this area to*
> *this work I do tonight.*

See/imagine the energy of the ritual area become even more bright and clear and pure.

Return to the altar and place the incense on it. Say:

> *Behold, this space is cleansed*
> *and consecrated.*

Stand quietly at the altar for a minute. Put the black candle for the Goddess into its candleholder and place it on the left side of the altar, to the back and slightly toward the center of the altar. Put the white candle for the God into its candle-holder and place it on the right side of the altar, to the back and slightly toward the center of the altar. If you have statues of the Goddess and the God, place them in front of their respective candles.

Pick up the athame, and hold it to your heart for a moment. Say:

*May my mind and my intentions
for this ritual be clear.*

Then place it on the east side of the altar.

Pick up the wand, holding it to your heart, and say:

*May my will be focused for this rite
and be in line with my Higher Self.*

Then place the wand in the south of the altar.

Pick up the chalice, hold it to your heart, and say:

*May my heart be fully present
and aligned with the purpose for
this rite. May all that I do here
tonight come from my heart.*

Place the chalice on the left side of the altar.

Now pick up the stone or crystal cluster, hold it to your heart, and say:

*May the energies of the
north and the earth manifest
my will here tonight.*

Place the stone or crystal cluster in the north.

Place the pentacle in the center of the altar. Place your hands on it, and be aware that the pentacle is the spiritual battery of the altar and the doorway between the worlds. Say:

*I stand at the doorway to all
worlds and all dimensions. I am
at the center of all time and all
space. I am one with all things,
and all things are one with me.*

Take the athame in your dominant hand, go to the east, imagine the blue flame flowing from it, and point the flame at the edge of the circle you want to create. Walk clockwise around the circle, and see/imagine the blue fire defining the boundary as you cut it. Say:

*Behold, I do cut apart a boundary
between the worlds, apart from
time and space, that shall focus and
contain all energy I raise herein.*

Now see/imagine the circle of blue flame extending above and below the ritual space,

becoming a sphere of blue, flaming light. Let the blue flame dissolve, but know that the circle/sphere is there. Say:

Behold, this circle is now cast.

Take your wand, and go to the east. Point your wand at the east, and draw up a pillar of white light from the floor. Imagine this pillar as tall and strong, glowing vibrantly with energy. Now say something like:

*Power of the east, element of
air, with love and with respect,
I invoke and invite you to be
with me in this, my circle. Lend
your guidance, your wisdom,
and your power to this work I
do tonight. Hail and welcome.*

Take a moment to feel the presence of the power of east as it enters the circle.

Then go to the south. Point the wand at the south, and draw up a pillar of white light from the floor. Imagine this pillar as tall and strong, glowing vibrantly with energy. Now say something like:

*Power of the south, element of
fire, with love and with respect,
I invoke and invite you to be
with me in this, my circle. Lend
your guidance, your wisdom,
and your power to this work I
do tonight. Hail and welcome.*

Take a moment to feel the presence of the power of the south as it enters the circle.

Go to the west. Point the wand at the west, and draw up a pillar of white light from the floor. Imagine this pillar as tall and strong, glowing vibrantly with energy. Now say something like:

*Power of the west, element of
water, with love and with respect,
I invoke and invite you to be
with me in this, my circle. Lend
your guidance, your wisdom,
and your power to this work I
do tonight. Hail and welcome.*

Take a moment to feel the presence of the power of the west as it enters the circle.

Go to the north. Point the wand at the north and draw up a pillar of white light from the floor. Imagine this pillar as tall and strong, glowing vibrantly with energy. Now say something like:

*Power of the north, element of
earth, with love and with respect,
I invoke and invite you to be
with me in this, my circle. Lend
your guidance, your wisdom,
and your power to this work I
do tonight. Hail and welcome.*

Take a moment to feel the presence of the power of the north as it enters the circle.

Return to the altar.
State your purpose for this ritual:

*I am here tonight to honor the
Goddess in her form as wise Crone
and keeper of the mysteries. I
wish to penetrate the veil between
the world of the living and the
Otherworld. Tonight I dedicate
my working/ritual altar and
scry with my magic mirror.*

Pick up the lighter or matches, and invoke the Goddess:

*I invoke and invite you, O wise
Crone of the Waning Moon,
Goddess of the Dead and of the
Otherworld, Queen of Dreams,
and Mother of Mysteries. I ask
that you share your wisdom and
your magic with me this night.
I call upon you as the patron of
Witchcraft, you who hold the
secrets of life and death within
your being. Fill my heart with your
wisdom. Come forth and be here
now, and I do say hail and welcome.*

Light the black Goddess candle. Take a few minutes to feel her presence. Be aware of the way her energy is different from the Maiden and the Mother.

Still holding the lighter or the matches, turn to the God candle, and say:

*I invoke and invite you, O
Horned One, guardian of
the gate between the worlds,
patron of shamans, priests, and
sorcerers, of magical and spiritual
knowledge, lord of dreams and
visions, come forth and be here
now. I do say hail and welcome.*

Light the white God candle. Take a few minutes to feel his presence. Be aware of his power and his wisdom. Be aware of the way his energy is different from the God as Lover and as Father.

Now you will dedicate your altar. Place your hands on the altar. Imagine it filled and surrounded with the yellow/white light that absorbs and transmutes all negativity. When the altar feels cleansed, see/imagine it filled and surrounded with the clear, vibrant, purple light of the highest spirituality. Say:

*I dedicate this altar to the Goddess
and the God. I swear that I will
use it always for the highest
good, and with harm to none.
As I have sworn, so mote it be.*

Now you will draw the energy of the waning moon inside yourself. Sit in your chair in front of the altar. Close your eyes,

and imagine yourself in a clearing in a dark forest. Far above, you see the thin, silver crescent of the waning moon. You feel the earth beneath you and are aware of the smell of decaying leaves and grass beneath you. You know that the decaying leaves and grass will become compost for new growth in the forest.

Feel the energy of the waning moon fill you with its potent darkness. Bask for a while in the quiet of this darkness. Think of the things within your self and your life that need to be released at this time to make way for new growth. Feel them fall away from you and fall to the forest floor to become compost for your new growth.

Feel the wisdom of the Crone and the Horned God fill you in this darkness. They may have something to tell you; listen for this. Feel the magic of this time penetrate and fill every atom of your being. Thank the Crone, the Horned God, and the waning moon for this time spent together. Open your eyes.

Stand your magic mirror in front of you on the altar. Place a black candle on either side of the mirror and the white votive candle in front of it.

Light the black candles. Sit and gaze gently into the mirror. Say:

I call upon my inner vision
to show me what I need
to know at this time.

Light the white votive candle.

Continue to gaze into the mirror for five or ten minutes. Keep your eyes on the mirror. It is okay to blink when needed. Relax, and release expectations. It may take several times using the mirror to see anything within it. You may see something tonight. You are building neural pathways from your inner self to your conscious mind. The mirror is the screen on which the pictures will show when they come. When you are finished, extinguish the candles you lit for the mirror. Wrap the mirror and place it back into your magical toolbox.

Once your inner vision is developed with the magic mirror, you can ask specific questions of it. You can use it without being in ritual space, although at least having sacred space is recommended for it. The waning moon ritual is an excellent place to use it on a regular basis.

Sit and enjoy the beauty of the altar for a few minutes. When you are ready, it is time to close the circle.

Stand up and face the God candle. Say something like:

I thank you, Horned One, guardian
of the gate between the worlds,
for your presence and your aid
this night. May there be peace
between us now and always.

With love and with respect,
I do say hail and farewell.

Extinguish the God candle. Be aware of the presence of the God leaving the circle. Turn to the Goddess candle, and say:

O Holy Crone, Goddess of the
Dead and of the Otherworld,
Queen of Dreams and Mother of
Mysteries, I thank you for your
presence and your aid this night.
May there be peace between us now
and always. With love and with
respect, I do say hail and farewell.

Extinguish the Goddess candle. Be aware of the presence of the Goddess leaving the circle.

Take the wand to the north. Take down the pillar of light, imagining it sinking down, down, into the earth. Now say something like:

Power of the north, element of
earth. Thank you for your presence
here tonight in this circle. May
there be peace between us now
and always. With love and with
respect, I do say hail and farewell.

Take a moment to feel the energies of the power of the north leave the circle.

Go to the west. Take down the pillar of light, imagining it sinking down, down, into the earth. Now say something like:

Power of the west, element of
water. Thank you for your presence
here tonight in this circle. May
there be peace between us now
and always. With love and with
respect, I do say hail and farewell.

Take a moment to feel the energies of the power of the west leave the circle.

Take the wand to the south. Take down the pillar of light, imagining it sinking down, down, into the earth. Now say something like:

Power of the south, element of
fire. Thank you for your presence
here tonight in this circle. May
there be peace between us now
and always. With love and with
respect, I do say hail and farewell.

Take a moment to feel the energies of the power of the south leave the circle.

Take the wand to the east. Take down the pillar of light, imagining it sinking down, down, into the earth. Now say something like:

Power of the east, element of
air. Thank you for your presence
here tonight in this circle. May

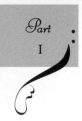

*there be peace between us now
and always. With love and with
respect, I do say hail and farewell.*

Take a moment to feel the energies of
the power of the east leave the circle.

Return the wand to the altar. Pick up
the athame, and go to the east. Point the
athame at the east boundary of the circle/
sphere, and walk counterclockwise around
the circle. See the blue flame of the circle
enter back into your athame as you walk.
Say:

This circle is open but never broken.

When you are back at the east, be certain that all the energy defining the circle/
sphere has returned to the athame. Return
the athame to the altar. Place your hands
on the pentacle, and say:

*The doorway between the
worlds is now closed.*

Release excess energy. Ground, center,
and shield.

Turn the lights back on, and extinguish
the working candles.

Write your experience of this ritual and
any insights into your Book of Shadows.

Lesson 9:
Communicating with the Dead

One of the most important things in the Wiccan religion is our belief that life is eternal; death is only a transition. We believe that the soul lives many lives, reincarnating many, many times. Between incarnations, the soul often rests in the Otherworld, often called the Summerland. However, some souls maintain close connections with the world of the living, even from the Summerland. These souls help and advise the living. Sometimes, the people they help are people they knew, such as members of their families. Other times, the soul helps people it never knew in life but to whom it has some other kind of connection—perhaps from earlier lives or through shared interests.

These souls do not do this because they cannot "let go" or cross over into the Summerland. Some souls do have that problem, becoming caught between this world and the next. However, the souls we are talking about have crossed over fully but continue to work with the living out of love and because they have wisdom to share. It is easy to communicate with those souls who stay close to us. The easiest way is to talk to them, out loud or silently, as

though they were right there with us. They will answer in return, though we may not be consciously aware of it. In future lessons, we will talk at greater length on how this kind of communication with ancestors and guides can be developed and deepened. But for now, know that it is possible, and feel free to talk to your departed loved ones—they *will* hear you.

Because we work with the spirits in this way, Wiccans have first-hand knowledge that life does extend beyond death, just as it precedes birth. This gives us a very different relationship to death and the grieving process than people who do not have this knowledge. Of course, anyone is sad when they lose a loved one, but the certainty that they are still with us in Spirit gives Wiccans a serenity in the face of death that few others religions have.

If there is a family member who has crossed to the other side whom you were very close to but have not been able to communicate with, there may be many reasons for this. If the person was ill for a long time, they may be resting or not even be aware of where they are. You can help this person (and all who are dead) by praying for their well-being, their awareness, and their continued growth on the other side. You can also light a candle on your ancestor altar with the intention of sending them love and healing. There can be a period of transition where the person who

has died becomes gradually aware of the change in their circumstances.

Deep feelings of grief and loss on your part, while natural, can be a barrier to communication. It is necessary to work through the grieving process, which cannot be hurried but must be experienced step by step. Once this has been worked through (this can take as long as three years to process, in some cases longer), you will probably be able to communicate with them.

In rare cases, the person who has died has no interest in communication but is caught up in their life on the other side. This must be respected, but love and prayers sent to them are still helpful.

A good way to build strong connections and communication with the dead is to have an ancestor altar. This can be a very simple altar where you place the names and pictures of family members who have died. You can include ancestors who died before you were born, thus honoring your lineage. Some of your guides (whether you are aware of them or not) may be these very ancestors. You can also include candles and incense. Having an offering dish to place rice, sugar, cornmeal, or some other food to "feed" the ancestors is an option. This is a way of offering them energy. You can place anything else on this altar that you want.

Try to spend a few minutes each day at this altar. Light incense and candles. Talk to your ancestors as though they are there with you. If you have problems or concerns, you can discuss these. You can share your happiness with them. Mostly this is quality time, enjoying the presence of the ones you love who have died.

When you are finished, thank them for this time together, and give them your blessings. Extinguish the candle/s and the incense. Go about your day renewed and refreshed by this companionship.

· · · ·

Starting a Dream Journal

In this lesson, we will begin the discussion of understanding your dreams. In subsequent lessons, we will build on what you have learned previously. Understanding your dreams can give you greater insight into yourself. To begin this process, you will need to start a dream journal.

For beginning purposes, do not worry about what your dreams might mean beyond asking yourself if the dream might have a literal meaning. An example of this could be dreaming of meeting a friend you haven't seen for a long time. If you do meet them within a short time after dreaming about it, the dream was literal. Dreams are an important part of spiritual growth and development. We will talk about dreams more in future lessons, but for now, just record them, and reread them once a week.

Be especially aware of dreams that come close to a sabbat, as they may contain spiritual guidance and information.

A simple technique to aid you in remembering your dreams is to repeat to yourself before bedtime that you want to remember. Keep pen and paper nearby for writing what you remember when awake. You will forget your dreams quickly otherwise. Be sure to date them. You can also record what phase the moon is in at the time of the dream. You may find you have certain kinds of dreams when the moon is in a particular phase.

Lesson 10:
Spells

In this lesson, we are going to talk about spells. Spells are among the most well-known aspects of magic, but most people have a very mistaken idea of what a spell really is. The word *spell* means "to speak," and in its simplest form, a spell is nothing more than declaring one's magical intent that a certain thing shall happen and focusing on manifesting it into physical reality. For example, if you are looking for a job, you could simply say: "The job I want is mine now, for the good of all and with harm to none."

Often, spells involve a variety of physical props, which are used to help focus a person's magical ability toward the given goal. These physical props operate on a symbolic level, bypassing the conscious mind to appeal directly to the Higher Self. Some people have described spells as "prayers with props," which is a very handy way of summing it up, but it is also important to remember that these physical props are not necessary to the process, merely helpful.

When we do a spell, we really are offering a kind of prayer: we are asking Deity and our own Higher Self to bring about certain conditions. People who do not understand the ideas behind spellwork sometimes think that it involves trying to go against the will of Deity, but this is not so. Rather, in spellwork, we are trying to use all available tools to align ourselves with the will of Deity and to be an active partner in that will, helping to create our lives rather than merely passively accepting what comes. We believe that Deity wants us to take responsibility for our own lives and play an active role in their creation. We already play this role unconsciously—we create our own reality every day of our lives on a spiritual level. Magic is simply the process of doing this consciously, and spells are merely a technique to help in that.

We do spells for many reasons. Often, spells are meant to draw certain things into our lives: prosperity, healing, love, a new job, etc. Other times, spells are intended to help us release things we have outgrown or do not want in our lives. Sometimes we do spellwork to protect ourselves or our loved ones. However, in such matters we must always be mindful of the Wiccan Rede—spells should be used to help create good things in our lives, never bad things, and above all one should never use spellwork in any way that will harm another person.

The classic example of this is the love spell. It is perfectly fine to do a spell to draw love into your life. It is completely wrong to do a spell intended to make a specific person fall in love with you.

Do spells always work? Of course not. If spells always worked, most Wiccans would have won the lotto by now. There are several reasons why a spell may not work. Most often, a spell fails because the person has mixed feelings about it; either they are not sure they really want it or consciously they may really want it but subconsciously they believe that they cannot or perhaps should not have it. Here is a simple technique for dealing with this problem if it arises.

Do a paper-burning spell to determine your True Will about what you have asked for in the failed spell. Within a few days, the answer should come to you—perhaps in a dream, by some kind of sign, or as a sudden realization. You may be surprised by what it is. For example, say you did a spell to bring love into your life, with no result. By seeking your True Will, you may discover that your feelings about love are not what you had thought. You may have had negative experiences in the past that have made you unconsciously unwilling to accept a love relationship, even though your conscious mind desires one. This kind of "crossed wire" can block the success of your spell. How do you "uncross the wires"? In situations like this, you should do soul retrieval (see lesson 7) to heal these issues and any blockages involved with them.

In this lesson, we will focus on the simplest form of spellwork: gemstones.

· · · ·

Magical Properties of Stones

One of the easiest spells you could ever ask for is simply to carry a gemstone with you, so that its magical qualities will aid you in a given area of your life. All stones have special qualities, and carrying them, wearing them, or otherwise using them can help to bring these qualities into your life. The energy of the stone will automatically help to attune you to its special qualities, and thus draw these into your life. Say, for example, you wish to improve your communication skills. Tiger's-eye is a stone with the special quality of promoting good communications and improving interactions with others. Carry a tiger's-eye in your pocket, or wear a tiger's-eye ring, or have one on your altar or keep one on your night stand while you sleep. The special energy of the stone will help you with your goal of improving your communication skill.

Below is a list of the special properties attributed to a wide variety of common stones:

Amethyst: Protects against psychic attack, is calming, relieves stress, aids in meditation and spirituality

Bloodstone: Healing, increases courage, creativity, insight

Carnelian: Physical health and vitality, personal power

Garnet: Enhances awareness and manifestation, creativity, attracts loyal love, money, protection

Moonstone: Psychic development, facilitates change, insight, enhances perception and aids in decision making, creativity, protection when traveling, rejuvenation of the body, and connects the physical, emotional, and intellectual bodies

Quartz crystal: Amplifies energy, can be programmed to direct energy for specific purposes—some quartz crystals are record keepers or can amplify body energy and thoughts

Ruby: Wealth, optimism, manifestation, protection

Eventually you may end up with many stones. Stones like attention; they want to be held and admired. Once a month, you should cleanse your stones in a dish of water, dry them with a soft cloth, and admire their beauty.

All stones have energy—river rocks, found stones, pebbles, etc. It is good to experiment with these stones, too. Collect a variety of found stones, of different sizes and composition, being sure to ask their permission before you take them. Hold a stone in your hand, first in your dominant hand for a few minutes, then in your other hand. Some stones radiate energy outward, others seem to absorb it. Test each stone to see which it is, and put them into two piles. If you choose, you can put the stones that radiate energy into a basket or dish and place them in a room or area where extra energy would be helpful. The ones that absorb energy can be put in areas where you want to relax and de-stress, such as under your bed or in your meditation area. Try holding one stone for an extended period of time—while you are reading, for instance—and see what additional energy you can pick up.

• • • •

Water Magic

Here we will offer a simple form of water magic that is important for many uses: lustral water.

The term *lustral* comes from the Latin *Lux*, or "light." Lustral water is water that has been blessed by light and that has been infused with the qualities of that light. Lustral water is most commonly blessed with moonlight or with sunlight.

Here we will be discussing lustral water blessed by the moon.

Lustral water can be used in spells to cleanse, consecrate, and charge items to be used, such as candles, stones, etc.

Lustral/Moon Water

This form of lustral water is also called moon water. This water should be in a clear glass container that has been exposed to the light of the full moon for three nights.

To create this kind of lustral water, you will need:

- A fragrant anointing oil, preferably floral, that you resonate with (rose is good, also honeysuckle, jasmine, or whatever flower you feel drawn to)
- Water—spring water if possible, but any clean water will do
- A pinch of salt, preferably sea salt
- A container made of clear glass (this can be a Mason jar)
- A decorative glass jar or bottle in which to store the lustral water

Be sure the glass container and the jar or bottle are clean. On the night before the moon is full, pour the water into the clear glass container, add the pinch of salt and a few drops of the oil, cover it, and set it outside or on a windowsill where it will be bathed in the light of the full moon. In the morning, remove it and store in a cool, dark place.

Set out the jar of water where it will be bathed in the moonlight for three successive nights. By the third night, the water will have absorbed the energies of the moonlight and can be considered charged by them. It is now lustral water.

Pour the lustral water into the decorative jar or bottle in which it will be stored.

Now consecrate and charge it, either as part of a ritual or in sacred space.

Some people make lustral water in this way when they know that the moon is in certain astrological signs, believing that the energy of the given zodiacal sign as well as of the full moon itself will be absorbed by the water.

. . . .

You now know how to do new moon, full moon, and waning moon rituals. You should try to do these esbats every month. This will connect you more deeply to the energy of the moon and increase your psychic abilities. It will also deepen your connection to the Goddess and the God. It will also make you familiar with circle casting and closing. In future rituals, this will not be included but will begin with the circle casting and the altar setup. If you wish, you may place real or artificial flowers of the appropriate color on the altar for the esbats—red for the Maiden, white for the Mother, and black for the Crone, if you can find black flowers to use.

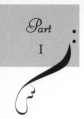

Lesson 11:
Correspondences

Because everything is energy, the correspondences used for spellwork are literal. So when it is stated that "red is the color of Mars, its day is Tuesday, its attributes are passion, aggressiveness, vitality, and the life force," this is true, because all these things vibrate at the same frequency. Every correspondence to a goal adds its energy, what the Native Americans call its "medicine," to the force of the spell.

You may wonder why anger and war are not listed under the attributes for Mars, as is commonly done. This is because we are concentrating on the positive qualities of Mars. Mars is essentially the life force, which in its positive form expresses as passion, positive aggressiveness, and vitality. It is when the life force is blocked or suppressed that it manifests as anger, negative aggressiveness, and war.

The timing of a spell can add to its effectiveness. The energies of the day of the week and the phase of the moon are currents that work with a spell or against it. Below are listed these energies and the spells that work best within them:

Monday: Ruled by the moon. Do spells that involve the element of water, psychic goals, and anything to do with emotions, dreams, home and family, astral travel, and healing.
COLOR: white or silver

Tuesday: Ruled by Mars. Do spells that involve the element of fire, passion, enthusiasm, courage, and energy.
COLOR: red

Wednesday: Ruled by Mercury. Good for spells that involve communication, knowledge, the mind, the element of air, and creativity. Clear focus and intention are important here. One of Mercury's aspects is the trickster. Don't leave room for unexpected consequences.
COLOR: yellow

Thursday: Ruled by Jupiter. For spells involving business, growth, success, expansion, good luck, and generosity.
COLOR: purple or royal blue

Friday: Ruled by Venus. Do spells that involve beauty, love, pleasure, passion, and money.
COLOR: green or pink

Saturday: Ruled by Saturn. Good for spells that involve the element of earth, banishment, protection, release, removing obstacles, binding, manifestation, and resolving issues. Saturn is the planet that brings

unfinished issues and business to our attention so we can deal with them.
COLOR: black

Sunday: Ruled by the sun. A day for spells that involve happiness, joy, well-being, prosperity, success, and abundance.
COLOR: gold

The phases of the moon important to spells are the new moon, the waxing/full moon, and the waning/dark moon.

New moon: Spells that involve beginnings, creativity, healing, independence, and animals. This is the time of the Maiden.

Waxing/full moon: Spells that involve spiritual learning and growth, psychic development, abundance, love, home and family. This is the time of the Mother.

Waning/dark moon: Spells to release, remove, bind, protect, and banish. This is the time of the Crone.

One last note: if you really need to do a spell and the timing is wrong, before you do it, say: "May all conditions be right for this working." Say it firmly and with the belief that it is so.

· · · ·
Color Correspondences

Below are the color correspondences that can aid in spells. Using candles in these colors helps to power your spell.

Pink: romantic love, affection, compassion, emotional healing, nurturing

Deep pink: deeply committed love

Green: prosperity, fertility, healing, Earth Mother, growth

Red: passion, vitality, life force, strength, courage, career goals, survival

Blue: healing, peace, communication, creativity

Orange: creativity—a person who likes orange is usually friendly and outgoing

Yellow: intellect, happiness, success, memory

Purple: spirituality, psychic ability, occult knowledge

White: all-inclusive, innocence, manifestation, the Goddess, purity

Silver: intuition, psychic ability, the Goddess, astral energies, receptive

Gold: money, the God, success, attracts wealth

Brown: the body, earth, sensuality, animals, manifestation

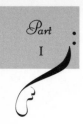

Black: banishing, magic, mystery, psychic, wisdom, guidance, protection

• • • •

Spoken Spells

Spoken spells are exactly that: spoken. These spells work best for people who love words and poetry, people with a lot of air in their personality. These people do well with prewritten spells if the spell resonates within them.

This can be a favored method for those who have learned how they create their reality. When you do a simple spoken spell, you phrase it in the present moment: " I have the money I want now," not " I will receive the money I want." You believe it when you say it, then you release it to the universe to become a reality in your life.

This can be combined with simple candle magic. You would say this while you light a green candle, and end by saying: "As this candle burns, so my desire comes to me."

An example of a spoken spell combined with candle magic is the following love spell. For this, you need three candles: one pink, one deep pink, and one red. The pink candle is for romantic love, the deep pink one is for deeply committed love, and the red one is to add passion to the relationship.

Light the pink candle, and as you do so, speak the following, saying it with intent and from your heart:

O Spirit, send to me who's best
To kindle love within my breast
I do not know who it will be
But let it be one right for me.

Now go on to the deep pink candle. Light it, and say the following:

O Spirit, let our love be true,
Committed, deep, and lasting too;
A love to trust and safely hold,
A love to treasure and enfold.

Now go to the red candle, and light it. Say:

O Spirit, let this love inspire
Lasting passion and desire
That in each other's arms we will
Find that which our hearts fulfill.

Now focus on all three candles. Say:

Even as these candles burn,
may love come to my life—the
perfect love for me at this
time in my life. With harm
toward none, may it be so!

Let the candles burn down completely. Mini candles are great for spells, as they burn down more quickly.

Candle Magic

Choose a specific goal to manifest. Check the days of the week on pages 64–65, and see which day is best for the goal of your spell. Do the spell on that day.

Check the list of color correspondences on page 65, and choose the color of candle that is best suited to your purpose.

More elaborate candle magic involves "dressing" the candle. This is done by rubbing it with a fragrant anointing oil to either draw something toward you, such as health, love, etc., or to repel something, such as banishing gossip or other negativity. To draw something toward you, apply the oil from each end to the center of the candle. Think intensely about your goal while you are doing this, and see your goal as accomplished.

For spells that repel or banish, apply the oil from the center of the candle to each end, again thinking intensely about your goal and seeing it as accomplished.

You only need a little oil for this. Too much creates a danger of starting a fire.

Write a statement or simple poem that states your desire as accomplished.

On the day for your spell, assemble all the items you will need, and decide whether you will do this as a paper-burning spell or as a candle-burning spell.

Sit or stand at your altar, create sacred space, and then perform the spell. Write the spell, the purpose of the spell, and the date in your Book of Shadows. Leave room to note when and how the spell is manifested.

You can buy anointing oils from a metaphysical shop or a catalog. Such anointing oils acquire their special qualities from the herbs with which they have been made. Below are listed the properties of many herbs. Pick an oil of the herb or flower that is suited to your goal, and use it in dressing the candle.

You can also make your own infused anointing oils. Start with a small amount (one or two ounces) of carrier oil, such as sunflower, safflower, or almond, and put ½ to 1 teaspoon of the herb into the oil. Let this stand for a week in a dark, cool place, then strain the oil, and store it in sterilized, opaque bottles. Keep them in a cool, dark place, away from heat or moisture. These oils won't have the scent of the flower or herb, but they will have the magical energy, and that is the important part. By making the oil yourself, you add your personal energy to the oil and thus to the spell.

. . . .

Magical Correspondences of Common Herbs and Spices

Acacia: protection, clairvoyance

African violet: spirituality, protection

Alfalfa: prosperity, anti-hunger, money

Allspice: money, luck, healing

Almond: prosperity, wisdom, money

Aloe: protection, luck

Amaranth: protection, healing a broken heart

Anemone: healing

Angelica: protection, exorcism

Anise seeds: protection, purification

Apples: healing, love

Apricot: love

Ash: protection

Avocado: love, lust, beauty

Balm of Gilead: protection, intellect, manifestation

Banana: fertility, prosperity

Basil: love, wealth, protection, purification, exorcism

Bay leaf: wisdom, protection, psychic powers, clairvoyance, exorcism, purification, strength, healing

Betony: protection, purification

Birch: cleansing

Blackberry: healing, money

Broom: protection, purification, wind spells

Burdock: protection, purification

Cactus: protection

Caraway: health, lust, intellect, protection

Cardamom: love, lust

Carnation: protection, healing, energy

Catnip: cat magic

Cedar: purification, healing

Celandine: protection, escape

Celery: intellect, psychic powers, lust

Chamomile: prosperity, meditation, relaxation, induce sleep

Cinnamon: spirituality, healing, cleansing, protection, passion, success

Cinquefoil: protection, love, prosperity, healing

Clover: money, love, luck, protection, repel negativity, stop gossip

Cloves: protection, love, money, healing

Comfrey: protection in travel

Coriander: love

Cornflower: psychism

Cucumber: healing, fertility

Cumin: protection

Cyclamen: love, fertility, protection

Cypress: protection, consecration

Dandelion: psychic powers

Dill: protection, money, lust, love

Elder: purification, love

Eucalyptus: healing

Eyebright: clairvoyance

Fern: protection, love

Frankincense: protection, purification, consecration, exorcism

Gardenia: love, passion

Garlic: protection, healing, exorcism

Geranium: love, healing, protection

Ginger: money, success, power

Hawthorn: protection, good fishing

Hazel: fertility, protection, mental powers

Heather: protection, rain-making

Heliotrope: clairvoyance, healing, exorcise, prophetic dreams

Henbane: love

High John the Conqueror: prosperity

Holly: dream magic, protection, balance

Hollyhock: prosperity, protection

Honeysuckle: prosperity, clairvoyance, protection

Hops: healing

Horehound: protection

Hyacinth: protection, happiness, love

Hyssop: purification, protection

Iris: purification, wisdom

Ivy: protection, healing

Jasmine: love, money, prophetic dreams

Juniper: protection, love

Lavender: love, protection, purification

Lemon verbena: protection, love

Lilac: protection, beauty, love, exorcism

Lovage: love, purification

Mace: psychic ability, intellect

Mandrake: protection, fertility

Maple leaves: love, money, longevity

Marigold: dreams, business, legal affairs, love, clairvoyance

Marjoram: love, happiness, health, money, protection

Mastic: clairvoyance, manifestation

Meadowsweet: love

Mint: money, luck, travel

Mistletoe: protection, fertility, healing, psychism

Mugwort: protection, clairvoyance

Mullein: courage, protection, health

Mustard seed: fertility, protection, intellect

Myrrh: protection, purification

Myrtle: love, fertility

Nettle: protection, exorcism

Nutmeg: money, luck, health, faithfulness, clairvoyance

Oak: fertility, protection, longevity

Oatmeal: money, prosperity

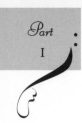

Onion: prosperity, purification, protection, exorcism, healing

Orange: love, happiness

Orris root: divination, love

Pansy: love

Patchouli: love, passion

Pennyroyal: protection, exorcism

Peony: healing, health, prosperity, communication with ancestors

Peppermint: healing, purification

Pine: fertility, purification

Plantain: healing, strength, protection

Poppy: fertility, prosperity

Primrose: protection

Rose: love, psychic power, divination, fertility, clairvoyance

Rosemary: love, power, healing, sleep, purification, intellect

Rowan: protection, healing

Rue: protection, purification, exorcism, intellect

Sage: protection, wisdom, healing, prosperity

Sassafras: money, health

Star anise: psychic ability, luck

Tea: wealth, courage, strength

Thyme: healing, psychic powers

Tulip: prosperity, love, protection

Willow: love, divination

An excellent book for further study on this and other fascinating folk uses for herbs and spices is *Cunningham's Encyclopedia of Magical Herbs* (published by Llewellyn).

• • • •
Protection Spell

A simple form of protection or banishing spell using water is to place a glass of water in a room, such as the bedroom, to protect from any negativity that may be there or come there. The water absorbs the negativity, and you simply pour it down the drain the next morning. Be sure not to drink the water. Some people place a pinch of salt into the water as added protection.

Bath Salts

Bath salts can be used as a form of water magic to add energy to a spell. When making the salts, you can use a scented oil that has the properties of the results that you want, such as honeysuckle for prosperity and green food coloring to add the energy of color.

To make bath salts, you will need:

- 3 parts Epsom salts
- 2 parts baking soda
- 1 part table salt or Borax
- Essential oil of your choice
- Food coloring

Combine the first three ingredients thoroughly. Add the food coloring in drops, sparingly, stirring well, until the desired color is reached. You can combine colors, such as red and blue to make purple. For uniformity of color, do this before you add it to the salts. Then add the essential oil, a few drops at a time, until it pleases you.

Add ¼ to ½ cup to a full bath tub, and soak in it while thinking about your goal. Feel the energy of the salts soak into your body. You should do this right before doing the actual spell so your energy will be congruent with your purpose.

In lesson 9, you began to keep a dream journal. Continue this with two additions: for each dream, write the basic feeling of the dream—happy, sad, detached, intense, etc.—and make a separate sheet in the back of your journal to keep track of the location, or setting, of each dream. The location of each dream and/or recurring symbols within the dream can be signposts that signal a change in consciousness for you, or a shift from one dimension to another. We will explore this more deeply in later lessons. For now, go back and record the locations of the dreams you have already recorded.

. . . .
Omens

Omens are messages from Spirit that come to us in symbolic forms. There are traditional meanings for omens, but anything can be an omen if you understand how to receive it. Say, for example, you are thinking about a situation in your life or something you are planning, and something you see or hear clicks for you with an "ah-ha" feeling. This can be words from a song, something you read on a bumper sticker, or something you read in a book. An omen connects you to knowledge deeper than your own, if you pay attention.

You can also use omens as a form of divination. Let's say you need to make an important decision and don't know what to do. Ask the question of the Lady or Lord, or Spirit, or the universe, and stay open to what happens. You may hear something on the radio or on television, or again, see a bumper sticker that brings the "ah-ha" feeling to you. When this happens, pay attention.

You should practice this form of divination on a regular basis. Then, when you need it for something important, it will be second nature.

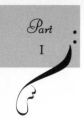

Lesson 12:
Designing a Spell

We have discussed the Wiccan belief that all things come from and are composed of Spirit, and that therefore all things are ultimately one. All things think of themselves as existing separately and independently, but in reality all are connected, all are part of the one. To us, Earth is a living being with its own consciousness, of which we are all a part. The universe, too, is a living being, of which Earth and all other planets and stars are part. All existence is one being, and this being is Spirit, or Deity. This gives us a very different relationship to the world around us.

Living the Wiccan life requires full participation in all areas of your life. Use magic to receive the gifts of life, and give back to life in whatever way is right for you to keep the flow of energy moving freely.

It is now time to design a spell for a purpose of your choice. Review the correspondences in the last lesson. Once you have your goal in mind, decide which day of the week is best and which phase of the moon is correct. Use the color of the day and/or the color best suited to your goal for the color of your candles. Add an herb or infused oil to your ritual bath mix or your bath salts to add its energy to the spell.

Choose a gemstone appropriate for your goal, and hold it during the reading of the spoken part of the spell or the reading of the poem you wrote especially for this purpose. Cleanse and consecrate the stone before you do the spell. Carry the gemstone with you until your goal manifests.

Choose an incense whose scent matches your goal, if possible. If you can't, choose one whose scent pleases you, and burn it during the ritual.

This spell will be done at your altar. Check the previous herb listing for an herb that may have correspondences to your goal. If you find one that corresponds to your goal, fix a meal that includes it to enhance the spell.

Engage every sense that you can when doing this spell, and be aware of the difference it makes in the way you feel while doing it.

Write the spell in your Book of Shadows, including the date and the way the spell manifests.

. . . .

Visiting the Hall of Consciousness

You are now going to visit your Hall of Consciousness for a specific purpose. Think about a decision you could make in your life, whether you are really considering it or not. The purpose of this visit is to see the probable outcome of choosing to do what you are considering.

As before, be sure you will not be disturbed, then ground, center, shield, and enter your stillness.

From this relaxed, focused state, close your eyes and imagine a spiral staircase going down. Let this staircase be wooden, or stone, or whatever you like, but see/imagine it in detail. Feel the smoothness of the wood or the coolness of the stone. See what color the walls are around you. Be aware of any smells. Feel your feet on each step as you go down. Count from one to ten as you descend. Say:

> *One—I am going down;*
> *Two—deeper and deeper;*
> *Three—I am relaxed;*
> *Four—deeper still;*
> *Five—here I am safe*
> *and protected;*
> *Six—I am focused;*
> *Seven—deeper and deeper;*
> *Eight—I am relaxed and aware; I*
> *will remember all that I experience;*
> *Nine—deeper still;*
> *Ten—I am in my personal*
> *Hall of Consciousness.*

Enter your Hall of Consciousness. Each time you come to the Hall of Consciousness, it may look different—always take note of how it looks, as this is a symbol of your inner state. Along either side of the hall you will see many doors. These too may be different each time. Think about the decision you are considering, and ask that you be shown the outcome. Now move through the hall, looking at the doors. One of the doors will be different from the rest—it will be set apart somehow so as to let you know it is the door you need. When you come to this door, open it and go through it. You will step into a room. On the walls of the room, you will see pictures or symbols of the outcome of making this decision. Pay close attention to these symbols and see what they tell you. Take as much time as you need here. When you are ready to return, tell yourself you will remember everything. Then return through the door back to the entryway of the Hall of Consciousness.

Now return by starting up the spiral staircase, counting from ten to one. Again, be aware of the details. Feel your feet on the stair steps. Feel your hands on the railings, if there are any. If not, be sure to touch the walls as you go. Make this experience as clear as you can. Say:

Ten—I am going up;
Nine—I will remember all I have
experienced;
Eight—higher and higher;
Seven—I am returning to my
normal state of consciousness;
Six—higher still;
Five—and yet higher;
Four—coming back to myself;
Three—almost there;
Two—when I reach the
count of one, I will be
fully awake and present;
One—I am back in my normal
state of consciousness.

Ground, center, and shield. Write your experience in your Book of Shadows.

Later you can make a similar journey to your Hall of Consciousness to see the outcome of *not* making the decision.

You can use this technique for many things. The Hall of Consciousness opens to all times and places. You can have a door for any purpose you like. You can visit the past or the future. You can visit the Goddess and the God. You can ask for a personal teacher for spiritual guidance.

Continue to experiment with this technique, and always write your results and the date in your Book of Shadows.

. . . .
Aspects of Deity

Aspecting a goddess or god is a way of working with their energy. Basically, you align yourself with the pattern of their particular energy, which then expresses itself in your life. One way of doing this is to write their symbol on a stone or a piece of paper, and place this on your altar.

You can do this in ritual, and call upon the form of the goddess or god who embodies the qualities you want to develop or experience. Ask the deity of your choice to share his/her energy with you for this purpose. Stand with your arms raised, palms up, and feel the energy of the deity fill you. Be open to any message, guidance, or requirement that may be made of you for sharing their energy. Thank the goddess or god for sharing with you. Then stay aware of the way this energy manifests in your life. Research the deity you choose, noting all of their attributes. Aphrodite, for instance, is a goddess of love and beauty. She is also very sexual in nature, open to many partners. Unless this is the energy you want, be prepared to channel the energy in other ways.

Only work with one form of Deity at a time, and as always, write what you do and the results in your Book of Shadows.

Connecting with
the Goddess

It is now time to add a red candle to your altar. This is for the eternal flame, the flame of the Goddess that is at the center and the heart of everything. This is the flame of divinity that burns in your heart. This same flame burns within the center of the earth and the sun, and is at the heart of every star. The Greek goddess Hestia personified this divine fire, as did the Roman goddess Vesta. The Celtic goddess Brigid also represents this divine fire. The Greeks and the Romans honored this energy at a hearth altar. This was placed in the energetic center, or heart, of the home. This is what the red candle represents on your altar.

Light this candle every day, and think about this fire at the heart of creation. Feel it burning inside of you, and then feel it burning at the heart of all that is. Now consider your home as a sacred altar that shelters this flame. Consider your home as the shelter, the sanctuary, and the divine altar of this sacred flame. Carry the awareness of this with you as you go through your day.

Part I Review

This is the last lesson of Part I of *Living the Wiccan Life*. Lesson 13 begins Part II. Before continuing to Part II, reread the previous lessons. Read your Book of Shadows, and see how far you have come in your understanding of Wicca. Think about the ways you have grown and changed, and enter these into your Book of Shadows.

Part

II

Lesson 13:
Increasing Psychic Ability

If you have been doing the work in these lessons, you should have experienced an increase in your psychic ability. Everyone is psychic, some people naturally more than others. Your psychic, or sixth, sense is your inner, or spiritual, sense.

There are different expressions of psychic ability, also called extra-sensory perception or ESP. Precognition is knowing something before it happens. Telepathy is mental communication, both sending and receiving. Psychometry is holding an object and picking up information about its present or past owners. Clairaudience is hearing a message in your mind. Clairvoyance is "clear seeing"—knowing something you couldn't with the five physical senses. Many people experience ESP in dreams. This includes precognition, astral projection from the dream state, past-life memories, time travel during astral

projection, and receiving needed guidance and information. You can ask for guidance or information from dreams by asking for this as you go to sleep. It may take two or three nights of doing this to receive an answer, but it works. There are other forms of psychic experience, but they are all expressions of the same energy.

Everyone has what can be called a psychic profile—the ways their psychic ability expresses itself most easily.

Take a few days to list the ways you are psychic. Write them down as you remember them. This list will show you where your psychic strengths are and the areas you can improve if you choose to.

If you feel that you are totally non-psychic, be patient; continue doing ritual and altar work, meditate every day (this is very helpful), continue to scry with your magic mirror, and consider the suggestions given here.

When you get a feeling that you should or should not do something, such as check if you left a stove burner on, lock the door, or take a different route to work, always listen to it. You won't always be right, but the fact that you pay attention to these feelings is a signal to your inner self that you are taking your intuition seriously. The more you act on these feelings, the more accurate they will become.

Every night before sleep, mentally review the events of the day, working backward from night to morning. If there are things you wish you had done differently, imagine in detail what you should have done, and let it go. Done consistently, this simple exercise has powerful effects.

Be consistent in your efforts to develop, but don't try too hard. Trying too hard will shut your abilities down.

Don't use ESP as a substitute for making your own decisions. Giving up responsibility for your life will close your ability down.

• • • •

Setting Boundaries

We have discussed the Wiccan Rede: "And it harm none, do as you will." The Rede arises from the belief that what we do comes back to us, that what goes around comes around—therefore, we must be mindful of what we put out because in time it will come back. Because of the Wiccan Rede, we try hard to do only good things. However, this does not mean that we must be doormats for other people. It does mean that when other people hurt or threaten us, we protect ourselves rather than trying to harm them. We do this with warding (setting magical boundaries), protection, and binding spells, whose purpose is to stop negative people or energy from harming us and our loved ones and to keep our lives running smoothly. This is done in a positive way that prevents others from harming us. We do not try to influence, control, or manipulate others; we simply defend our own space. If you are consistent in warding and protection spells, you will rarely need to use a binding spell.

A simple form of warding spell that you can use for your home is to place large stones, charged for protection, in each direction at the boundary of your yard or property. At the entrance or sidewalk to your property, place a stone on each side at the boundary. If you live in an apartment, place the stones inside, one in each direction. To charge a stone for warding (shielding and protecting), cleanse and then consecrate it by placing both hands on it and seeing it filled with the intense purple light of spirituality. Say:

I charge this stone to protect this property, guarding it from all harm. By my will, this is so.

Ask for the permission of the stone before using it.

A binding spell to prevent someone from harming you in any way requires the person's name to be written on a piece of paper and an empty container, such as a prescription or vitamin bottle. Put the paper with the person's name on it in the bottle, fill the bottle with water, hold it, and say something like:

This person is bound from harming me in any way. May their life be blessed in all other ways. So mote it be.

Put the bottle in the freezer. You have literally put them on ice. Keep the bottle in the freezer as long as necessary.

To do the same thing inside of your house or apartment, place a cleansed, consecrated, and charged piece of obsidian or quartz crystal in each corner.

. . . .

Banishing Negativity

Banishing negativity or removing stagnant energy from a room or building can be easily done by going counterclockwise around each room with a bell, ringing it as you go. Then ring the bell three times in the center of each room. Sound affects energy, and this kind of action breaks up negative energy patterns and cleanses them. Drumming is also used for this purpose and can be done in the same way. Another thing you can do is hang wind chimes near your outer door to break up and release any negative energy that may try to enter in.

. . . .

Improving Psychic Ability

Here, you will be focusing on your ability to concentrate, which will in turn improve your psychic abilities.

For your first exercise, take an object—a pencil, a glass, or a single flower—and keep your attention focused on it for as long as you can. If your mind wanders, and it will, bring it gently back to the object. Do this for a full minute at first, then increase your time each day until you can concentrate for five minutes. Be patient with yourself. This may take months to achieve.

You may find that doing these exercises may lead to some degree of physical fatigue. This next exercise will help you conserve and make the best use of your energy. Do this on your bed or on the floor, whichever is more comfortable. Allow about an hour to an hour and a half. You will lie down with your head toward each direction for fifteen to twenty minutes. This will allow you to discover how the energy from each direction affects your personal energy. Start with your head toward the north, and move clockwise to the other directions. Relax but don't sleep, and be aware of how your energy is affected.

- - - -

Invisibility Cloak

Another example of advanced psychic work is creating an invisibility cloak. To create your own invisibility cloak to protect you from harm, imagine that you are completely surrounded by an impenetrable mist. You can see through it but others will not notice you. Put as much energy as you

can into this image. Practice this in non-threatening situations, and see how many people are aware of you. This can be useful if you see someone approaching you that you don't want to talk to.

If you find yourself in a dangerous situation, always, if at all possible, leave. If you cannot and haven't been noticed, do the invisibility cloak.

Another way to do this is to imagine that you are surrounded by a thick black curtain.

- - - -

Lucid Dreaming

A lucid dream is a dream where you become aware that you are dreaming. This can be an important skill, and we will now discuss how to develop it.

To start, three or four times a day, look into a mirror, and ask yourself if you are dreaming. Then walk away and don't think about it. At bedtime, tell yourself four or five times that you will dream of looking at yourself in a mirror and become aware that you are dreaming. Eventually this will happen.

When you wake up, stay in bed a few minutes and see if you recall your dreams. If you do, make a note of them. This helps you to remember your dreams, including lucid dreams.

Being lucid in a dream feels very different from a regular dream. It is an unmis-

takable feeling, but it is easy to slip back into a dream from the lucid state. It takes practice to remain lucid.

Astral projection is where your astral or emotional/mental energy body leaves your physical body and travels either to another place in the physical world or to other dimensions. Your astral body is able to see and hear with your inner senses. Once you are able to remain lucid in a dream, you can astral project from that state.

Everyone astral projects naturally every night. Because you use your inner senses and are in an altered state of consciousness, you rarely remember these experiences. By learning to dream lucidly and then to consciously astral project from this state, it will be easier to remember them.

Be sure to write your experiences in your Book of Shadows.

Lesson 14:
Divination

Wiccans use divination to see the patterns of energy in their life so they can direct or redirect them to accomplish their goals. Many Wiccans use divination before doing spellwork to see the probable outcome of the spell and whether or not they should do the spell at all. A spell can be successful and still not give you the outcome you really want. This is a case of climbing to the top of the ladder only to find that the ladder was propped against the wrong wall.

Divination can show the probable future, but that is not its best use. We use the term "probable future" because the future is never set in stone; your actions can change the outcome of almost any situation. The best use of divination is to see the issues surrounding a situation. These may be your true feelings about the situation, habits, attitudes and behaviors of yours or someone else's that affect the situation, and whether taking a specific action will help or hinder what you really want.

Divination is a technique of using symbolic systems to reveal information about situations that is not otherwise known to the conscious mind. As stated above, this information can be the probable outcome, but it can also be the underlying issues, as well as other influences on the situation. There are many systems of divination, and each one would fill a book of its own. In these lessons, we will only offer a brief introduction to several forms of divination, and in this lesson, we will discuss one of the most common forms of divination: tarot cards.

Tarot cards are probably the best-known form of divination. The standard tarot deck consists of seventy-eight cards—twenty-two major arcana and fifty-six minor arcana. The major arcana describes the journey of the soul through life and can represent spiritual issues that are part of the situation. They also have meanings that refer to everyday life.

The minor arcana deals with everyday life. It is divided into four suits: wands, swords, cups, and pentacles. In some decks, the suits have different but similar names, such as rods, knives, bowls, and discs. Wands represent the element of fire and the qualities of will, energy, passion, action, and creativity. Swords represent the element of air, the mind, knowledge, choice, decisions, and the ability to discriminate between things. Cups represent the element of water, emotion, cleansing, and, to some readers, Spirit. Pentacles represent the element of earth and money, possessions, security, and business.

A question is "shuffled" into the cards, and they are laid out into a spread (a pattern with specific meanings for each placement of the cards). The meaning of each card is then combined with the meaning of the placement of the card. The most common tarot spread is the Celtic Cross spread, which has a place for cards representing the situation, what opposes the situation, the foundation of the question, the immediate past as it affects the present, the energy that affects the situation, the immediate future (usually six to eight weeks), the questioner, the environment surrounding the questioner, the hopes and fears of the questioner, and the probable outcome of the situation.

There are many other spreads, or you can design your own. Let's say you want to know how a situation or a choice will affect you mentally, emotionally, creatively, and financially. You would design a placement for each, shuffle the cards, and lay the cards in the positions you have chosen. You would then balance the meaning of the card with the meaning of the placement of the card.

You can also use tarot cards for spells. You would charge the card that represents your goal and keep it on your altar, taking a few minutes each day to meditate on the card.

There are literally hundreds of different tarot decks available today. Some suggest-ed decks to start with are the Rider-Waite Tarot (also called the Waite-Smith Tarot), the Robin Wood Tarot, or the Hanson-Roberts Tarot.

The really important thing is to pick a deck that you feel pulled toward and work with it, giving yourself the time to learn it.

· · · ·

Connectedness

We are now going to return to the theme of our connectedness to All That Is with an exercise that will help to strengthen your sense of connection to the world around you. We are going to start connecting with the energy of your area. This includes the yard, plants, trees, flowers, sidewalks, streets, alleys, and driveways. You can do this easily from inside your house or apartment, day or night. Walk a one-block-square area around your home. If you live in the country, walk an area around your house that is comparable. Notice grass, trees, plants, flowers, shrubs—whatever is there. Let your attention flow to whatever you are observing almost as though you were physically touching it. Don't strain or try too hard to "feel" anything; let this be easy. Do this once a day for a week.

Now take some time each day when you won't be disturbed, perhaps at bed-time, and mentally walk the area again. Walk the entire area, observing as much as you can, though you are doing this from

memory. As you walk, send blessings to the area and the individual beings within it (trees, plants, etc.). Then pick some part of the area to explore more deeply. Extend your consciousness to a particular tree, for example, and feel/imagine the energy of the tree. Is it easy to sense, or do you feel shut out? If you do, pick something else. When you find something whose energy you can sense, mentally place your body there. If it is bushes, lie down under them or sit at the base of a tree, or sit with your back against the house and observe your yard.

Even sidewalks can welcome you with loving energy. Explore your area, and see what you are able to experience.

· · · ·

Spiritual Healing

Wiccans use various magical techniques for the purpose of spiritually healing themselves or others. This can be done in person, but it can also be done from a distance. It should be noted that this kind of spiritual healing is meant to help with physical healing but should not be relied on to bring this about by itself; rather, it should be used as an adjunct to normal medical treatment.

Before we explore healing methods, we need to talk about illness and its causes. What we believe about health, illness, germs, and our resistance to germs and viruses directly affects our health. Every-

one has various germs and viruses in their systems and rarely becomes sick from them. If you believe your resistance is good and that you are basically healthy, you will rarely become ill. If you think that powerful germs are everywhere and that they are stronger than you, you will be ill a lot.

Another cause for illness is when we don't deal with problems and situations in our lives but continue to submit ourselves to unhappy or abusive situations and people; our bodies express the dissatisfactions we are feeling as illness in some form. It is said that more heart attacks occur on Monday morning, the start of the work week, than any other time, a prime example of the body expressing dissatisfaction with a job.

There are rare occasions where a serious condition is a result of a pre-birth choice of the soul for a learning experience. Because this is a decision taken at the deepest level of the soul, it can be difficult to affect the situation in any way. Even in these cases, however, the condition can sometimes be lightened or sometimes reversed through serious magical working.

Soul loss can contribute to illness. When traumatic events occur, parts of our soul sometimes become blocked by them, and that part of our energy is cut off from us. Sometimes a great deal of our energy becomes blocked in this way. This can be reversed by a technique called soul retrieval, which we will discuss in future lessons.

To heal yourself or someone else, even at a distance, enter your stillness, then imagine your body or theirs, and mentally examine it. If you feel or sense a blockage or problem, mentally heal or remove it. For instance, a blockage may feel like coal, hard and immobile. To remove this, you might imagine a small jackhammer to crumble it, and then hot, soapy water to flush it away until the area is clean and healthy. Sometimes a blockage feels like thick gelatin or fish scales. To remove this, you would actually use your hands (or if at a distance, imagine using your hands), pulling and removing the blockage from the body, flicking it to the side to go into the earth and be neutralized. Do this until it is gone, and then mentally flush it with warm water to remove it thoroughly.

Do whatever seems needed to unclog, heal, or remove whatever is needed for healing.

The best form of healing is prevention. A way of maintaining good health is through regular maintenance of your personal energy. Your aura (the ball of spiritual energy surrounding your physical body, usually about six feet in diameter) is a barometer of your personal energy. Traumatic events or emotions can cause tears or holes in your aura that allow your energy to leak away, leaving you depleted and unmo-

tivated. To repair this condition, release, ground, center, and shield. Now imagine your aura as it surrounds you. Imagine the aura as a ball of clear white light extending several feet in all directions. Imagine that you are inside your aura and can see it in its entirety. Take stock of your aura, and look for any holes or tears that may be present. When you find a hole or tear, fill it with white light and mend it. Fill the hole with as much white light as it will take until it is fully repaired. Do this for every hole or tear you find. When you have completed this, you should feel a shift in your energy.

• • • •

Dream Interpretation

Dreams give you insight and guidance about your life, goals, health, and spirituality. There are many books on dream interpretation, but those with definite meanings for symbols are not to be taken literally. Symbols mean different things to different people. Your personal meanings, even if you think you don't have them, are the ones that have meaning for your dreams. It is helpful to begin a journal of personal dream meanings. If you have a recurring symbol you don't understand, keep working with it. Eventually it will make sense to you.

In a dream, your house represents your life. This does not necessarily have anything

to do with the house you physically live in during your waking life, but rather any house you dream that you are living in. The ground floor is your daily life. The front, or living, room is your daily activities and/or your interactions with other people. The kitchen is health, diet, nurturing; the bathroom is cleansing and releasing. The bedroom is your personal self, secrets, rest, and sex. If you are married or in a relationship, your bedroom can represent that. Closets are storage, which can be memories as well as abilities you have but aren't using.

The second floor is your mind, your attitudes, and thoughts that you have. If you are doing something on the second floor, and the mood and furnishings are pleasant, with a solid floor, what you are thinking or planning in your daily life is sound. If the room is dark, oppressive, cluttered, and/or dirty, your attitudes or your thoughts and plans are not good. If the floor is shaky, has missing boards, or slants dangerously, your plans have a poor foundation, and you should examine them.

The attic, or third floor, refers to your spiritual life and ideals. It can also be a place of initiations. If this floor is neat and pleasing, all is well; if it isn't, or if something is needing repair, you should pay attention to it.

A basement is the subconscious mind and occasionally refers to past lives. Sometimes, you will dream of coins or jewels in a basement. These may be past-life skills that are available to you.

Using these guidelines, get a book on dream interpretation and begin to work with your dreams. These are the first places to look when you seek the meaning of your dreams. Dreams usually are about your present life and often comment about the day that just ended. Dreams occur at many levels—a dream can comment on something in your daily life and the quality of your goals at the same time. Reread your dreams once a week to check for ESP. This can be about something very mundane, such as bringing cheeseburgers to the house of a friend. If you don't record it, you won't realize that it was precognition.

It is also important to remember and record all spoken words in a dream. Their meaning may not be immediately clear, but as you reread your journal, it is possible to glean some insight from them.

When you begin to seriously work with your dreams, you may find that you have more dreams than you have time to work with. If this happens, work with the last dream you have each night, and tell your inner self to send the more important dreams on the weekend, when you have more time to work with them.

• • • •

Guided Visualization

The following is a guided visualization
where you will pick a place that you are
familiar with—this can be a place you
go to in the present or somewhere from
your past, whether it still exists or not.
Sit where you will not be disturbed, then
release, ground, center, and shield. Enter
your stillness. Now see yourself at the place
you have chosen. Walk around this place,
and experience it as intensely as you can
with all of your senses. Spend at least ten
minutes here, then return to normal consciousness. Record your experience in your
Book of Shadows.

This, as is the case with all guided visualizations, is a real journey. Practice doing
this one or two more times this week. This
will increase your concentration and visualization skills.

Lesson 15:
Labyrinths

Labyrinths have been around for over 4,000 years and are found in almost every major religious tradition in the world. They have also been an important part of many cultures, such as the Native American, Greek, Celtic, Cretan, and Mayan. Labyrinths are considered to be sacred space and a path for prayer and meditation. They can have a tremendous healing effect, clear your mind, give you insights, and increase your creativity.

People have different experiences walking the labyrinth. There is no "right" experience. You may feel a sense of peace or find yourself thinking about a present situation or feel nothing at all.

If you do not have access to a large labyrinth, lap, or finger, labyrinths can be used for the same purposes. You can use the ones below or draw your own. Don't worry for now about what effect this is supposed to have. Just sit once or twice a day and trace the path of the labyrinth slowly with your finger. Trace into the center and then back out. Give yourself about half an hour after doing this to notice any effects, and then write about anything you experience in your Book of Shadows.

After you do this for a while, take a problem or question with you into the center of the labyrinth. While you are in the center, think about the problem or question from all sides, then leave it in the center when you depart. Be alert to any guidance you receive in the next day or two.

Diagram of a labyrinth, left, and a more classic version, right

Self-Discovery Collage

Self-knowledge is extremely important to a Wiccan or to anyone on a magical path. This is because we seek to play an active role in the creation of our world, but we cannot do that well if we do not know what we want. Therefore, we will now discuss a simple way of increasing our self-knowledge. This technique involves making a treasure map of our desires to aid in their manifestation. This is a way to connect with your inner longings so as to be better able to focus on fulfilling them. We will do this by making a timed collage. For this, you will need:

- White poster board, about ten by twelve inches
- A glue stick
- Scissors
- Two or three magazines with lots of pictures
- A timer

Assemble everything within easy reach. Set the timer for half an hour. You have exactly one-half hour to go through the magazines and tear out every picture that appeals to you (don't use your conscious mind here—if a picture pulls you, tear it out). Cut out the images that you like, arrange them on the poster board, and then glue them in place. You probably won't use all the pages you tore out, but that's okay.

After you begin to arrange them, you aren't allowed to tear out more. By timing this exercise, you bypass your conscious mind and let your inner feelings show.

When you are finished, look at the collage and see what you have. Did you choose pictures of exotic places, or jewelry and clothes, or a house and/or a garden? Maybe it was cars on a highway. Look for a common theme, then ask yourself what it is you really want at this time. Pictures of exotic places may mean you want a vacation or simply to get away, or something new and exciting in your life. Jewelry and clothes are self-explanatory. A house and/or garden may be a longing for your own home or to remodel your current living space, or simply for security and family, and the peacefulness associated with them. Cars on a highway are similar to exotic places—a desire to go, whether toward or from something.

This collage is a treasure map; it shows what your inner self is asking for. Now, you should take time to think about the themes you see, and ask yourself how you feel about them. These are things your inner self desires, but are these things you want to work on manifesting into your physical life at this time? If the answer is yes, then use the magical techniques you have been learning in this course. If the answer is no, then you have a "crossed wire" between your inner and outer self. In that case, you

will need to use the techniques you have learned in this course to help resolve the division between what you consciously want and what your inner self desires. But fear not: resolving a "crossed wire" is not as hard as you might think once you know it is there, and a simple paper-burning spell with the intent of resolution may be quite enough.

• • • •

Introduction to Runes

The topic of runes is very complex, and the discussion below is not meant to be exhaustive but just a brief introduction. Runes derive from the Nordic and Germanic tribes of northern Europe. Originally they were a magical system of pictographs that represented the very real forces of nature. Eventually they became a runic alphabet, the most common of which is the Germanic, or Elder Futhark, named after the first six letters of the alphabet. They still offer access to the very real forces of nature. If used for magic, they should be used with caution and respect.

There are twenty-four runes, divided into three groups of eight: Frey's Eight, which deal with creation, daily life, money, and happiness; Hagall's Eight, which deal with transformation related to daily life; and Tir's Eight, which deal with spirituality and mental growth. Modern rune sets contain a twenty-fifth rune, called Wyrd.

Wyrd represents unknown influence, the will of the gods, fate, karma, and destiny.

In ancient times, runes were widely used for magical purposes. They were not, however, used for divination in the way that they are today. That is just fine, because life is about growth and developing new ideas and new techniques.

For divinatory purposes, runes are commonly made into runestones—small tokens, each bearing the image of a single letter from the runic alphabet. Runestones can be made from many substances. They can be made from the branch of a tree cut into coin-sized pieces with the symbols carved or painted onto them. They can also be drawn or painted onto stones and clay. As a rule, the runestones are then kept in a small bag, from which individual runestones are drawn for divination.

Generally, runestones are drawn in response to a question. Usually one to three runestones are drawn and the meanings of the runes applied to the situation. Runestones give a more general meaning than tarot cards, so it is necessary to think about the way the rune drawn relates to the question.

• • • •

Chakras

Beginning in this lesson, we are introducing the topic of chakras. For the next several weeks, each lesson will contain more in-depth information about chakras. Chakras are the energy centers in your body. There are seven major chakras and numerous minor chakras. Chakras are transformers of spiritual energy that reduce that energy to a level the body can use without harm.

It should be noted that while the word *chakra* is Sanskrit, and a highly developed system for working with chakras exists within Hindu tradition, the use of the term chakra in modern Western metaphysics often refers to ideas that can be quite different from those of Hinduism. Western ideas about chakras are similar in many ways to Eastern ideas, but they are not identical. Many different cultures have had or do have teachings about energetic centers in the body—"chakra" has simply become the default term for this. Again, this is a natural result of the process of growth and development.

Each chakra deals with a particular kind of energy.

The first chakra is the base, or root, chakra. Its color is red. It is found at the base of the spine. This chakra deals with survival, your basic feelings of security, and your will to survive. An imbalance here can be experienced as leg pain, lower back pain, or a feeling of fearfulness. It can also manifest as greediness (coming from a feeling of not having enough) or a poverty consciousness that isn't related to how much you do or don't have. The plan-

etary correspondence of the first chakra is Saturn.

The second chakra is the sacral chakra. It is found at the sexual glands, just below the pelvis in men, in the area three to five inches below the navel in women. Its color is orange. This chakra deals with sexuality, creativity, and friendliness. An imbalance here can be experienced as sexual dysfunction, depression, blocked creativity, self-criticism, low energy, and extreme introversion. The planetary correspondence of the second chakra is Mars.

The third chakra is the solar plexus chakra. Its color is yellow. It is found in the area between the naval and the diaphragm. This chakra is about your sense of personal power and how you present yourself to the world. It can also be a reservoir of personal energy you can draw on when you need it. It is your sense of self. An imbalance here can manifest as a feeling of alienation, powerlessness, and low self-esteem. The planetary correspondence of the third chakra is the sun.

The fourth chakra is the heart chakra. It is in the area of your heart. Its color is green. This chakra deals with your ability to give and receive love, your openness to life and experience. An imbalance here can manifest as anxiety, fear of relationships, a hoarding of self and emotions, and mistrust of others. The planetary correspondence of the fourth chakra is Venus.

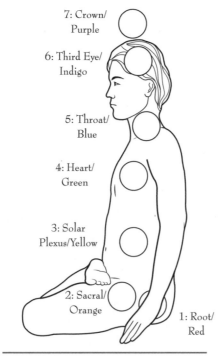

7: Crown/
Purple

6: Third Eye/
Indigo

5: Throat/
Blue

4: Heart/
Green

3: Solar
Plexus/Yellow

2: Sacral/
Orange

1: Root/
Red

The seven chakras and their colors

The fifth chakra is the throat chakra, located in the area on or just below the Adam's apple. Its color is blue. This chakra deals with communication and your will. An imbalance here can manifest as a feeling of fullness in this area, or as a sore throat. This is usually caused by not saying something that needs to be said or from failing to honor your personal truth. The planetary correspondence of the fifth chakra is Mercury.

The sixth chakra is the third eye chakra. It is located on your forehead, usually between or just above your eyebrows. Its color is indigo. This chakra deals with your psychic/spiritual abilities. An imbalance in this area can manifest as blocked psychic ability and headaches. The planetary correspondence of the sixth chakra is the moon.

The seventh chakra is the crown chakra. Most writings list this chakra as being at the top of the head, but actually it is about an inch above the third eye chakra. There is a chakra at the top of the head, or just above, but it is the transpersonal chakra, and we aren't dealing with it here. The color of the crown chakra is purple or violet. An imbalance here manifests as a feeling of spiritual restlessness, as being disconnected from the divine. The planetary correspondence of the seventh chakra is Jupiter.

To learn where your chakras are, sit where you won't be disturbed. Release, ground, and center. Starting with your root chakra, put your awareness gently in the general area of the chakra and rest it there. Be aware of any response you may have there. Your chakra thus focused on should feel good, slightly "dizzy," or subtle, or you may experience a different but definite response. Once you have located the chakra, keep your awareness there for a minute, then move on to the next chakra. Do this for all seven chakras.

Another way to balance the chakras is to use stones for this purpose. You start with the first chakra, and balance it by lying with a stone on this chakra for half an hour. Each chakra has certain stones that are balancing for it.

Before we do that, however, use a rose quartz for each chakra, one at a time, beginning with the root chakra. Lie down where you won't be disturbed. Release, etc., and enter your stillness. Place the stone on your root chakra, and relax for half an hour. Later on, or the next day, do the same thing with your second, or sacral, chakra, and continue through the week until you have used the rose quartz on every chakra.

You start with rose quartz because it is a healing stone, especially for emotions and childhood trauma. Use it and the other stones that will be recommended in future lessons on every chakra, because all the chakras are connected. Start with the first chakra because each chakra is influenced by the others, and the chakras below each chakra are the foundation of the chakra; if the foundation is poor, the chakra can't function properly.

As always, record your results in your Book of Shadows.

When your chakras are balanced, you function better and have increased health and energy. A way to balance them is to take some time each day to surround your body with the color of the chakras, in order. Start with red, then orange, yellow, green, blue, indigo, and purple or violet. By surrounding your body with each color in turn, the body will use the color it needs, where it needs it. Although each chakra has a color, sometimes a chakra needs a color from another chakra to balance it.

Do this exercise once a day, every day.

Lesson 16:
The Broader View of Wicca

You may have wondered what communicating with trees and plants and working with labyrinths, chakras, etc. have to do with Wicca. Some books on Wicca make Wicca appear to be a very narrow and limited philosophy, and some traditions of Wicca look at it that way. Here we are clearly advocating a very broad view of Wicca.

There is a belief that present-day Wicca evolved from the religious practices of the indigenous peoples of Europe. These beliefs survived from ancient times in an often rather disorganized state, often under a thin gloss of Christianity. You see a similar state of affairs in much of Central and South America today, where indigenous religious ideas remain alive and well under a gloss of Catholicism.

In the nineteenth century, this gloss began to be peeled away, and the movement which would become Wicca started to coalesce out of these older things. By the early twentieth century, much of modern Wicca was already well developed on both sides of the Atlantic, as was the schism between American and British Wicca, which has persisted ever since. Today, in the twenty-first century, Wicca has count-

less traditions and forms, some quite old, others very new. But our roots remain with the experience of the indigenous peoples of Europe.

Like native peoples everywhere, they were taught by the beings and energies of their place, that particular spot they called home. They had an active relationship with the land and the beings of that land, seen and unseen, that shaped their lives and their spiritual understanding. Due to their direct interaction with the land in their daily lives and their honoring of it in their religious practices, they were more easily able to experience other levels of reality. I believe that many, if not all, of their ceremonial sites were originally designed for access to these other levels, or dimensions, and intended to keep those points of access open and healthy. Their ceremonies were also designed to maintain the health of the people—and to many ancient peoples, "people" included all that is: the animals, birds, plants, trees, rivers, oceans, stones, winds, and beings of all dimensions.

As was written earlier, relationship is an important part of Wiccan practice. Wiccans are aware, as were ancient peoples, that an ongoing relationship with all beings and levels keeps all of the "people" healthy.

Connecting with Objects

For this exercise, pick a plant, tree, or rock near your home. Your intention here is to build an intimate relationship with whatever object you choose. Try to spend some time daily with this object. Touch it, smell it, taste it. Talk to it—you can do this silently—and listen for any response it may give you. Ask it for advice, if you need insight on a situation in your life. Spend extra time each night as you do your nightly mental walk around the block, giving energy.

If you aren't able to go out physically once a day, visit it mentally. Stay aware of any change in your feelings toward this object. You may find that the energy or spirit of this object may visit you from time to time. Write all of these experiences in your Book of Shadows.

Connecting with Spirits of Places

Every place is guarded and protected by spirits that inhabit it. To connect with the primary spirits of your place, you first need to define your place. Simply put, your place is the area where you live that you feel responsible to and for, and that you can affect, whether physically or by energy work. You can define this simply by the town or city where you live or by a natural

geographical feature. Mentally explore the boundaries of the area you choose and see if you feel an emotional connection also. If you do in some areas and not in others, rearrange your boundaries accordingly. Mark out the area on a map, and place it on your devotional altar or make a separate altar for it.

Now plan a journey to your Hall of Consciousness. As always, the hall will be lined with doors. Ask for a door that will lead you to the spirit or spirits of your particular place, and look for the door that is different from the rest. Be alert for any symbols you may see on the door or during the journey.

Open the door that is different from the others, and step through it. Where do you find yourself? It may be some physical region within your "place," or it may be a symbolic representation that represents the qualities of the spirit of the place. Look for the spirit of place. The spirit will be there, but you should have no preconceived notions as to how it will appear. It may appear as a person, as an animal, or as a natural feature such as a tree or stream.

Pay your respects to the spirit of place, and explain that you wish to deepen your relationship with it. It may speak with you or it may not. It is possible that it may give you an elaborate vision—or it may ignore you altogether. In any event, spend a few minutes in its presence, and feel its energy.

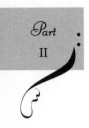
When you feel that you have been there long enough, thank the spirit of place for the experience, and return through the door to the Hall of Consciousness.

Return to normal consciousness, and write your experiences. You can draw the spirit of place or find representations of whatever symbols are connected with them. Place these on the altar. You can talk to them and should on a regular basis—during time spent at the altar or when you feel their presence. You do not worship them, but you honor them. They have more knowledge and power than you do.

• • • •

The Pendulum

The pendulum is a very simple tool for divination that can be made very easily by simply hanging a ring, stone, or similar object at the end of a chain or string. You can also purchase ready-made pendulums that are often quite beautiful. The pendulum can give you yes/no answers (determined by the direction of its swinging) or can be used with a chart (which you can make) to find answers to your questions.

To use the pendulum, hold it between your thumb and index finger, with your elbow resting firmly on the table or other flat surface.

To ask a yes/no question, you must first determine what constitutes a yes or a no answer. The pendulum can swing in any of three basic motions: forward and backward, side to side, and around in a circle. To determine which of these is yes and which is no, you would first ask the pendulum a question whose answer you already know to be yes, and observe which direction it moves in. You would then do the same with a question whose answer you know to be no.

The pendulum moves in response to your involuntary muscles, which are not under the control of your conscious mind.

The pendulum isn't the best tool for divining the future. It is often quite accurate, but you can't count on it. It is better suited to answers about present situations, especially in regard to what you really feel and want.

The pendulum can also answer other kinds of questions besides yes/no questions, but for this it needs the help of a chart listing potential answers. Such a chart can be made for any purpose, but be sure if you do make such a chart to include as many potential answers as possible.

Three charts for pendulums are included on the opposite page; one is for career choices, one for vitamins and minerals, and one for color choices.

To use the charts, simply hold the pendulum between your thumb and index finger, place it at the center of the chart at the bottom, and ask a question. For the vitamin and mineral chart, first do the yes/no

and ask if you need any of these, and if the answer is yes, use the chart and ask which one you need most. After you get your answer, ask if there is another one that you need, then ask again which one you need. Do this until you get a no on whether or not you need another one. This chart is only a sample chart. You would make a more thorough chart for actual use. For the color chart, ask what color you should wear today or what color will help a specific condition that you have.

The chart for career choices is self-explanatory.

If the pendulum appeals to you as a tool for divination, you can buy lovely pendulums that are more special than homemade ones.

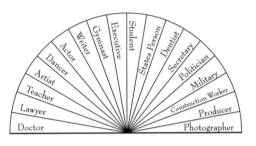

• • • •

Dream Symbology

We will now discuss a few symbols that may appear in your dreams—specifically, symbols that represent your body or your life in general. Cars and other vehicles often represent our physical body, and as such, they can inform us of our health. For example, dreaming of a beautiful car can be a very good sign for one's health, while a decrepit jalopy would be a warning of a need to take better care of one's self. A dream of driving a car and unsuccessfully trying to put on the brakes can mean something about our health is out of our control.

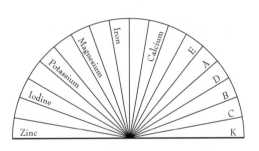

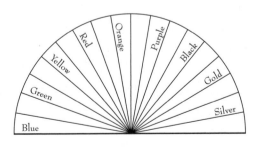

Examples of pendulum charts

Dreams of driving on a highway under construction can mean that your life is under construction or being restructured in some way. If you are driving and get lost, you may be "losing your way" in some manner in daily life.

When you dream of being in a car, notice who is driving. If you are, you are directing your life. If someone else is driving, someone else may be directing your life or the qualities of the person driving may relate to the way you are handling your life, since people appearing in our dreams often represent not the physical person we know but rather the qualities we associate with that person. If the person driving is someone you know to be irresponsible, then your dream may be telling you that you are making irresponsible decisions for yourself.

Because the people we dream about often represent specific qualities rather than specific individuals, it is helpful to make a list of the people who frequently appear in your dreams, and write the first quality you think of in connection with each of them.

Sometimes it can be helpful to make a drawing of dreams you have had. You do not have to be a great artist to do this— artistic skill is not the point. Often in the process of depicting the dream, you may remember parts of it you had forgotten or realize meanings that had not previously occurred to you. Because art expresses our inner self, this is also a good way to build up a closer relationship with your inner self.

Lesson 17:
Understanding the God and Goddess Relationship

Modern Wicca has a weakness in that the figure of the God is rarely discussed in any depth; the Goddess tends to get all of the attention. The main reason for this is that Wicca, with its focus on the Goddess, fills a void that has existed for women for millennia. Women have flocked to Wicca in response to a deity that is female, powerful, and valued. This validates women's worth and gives women a religion that is positive and life affirming. However, this should not obscure the importance of the God in Wicca.

In Wicca, the Goddess and the God are equal opposites, often described as two sides of a coin—the coin being Spirit. They are often likened to the Eastern idea of yin and yang, the inward and outward movement of Spirit in existence. Similarly, in Wicca the Goddess is thought of as inward and spiritual, the God as outward and physical in nature. What does this mean? On an existential level, Goddess is Spirit and all aspects of existence that are spiritual, emotional, internal; she is the origin and the essence of all things. The God is matter and the cycles of motion that regulate it—physical manifestation, action, time.

On a more personal and less cosmic level, the Goddess is loving, nurturing, and creative, while the God is expansive, passionate, and ecstatic. The God also deals with structure and form. Both have many aspects through which their characteristics are expressed.

As a suggestion, make it regular practice to take perhaps one day each week to commune with the God separately from the Goddess, and one day to commune with the Goddess separately from the God, so as to get a feel for their different energies.

. . . .

Power Animals

A power animal is a kind of spirit guide in the form of an archetypal animal. What kind of animal the power animal is depends on and corresponds to the energy of the person. Each kind of animal is considered to have certain archetypal characteristics. These archetypal characteristics would be shared with the person for whom a given animal was the power animal. For instance, a person whose power animal is a wolf has a talent for teaching. Such a person is territorial, family oriented, social, loyal, and intelligent. They are probably night people and actively pursue their goals.

As with other kinds of spirit guides, a person is born with one or more power animals, but may attract other power animals during the course of their lives. You may

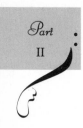

also invite power animals to work with you who have qualities that you wish to develop within yourself.

There are several ways to determine your power animal(s). One is by identifying which power animal comes closest to your own personal characteristics. Another is through shamanic journeying.

Shamans take shamanic journeys to discover their power animal. This means that they enter into the Spirit world, which they commonly describe as the Underworld, and this is where they meet their power animal. You can go to your Hall of Consciousness and designate a door to lead you to your power animal. When you go through the door, you will enter the shamanic Underworld to find your power animals. Once you enter, become aware of the many animals, birds, reptiles, and insects you will see there. These spirit animals look more or less like animals in the everyday world, although some may manifest unique differences in size, color, etc. One of the animals will come to meet you or will otherwise gain your attention. Sometimes they will speak to you as if they were human—for at the spirit level, we are all equally sentient. The animal, bird, reptile, or insect that shows itself to you three times is your power animal. Do not accept an animal that makes you uncomfortable or that bares its teeth or fangs. Once you have found your power animal and accepted it, hold

it in your arms and bring it back with you as you return to your Hall of Consciousness. When you have returned to your Hall of Consciousness, place your power animal in your heart and thank it for coming with you.

Some traditions say that insects are never power animals, but many people interact with insects as their power animals nonetheless.

To study animal totems in depth, you might read *Animal-Speak* by Ted Andrews.

• • • •

Tea-Leaf Reading

A very interesting form of divination, which also has the benefit of being quite relaxing and pleasant, is the reading of tea leaves.

For a tea-leaf reading, you should use a cup with a wide top and a narrow bottom, as opposed to a mug that is cylindrically shaped. This is important, because this shape of cup allows a wider range of meaning. You will also need a saucer.

Ground/release, shield, and center yourself. Put the water on to boil, and place about a teaspoon of loose tea leaves in the cup. When the water boils, pour it over the tea leaves, and let it sit until it is cool enough to drink.

Now take a moment to focus on your question. Drink your tea in a calm and relaxed manner, enjoying its flavor and aroma, and continuing to think about your question. When the liquid is almost totally gone, swirl the cup around three or more times while thinking of your question. Then turn the cup upside down onto the saucer and leave it there for a few minutes. This allows the remaining tea leaves to assume their final position.

Now turn the cup right-side up, and you are ready to read. The tea leaves will have settled in small clumps whose general shape will suggest symbols of various sorts. For example, a clump of tea leaves may resemble the image of a dog—this is taken as the symbol of a dog and interpreted according to whatever meaning you associate with dogs.

The area around the handle relates to you as the querent. This can be your attitudes, beliefs, habits, actions, or what is in your life right now. The farther away from the handle the leaves are, the more likely it is that the symbols refer to what is going on around you and the attitudes and actions of others involving the question. The left side of the cup is often the past, and the right side of the cup refers to the future. The symbols from the top half of the cup are the things that you are aware of and/or are visible in the world. The symbols in the bottom half of the cup are things that aren't visible—subconscious beliefs and attitudes, whether yours or someone else's,

or thoughts and actions of others that you aren't aware of.

Take time to observe the symbols and to notice your reaction to them. Decide which symbol is most important to you—the one that is the most obvious or that you have the greatest reaction to. This symbol is the lens through which to consider the other symbols. Consider each symbol as you would a dream symbol. Your personal meaning is the most important. If you don't have a meaning for the symbol, consult a book on symbols, such as a dream book, or any book on divination that uses symbols. If you can't find a meaning that satisfies you, make a note of the symbol and wait for future understanding.

Every symbol in the cup relates to the question or situation. This form of divination, even more than most, pulls symbols from your subconscious mind. Keep a logbook of these readings or put them in your Book of Shadows, dated, with room for the outcome of the reading. You are building a language that is a bridge between your conscious mind and your subconscious access to unlimited awareness. Working with symbols in this way will improve your understanding of your dreams.

You can also use this form of divination on a daily basis, such as in the morning to see what energies you will encounter during the day. The more you do this, the more

your subconscious mind will communicate with you in this way.

. . . .

Connecting with
Spirits, Continued

In our last lesson, we connected with the spirits of our place, the area where we live. By doing this, we open a dialog with them. Often this dialog will be continued. Just as we can talk to them, so too they can talk to us. Consequently, you may find the spirits communicating with you. You may feel their presence and be aware of receiving information from them mentally.

What are they likely to talk about? It may be issues directly relating to your local place, but it could just as likely be about other subjects. You may find they act almost like a guide to you, giving valuable insights and advice.

Be sure to write down all such communications, because you may forget otherwise. The reason for recording these communications is that all such communications are received in an altered state of consciousness, even though you may feel wide-awake. You are at a different level of consciousness then, one not easily remembered by the conscious mind. They may also come to you in dreams.

In preceding lessons, we have worked with ideas of connecting to place, communing with the energies of place, con-necting with the spirits of place. In this lesson, we will begin learning ways to heal your place.

In a moment, I will discuss how to work on healing a place energetically, but let me point out that one of the most important aspects of healing a place is by being physically involved in its everyday welfare. This means paying attention to ecological issues such as recycling, using energy sensibly, refraining from littering, and becoming involved in things like community clean-ups. This does not mean that you must sacrifice a modern lifestyle. By being conscience of your environment, you will often find that there is a more earth-sensible way to go about things that requires little or no extra effort.

This also means political involvement. Pay attention to what is happening politically at the local and national level—who is in office and how they are using that office. Elections exist to give the people power to choose their leadership; use that power and vote for people who support your values, people who will improve your place, your community, your world. This is also a part of healing your place as well as of healing the earth as a whole.

Now I will discuss energetic techniques for healing place. There are many ways to do this, but we will start with two that are fairly simple.

One technique for healing a place is to imagine that place strongly in your mind. Imagine all of its details clearly. See the colors, smell the scents, feel the sensations. You should take a moment to declare your intent to heal the place, and perhaps make a prayer to Goddess and God asking them to help with this. Now, imagine flooding the whole area with a yellow-white light—a very clear, strong yellow-white light that heals and cleanses all it touches. When you have filled the space with the yellow-white light and cleansed out all negativity, then flood the area with blue-white light to raise its vibration, refresh, and reinvigorate it. Finally, flood the area with violet light to align it to its own highest spiritual good. Record this in your Book of Shadows.

Another technique for energetic healing of place requires a map representing that place, as we have previously discussed. Over the top of this map, place a sheet of paper bearing a diagram of a classical labyrinth (see page 88). Again, you should declare your intent and perhaps make a short prayer. Now imagine your place as it would be if it were in its best, most positive ideal state. Imagine anything that is damaged, dirty, or otherwise wrong with your place as being healed and healthy and whole. Hold this image in your mind. Now use your index finger to trace the path of the labyrinth to its center. Once in the center of the labyrinth, imagine this heal-ing as being fully accomplished. See this as clearly as you can. Softly say: "This now is so." Travel back out of the labyrinth. Record this in your Book of Shadows as well.

Try both ways of healing, and see which one works best for you.

· · · ·

Balancing Your Root Chakra

Now that you have worked with rose quartz on all of your chakras, it is time to begin balancing each chakra with a stone that is specific for it. You will use each stone as you did the rose quartz, placing it on each chakra in turn, beginning with the root chakra.

Garnet, ruby, and bloodstone are rec-ommended for the root chakra. Red jasper can be used for this also. Choose the stone that appeals to you, and starting with the root chakra, place the stone there for half an hour. The next day, put it on the second chakra, and so forth.

Garnet brings power, prosperity, happi-ness, and peace. It purifies, protects against nightmares, gives patience, persistence, energy, vitality, and quiet sleep. It draws faithful love.

Ruby helps open psychic ability, aids in manifestation, draws prosperity, is physi-cally energizing and rebuilding, and gives courage.

Bloodstone offers courage, persistence, and stops bleeding.

As always, pay attention to the effects this has on your body and energy, and record them in your Book of Shadows.

Lesson 18:
Designing Rituals

In previous lessons, we have covered rituals for the esbats. We have also discussed the form and function of ritual. We will now discuss ritual for the sabbats; however, here I will not be relating rituals so much as discussing how you can create your own. The ability to create your own ritual is the true heart of the art of ritual.

There are many books on ritual which can be of aid in suggesting ideas, but in the end your ritual must have meaning for *you*. One of the better books on this subject is *Witch School Ritual, Theory & Practice* by Rev. Donald Lewis-Highcorrell. This book deals with group ritual but includes many good ideas that can be of use to the solitary ritualist as well.

In designing a ritual for a sabbat, you will have several important considerations. These include how best to incorporate the meaning of the holiday into the ritual, whether it is a solitary ritual or involves several persons, and whether it is indoors or outdoors.

If you are doing this ritual inside, you can do it at your altar. If you are outside and aren't comfortable doing a physical circle casting with your tools, etc., you can visualize this part of the ritual. Practice

this before doing the actual ritual. Visualize a complete ritual, from casting the circle, invoking the directions, and calling the quarters to lighting the incense and candles. Smell the incense, see the candle flame, and be aware of the energies of the elements, quarters, and deities entering and later leaving the circle. Smell the waxy scent extinguished candles have. This may sound difficult, but with practice it will become easy.

Below we discuss how to actually design your ritual.

. . . .

Ritual Checklist

When you design any ritual, you need to have a checklist of the elements of ritual. These are:

The Purpose of the Ritual: Why are you doing it? What do you want to accomplish? This is the most important aspect of the ritual. You need the utmost clarity of purpose here.

How You Will Accomplish this Purpose: Every step of the ritual should serve the purpose of the ritual. This includes all objects used in the ritual, all actions done, everything that is spoken or visualized.

A Well-Written Statement of Intent: This will be read during the ritual.

A Written List of Everything You Need for the Ritual: Include also each step of the ritual in order, beginning with the ritual bath. Read this list before you perform the ritual bath, and have everything ready to use as needed.

Sensory Details: How will you engage all of your senses to add to the energy of the ritual?

Deity and/or Spirit: Will you invoke deities as part of this ritual or will you invite the primary spirits of your place or both? Why will you do this?

Opening and Closing: The ritual begins with the casting of the circle and ends when the circle is opened. A definite beginning and ending is important in all rituals.

Always release, ground, center, and shield. A ritual should be an experience, not simply a mental concept done by rote.

. . . .

Manifesting

In this section, we will discuss manifestation. Manifestation is the way in which we create our reality. Manifestation shapes spiritual energy into the physical world on a constant, ongoing basis.

Manifestation might be described as the combination of belief, expectation, and desire, fueled by emotion and focus. We all manifest constantly in an unconscious manner. The main goal of magic is to learn to manifest in a conscious manner.

The greatest truth about manifestation is both the saddest and the most joyful, depending upon your extent of self-knowledge. This is that when creating our own reality, we do not always create what we desire, but we do always create what we expect and believe to be possible. To limit our expectations limits our possibility of results.

Fear creates negative manifestation. When we are in fear, we focus intensely on what we are afraid of, often in great detail, and we fuel this mental picture with our emotions. This is a perfect blueprint for manifestation. Let go of fear now. When you find yourself in a situation where it is hard to let go of fear, do soul retrieval (lesson 7) to release it.

An affirmation is a kind of simple spell, a statement spoken to create something you want, whether externally in the physical world or to change something internally about yourself. Unlike certain other kinds of spellwork, an affirmation specifically does not involve any external props. However, in order to create what you desire, you must believe it to be possible. If you don't believe the affirmation when you say it—if you believe that what you are trying to create is not possible—then it will not be possible. However, repeating the affirmation often enough will sink it into your subconscious and begin to change the limiting belief.

It is important to pay attention to your inner response to any affirmation you may do. For instance, if you affirm, "I now manifest the perfect job for me," but inside you think to yourself, "There aren't any openings for the job I want, and I could never get it anyway," then you have immediately blocked your affirmation. However, by becoming aware of this limiting belief, you can now work to change it, then repeat the affirmation more successfully. Remember, you get what you expect and believe is possible for you.

A good exercise to work with this is to write out something you wish to manifest as an affirmation. Now listen to your response to this affirmation—is it a positive response or a self-limiting, negative response? If you find a limiting belief, as in the example above, create affirmations to change the belief. For example: "I believe that I can have the perfect job for me." At first this may be hard, but if you can at least get the feeling that the new belief is possible, you can begin the process of change.

Finding and releasing the beliefs that limit you is the first step in conscious creation.

While you are doing this work, you can also practice manifestation. Spend some time each day seeing yourself enjoying having the goal you are working for. Imagine it in detail, feeling the way you will feel when you have it. Involve as many senses as possible while doing this. If you want a car, see it, feel the seat against you as you sit in it, smell it, hear the engine running. Imagine driving it down the road. Feel your hands on the steering wheel.

You need to be specific when you visualize what you want. It is helpful to know, if a car, what year of car you want and what price range you can afford, and be sure you include that the car is in good condition and runs well.

It is also important to give yourself the time you need to build your inner muscles. When you first begin to manifest, choose something a little out of your reach—but don't try for a million dollars the first thing, unless you can easily earn five hundred thousand dollars. Stretch your muscles gradually, as if you were lifting weights. As you get more experience and confidence in manifesting what you want, stretch yourself a little more.

We will return to the subject of manifestation in later lessons.

· · · ·

Dream Relationships

We will now expand on our dream learning. When you dream of a place where you have lived in the past, your dream is telling you that you are involved in an issue or repeating patterns of beliefs and behaviors that you had when you lived there. Relate what is going on in your life now to what was going on then.

Was your life there happy or sad? Are your beliefs different now than they were then? What issues are in your life now that were in your life then? What part of your past are you possibly repeating? Are you making better decisions now than you did then? Is there a lesson learned in the past that can be applied to your present life?

Working with this kind of dream symbolism takes some time, but it can clarify what is going on in your life now.

· · · ·

Balancing Your Second Chakra

The stones to balance the second chakra are carnelian and red-orange coral. Carnelian is protective and aids in past-life recall. It helps to remove sorrows and cleanses and rejuvenates tissues and cells.

Coral quiets the emotions and brings peace. It balances the sexual, creative energies and provides focus to achieve one's goals. It is a protective stone that connects one to the deepest spiritual energies.

As before, do the first chakra, then do the remaining chakras one day at a time this week.

Lesson 19: Spell Variations

In these lessons, you will be offered many ideas that can be used in spellwork. Although there are many traditional forms of spellwork, it is important to remember that what has meaning for you will work best, and you must never be afraid to experiment and innovate. Some people feel that magic must be handed down exactly as it was in ancient times, and never changed or altered, but this is unwise. All fields of knowledge, if they are to remain useful in a constantly advancing world, must grow and expand or be left behind. If the knowledge of the magical student does not in time surpass the knowledge of the magical teacher, then the teacher has failed.

• • • •
Magical Dolls

In this lesson, we are going to discuss the use of magical dolls. A magical doll is what it sounds like—a simple cloth doll made to represent yourself or someone for whom you are working. Such a doll can be used for healing, for cultivating traits you desire to develop in your life, for prosperity, for protection, and for love magic (to draw the perfect love for you, never directed at a specific person). There are many other potential uses of a magical doll, and no doubt you can think of quite a few.

If you are doing the spell for another person, make sure you have their permission to do it.

Choose herbs whose qualities match the purpose for which you are making your doll. You might also use some stones whose qualities are appropriate as well. Pick the day and the moon phase that correspond to your goal.

Have two pieces of fabric cut in the shape of a human. Prepare a written version of your spell, setting forth your intent —that is, what you want to happen. When you are ready to do the spell, ground/release, shield, and enter your stillness.

Sew the pieces of the doll together, leaving the top of the head open to add herbs, stones, etc. Concentrate on the purpose of this spell the entire time you are making the doll. You can add yarn or some form of artificial hair to match the hair of the person the doll represents, or you can use colored markers to draw hair on. If you want, dress the doll in clothing made out of something owned by the person. It is important that the doll represent the person it is supposed to be. If that is real in your mind, then you have made a successful doll.

Read the spell out loud and place all your items inside the doll, then sew the top of the doll together. Say something like:

*Behold, I have created this magic
doll and infused it with my will.
As I do will, so mote it be!*

Wrap the doll carefully and leave it on the altar until you manifest your goal.

Some people keep the doll after their goal is achieved, and some release the herbs, etc., back to the universe. Do what feels right to you.

Some people like to use the term "poppet" to describe a magical doll. There is nothing inherently wrong with this, but unless you are British it is going to sound rather affected.

· · · ·

Planting a Garden

Many Wiccans keep a magical garden in which they grow plants they plan to use in ritual or spellwork, or which they are cultivating because of the plants' specific magical properties. All plants have specific magical properties, whether they are being grown for that reason or not, and as these lessons progress, we will discuss these in great detail. The plants, flowers, herbs, and trees that grow in your yard can offer protection, prosperity, love, healing, and peace. If you are fortunate enough to be able to plant an outside garden, you have many options available to you. A Wiccan garden can be a formal, landscaped affair or a casual, seemingly random one.

If you can't plant an outside garden, you can grow many flowers and herbs inside on your windowsills and in hanging containers. While this is a more limited option, it still allows you to enjoy the benefits that come from the magical properties of plants.

Some plants and flowers are poisonous, either in part or the whole plant (for example, every part of the morning glory plant is poisonous). Make it a point to research any plant before you consider eating it, and do not assume that any plant is edible unless you are absolutely certain.

For magical uses of the many plants and flowers available, an excellent book on this subject is *Cunningham's Encyclopedia of Magical Herbs* by Scott Cunningham.

In our next lesson, we will discuss the magic of herbs, herb gardens, and the magical correspondences of trees.

When planning a garden, whether for magical, comestible, or ornamental purposes, consult the spirits of your place and enquire as to their wishes and advice. They may make recommendations to improve the garden that would not have occurred to you, or they may suggest changing its location or layout. The spirits of place have a better understanding of the energies of your area and may be of great help in things such as this. The spirits of place can also sometimes be of help energetically, either in directing you to which areas are energetically strongest or by helping you see how to strengthen a given area energetically.

You can do this through your Hall of Consciousness or through meditation at your altar. Make sure to thank the spirits of place for their aid, and perhaps make a symbolic offering to them of flowers, a stone, or anything that you feel may be appropriate.

• • • •

Personal Power

In this section, we are going to share a few words about how to increase our personal energy. The work and rituals you have been doing in these lessons should act to increase your energy automatically, because our energy, like our physical muscles, is increased through use. However, you can also increase your personal energy intentionally through a program of energetic exercises, and that is what is discussed here.

The more "congruent" you are—that is, the extent to which your life reflects your inner beliefs and values—the more energy you have. When we depart from our inner beliefs, it sometimes creates a kind of internal division, with parts of our energy becoming blocked or caught in these inner contradictions. Consequently, the more self-knowledge we develop, and the more we act from that self-knowledge, the less often such inner contradictions will arise to block our energy. Techniques for clearing such inner blockages when they do arise are discussed elsewhere in these lessons under "soul retrieval," a very important and useful practice.

Here is a simple way we can increase our personal energy. Ground/release, shield, and enter your stillness. Visualize a sphere of brilliant white light about six to twelve inches above your head. This is the divine light of the universe. Now feel this energy fill your body as a flowing, pulsing light. Do this until you feel energized. Keep what you need, and release the excess energy back to the universe.

Another way to increase your personal power is to put your personal stamp on your surroundings, whether at home or at work. This extends to the clothes you wear and the vehicle you drive. When you surround yourself with objects that express the inner you, these objects increase that energy and reflect it back to you. When decorating your house or buying clothes, ask yourself if your choices reflect your personal taste or what is "in" at the moment. Your surroundings and clothes are a genuine expression of yourself.

Dream Guardians

We will now discuss the idea of a dream guardian. A dream guardian, as the name might suggest, is an astral golem created to guard you while you sleep and aid in your dreaming. Such a golem can assist you in your dreams by helping you attract the kinds of dreams you desire, such as clear answers to questions, by protecting you from bad dreams, perhaps helping such dreams assume more positive forms when they contain a needed message, or eliminating them altogether in some cases, or by actually figuring as a character and/or guide in your dreams. Such a golem is an energetic construct you create and empower. The golem can be visualized in any form you desire—human, animal, or otherwise. Whatever form you give it should be one you see as comforting and protective. As a rule, the golem is usually represented by a physical object, such as a doll, statue, or painting—whichever form is easiest for you to work with.

Having created such a guardian, you should speak to it regularly and give it periodic offerings, such as lighting a candle for it, in order to keep your bond with it strong. If the golem is not regularly interacted with, it will fade away over time.

Your childhood home is often a dream symbol of your spiritual life, your spiritual progress, and the issues in your life that affect your spirituality. Dreams of being there are significant. Go through your dream journal and make a list of the different places you have dreamed of, paying special attention to any dreams of your childhood home and the issues of those dreams.

Also compare the different places with what was going on in the dream, and see if any particular place or symbol may be a signpost for a change in the level of consciousness or dimension in the dream. You would know this by the quality of the dream, the action in the dream (such as dealing with spiritual issues) the feeling you had in the dream, or extremely clear colors.

Balancing Your Third Chakra

This week, we will work on balancing your third chakra. Yellow and golden stones are used for this. Choose from citrine, yellow topaz, or amber. As before, start with placing the stone of your choice on your root chakra for half an hour, then the next day place it on your second chakra, and so on, until you have used it on all seven chakras.

Citrine regenerates the body, balances the central nervous system, and aligns the body on all levels—etheric, emotional, mental, and physical. It aids clarity and the intellect, and psychic and sexual energy.

Yellow topaz heals the etheric body, balances the central nervous system, and detoxifies and heals the sacral-cranial spinal rhythm. It assists treatment of insomnia and depression.

Amber is a stone of heat and quickness. It repairs the aura, protects against psychic attack, and calms.

Lesson 20:
Herbal Gardens

In botanical terms, *herb* has a very specific definition: that is, an herb is a plant that does not have a woody stem and that dies down to ground level each fall. However, in common Wiccan usage, an herb is any plant that has magical or ritual use, regardless of whether the local Master Gardener would recognize it as an herb or otherwise. It is not unusual to find items that are actually animal based, such as ambergris, civit, or musk, discussed under "Herbs" because they are used in similar ways.

Many Wiccans make extensive use of herbs, using them in cooking but also in incense, anointing oils, and magical charms, as well as using them in various ways in ritual. Many Wiccans like to make these things themselves, feeling that this imbues the items with their own personal energy and makes them more effective for magical usage. Many other Wiccans, however, buy their herbs, incenses, and oils from the local grocery or metaphysical shop, or nowadays online. Which of these alternatives you prefer is simply a matter of personal choice.

Herb gardens are common outside of the Wiccan community as well as inside it. Everyone can enjoy the beauty of growing herbs in a garden, as well as the wonderful scents that many herbs produce—but many Wiccans value their herb gardens because these gardens provide them with fresh ingredients for ritual and magical items. The magical energies of herbs, which will be discussed in detail below, can add their qualities to a yard (or porch garden, in the city) just by being there. Or we can harvest them and use the herbs in many ways.

Many Wiccans plant specific herbs for the purpose of bringing protection, tranquility, or prosperity to their homes.

Many herbs contain multiple qualities, such as magical, culinary, and healing. The number of herbs to keep on hand will depend on your individual needs. Below is a list of the magical properties of some common herbs:

African Violet: spirituality, protection

Allspice: courage, money, strength, healing, luck, energy

Angelica: meditation, divination, visions, protection, exorcism, health

Balm of Gilead: manifestation, protection, healing, love

Basil: happiness, love, wealth, mend quarrels, sympathy

Borage: courage, financial gain, psychic abilities

Caraway: protects against theft, improves health, aids the mind

Cardamom: lust, love

Catnip: beauty, love, happiness

Chamomile: love, meditation, calming (a tea of chamomile is relaxing and promotes sleep)

Clover: protects, attracts fidelity, love, prosperity, success

Comfrey: attracts prosperity, protects travelers

Coriander: healing, love

Dill: protection, money, luck

Fennel: healing, protection

Garlic: protects, guards against theft, useful for exorcism, healing, lust

Lavender: releases stress, gives peaceful sleep

Lemon balm: love, success, healing

Marigold: divination, for dreams, makes a healing salve, legal matters, use as a border in gardens to repel insects

Mint: purifies, heals, attracts prosperity and creativity

Mugwort: dreams, divination, protection, aids psychic ability

Rosemary: cleansing, purification, protection

Thyme: courage, protection, sleep

Valerian: love, sleep

Vervain: creativity, healing, prosperity, sleep, love

White sage: cleanses, purifies, protects

Yarrow: banishing, attracts love, aids psychic abilities

For an in-depth study of the properties of herbs, there have been a number of books written. Scott Cunningham is probably the best-known author, and his books are readily available at bookstores. The Internet is also a good resource.

Additionally, you may find it helpful to a have gardening book for herbs to help choose the right herbs for your specific climate. The shape of your garden can vary from traditional rows to anything you wish. A pentagram is an especially Wiccan garden design, as you might imagine.

If you don't have a yard, you can use window boxes, hanging planters, or place small pots on windowsills. Homegrown herbs will typically contain more energy than those you purchase.

Trees add energy to your yard and neighborhood. Below are some common trees and their magical correspondences:

Alder: strength, protection

Apple: aids magic, health, healing, fertility, love, occult knowledge

Ash: wisdom, spiritual knowledge

Beech: tolerance, a link to knowledge of the past

Birch: new beginnings, cleansing, purification, birth, rebirth

Cedar: prosperity, spirituality, healing, cleansing, protection

Cherry: death, rebirth, new awareness

Elder: healing, prosperity, protection, birth, death

Elm: protection, intuition

Hawthorne: protection, magic, creativity

Hazel: wisdom, divination

Holly: magic, protection, mystery

Juniper: protection, sociality

Maple: love, balance, psychic ability

Oak: magic, strength, endurance, healing, prosperity

Orange: emotional clarity, release of trauma

Palm: protection, power, peace

Pine: fertility, creativity, earth energy

Poplar: success, magic, protection

Rowan/mountain ash: magic, protection, intuition

Spruce: healing, intuition

Sycamore: love, communication

Walnut: protection, prosperity

Willow: clairvoyance, the Goddess, magic, healing, intuition, inner vision, dreams

You can use flowers, herbs, plants, and trees to surround yourself with the energies you want in your life. Now is the time for research and planning your garden.

• • • •

Creating Your Reality

They say that age is a state of mind. This is a truism because the physical is a manifestation of the spiritual—our inner qualities can, in fact, strongly affect the outer. Many people grow "old" not because their bodies have passed a certain point in years, but because their consciousness has passed a certain point in rigidity. Beliefs, attitudes, and habits have confined them in rigid patterns that cause them to limit their lives to what they think their lives "should" be. Inspiration and flexibility are rejected. It is a kind of spiritual rut. "Youth" in the sense that most people use the term is not about years so much as attitude—the willingness to continue growing and experiencing life, holding on to or recapturing the awe and joy of living.

How do we do this? Well, here's a start. If you are feeling "old," whatever your age, take a few minutes each day and focus on feeling "younger"—whatever that means to you. Imagine that you look and feel and act the way you *want* to look and feel and act. Imagine what that feels like, what it is like, and focus on that feeling. Concentrate on this feeling—but don't think about it, *feel it.* Then, after a few minutes, let it go and carry on with your day. Do this for a while and see how much difference it makes.

Be conscious of the way you look at yourself and the attitudes you have towards yourself. Are you focusing on limitations? Do you unconsciously believe that your physical age requires you to act "old"? If you are doing these things, stop. If you find yourself with a limiting idea about your age or health, replace that idea with a different, more positive one. This is especially important in terms of how you see yourself. What you focus on will tend to manifest, and conversely, you cannot manifest what you do not focus on—so focus on a positive image!

Stay involved in the present instead of longing for the past. See the many changes in the world as opportunities and challenges. Stay excited about life and learning. Youth and health begin in the mind, as does everything else.

· · · ·

Energetic Patterns

Each of us has a certain energetic pattern that is unique to us. You might think of this like the psychic version of DNA. It is our psychic fingerprint, the key to who we are. In many cultures, this pattern is represented by a symbolic image that is unique to the person—a vision image.

This image cannot be given to us by another person; it must come from Spirit. There are many ways to pursue the image, including the famous vision quest. In this case, however, we are going to pursue it through meditation.

This week, you will journey to your personal Hall of Consciousness, as we have discussed in previous lessons, to ask your inner self for a symbol that represents your personal pattern. Once you have done this, you should draw this symbol in your Book of Shadows. You do not need to be a great artist to this—it is the image that is important, not the skill with which it is depicted, so do not let that inhibit you.

Next, you should meditate with your symbol every day for a few minutes. Ground/release, shield, enter your stillness, and feel the energy of your symbol within yourself. Doing this will make it easier for you to clearly express your inner self and increase your effectiveness in the world.

· · · ·

Flow

The concept of flow means that things in your life move along smoothly and without struggle—they flow like a gentle river. This is also called serendipity. How do we create flow in our lives? To do this, we must work with Spirit and our own Higher Selves. First, we must try to align with the higher purposes of our lives and fulfill these. If we

are moving in the direction of our highest good rather than struggling to go in other directions, flow happens naturally. We can do this by setting the intent to move in sync with our highest purposes and through meditating on what these purposes are and then consciously bringing ourselves into alignment with them.

Another way we can promote flow in our lives is by talking to Spirit daily and telling Spirit what we desire from each day—leaving room for the unexpected as well—and asking Spirit to bring these desires to us in the best possible way for all concerned. As always, such desires must be with harm toward none.

A practical application of working with flow is to think of a difficult situation where you want or need to say something to someone and you are unsure about the approach. Mentally practice what you want to say. When you are with the person, the opportunity will arise, and the words will come easily, with little effort on your part.

· · · ·

Balancing Your Fourth Chakra

This week, you will balance your fourth chakra, the heart chakra. Green and pink stones are used for this purpose.

Rose quartz is one of the best choices, as it heals the emotions and childhood trauma, removing blocks that bind the free flow of loving energy. This includes self-love as well as love of others. You started with rose quartz on all the chakras before you began working on individual chakras. You can use it again or use one of the other stones recommended. Mother-of-pearl, while not an actual stone, is good for the heart chakra. It absorbs sorrow and pain and releases them from one's experience. It gives strength, endurance, peace, and joy. This works slowly but thoroughly. Blue aventurine and blue-green aventurine are good stones for the heart chakra. Both stones heal, soothe, and balance the emotions. Blue aventurine opens and mends a broken heart. Moss agate eases emotional pain and increases trust and strength.

As before, start with the root chakra and do one chakra a day.

Lesson 21:
Concept of Time

This week we are going to take a little time to talk about... well, time. It's about time that we got around to time; for most people, time is one of the most rigid and immutable aspects of life. There's never enough time. Time flies. Time slips away. Time waits for no man ... But magic is not about most people.

Magic works because the seemingly immutable physical and temporal world is created from the very mutable spiritual world. This apparent rigidity of the material world is actually an illusion. The material, created as it is from the spiritual, is actually very mutable, even fluid. And the material can be shaped and changed by those who realize that its seeming solidity is illusion. This is the heart of the mystery that is Witchcraft.

However, it is one thing to realize that the physical world is actually very mutable and another thing altogether to start changing it. Many people who want to study magic are not remotely prepared for the fact that it actually works—especially to the extent that it does. To learn that reality is not as you thought it was can be exciting; to experience that reality is not as you thought it was can be shattering if you are not prepared for it. This is why so much emphasis is placed on grounding and on knowing yourself—so that when you eventually start working with major magic, you will be working from a secure center.

The Cabalists have traditionally held that no one should be permitted to study Cabala unless they are married, have children, and are over forty years of age—on the premise that these things will provide the needed grounding as they explore the illusory nature of reality.

Obviously enough, we do not agree with this point of view, but in contemplating and eventually interacting with the illusory nature of reality, we cannot stress too much the importance of a strong center and a deep self-knowledge.

So saying, let us examine the nature of time. Time is an illusion. That doesn't mean that time has no reality, but rather that the reality of time depends entirely on the level from which you are relating to it. Time isn't nearly as rigid as we perceive it to be. It is possible to manipulate our experience of time—to shorten or lengthen our experience of it, and to travel backwards and forwards within it. You have already had some experience of this when you asked for the future outcome of various decisions. Some of these skills are easy to learn, others require effort and time, but all are worth it.

We are not going to discuss techniques of manipulating time at this point, but rather merely introduce you to the idea of time's mutability and the importance of approaching the illusory nature of reality from a strong base in yourself.

• • • •

Personal Symbols

Personal symbols expressed through masks, shields, or banners are a time-honored way of expressing aspects of our spirituality and our personal power. Such personal symbols can be made to express many different aspects of the self as well as many different roles we play in life. By externalizing these symbols, we validate these aspects of ourselves and reinforce them. Such externalization also allows us to focus on these aspects of ourselves by using the symbols which represent them for meditation, magic, and so forth.

We can also use masks, shields, or banners to symbolize aspects of ourselves that we wish to develop further, such as skills or abilities we would like to increase or new roles we wish to grow into.

Here we are going to discuss making a mask, but the same considerations could also be applied to a shield or banner. Because a mask is worn over the face, it speaks directly to issues of identity in a way that shields and banners do not, so a mask lends itself to dramatic ritual uses.

To make your mask, you will find the following list helpful:

- Paper, poster board, or a material such as papier-mâché
- A balloon
- Paint, crayons, or colored pencils
- Scissors
- Glue or rubber cement
- Beads, feathers, sequins, bits of glass, etc.

The basic mask can be cut out of paper or poster board. For a more three-dimensional mask, use an inflated balloon and cover it with papier-mâché. In the latter instance, wait until the papier-mâché has dried and then break the balloon to free the mask for use.

It is possible to use one of the preformed mask-faces available from craft stores, but this takes away a bit from the experience, and we advise against it, at least for the first ritual mask you make.

Now consider the qualities you are trying to express through this mask and how you perceive them in terms of visual depiction. You will find that the color or colors you use on the mask, and the patterns you use for the colors, have a great deal to do with the final effect. However, this is not really a thinking exercise so much as a feeling one—allow yourself to be guided by what *feels* right. Try to avoid preconceived notions, and let the mask tell you what it wants to be like.

Once you have painted the mask, you will want to add other decorations. Allow the mask to be as simple or ornate as it wishes. You will know what the mask wants to be by what *feels right*.

When the mask is complete, you should cleanse, consecrate, and charge it at your altar, as you did your sacred tools.

Keep it in a place where you can see it easily. If you feel it doesn't want to be in public view, keep it in your bedroom or somewhere else that is private.

By making this mask and seeing it on a regular basis, you strengthen the qualities it represents for you. You may find that the mask represents qualities you don't have yet, but the making and viewing of it will draw forth these qualities within you.

Building Your Relationship with Objects

In lesson 16, you were asked to build an intimate relationship with an object in your one-block area, such as a tree, bush, stone, etc. Now pick another object in your one-block area and build a relationship with it. Continue to do this with other objects as well as the first one you picked. In effect, you are becoming acquainted with your "family," the "people" who share your space. Remember to send them the blessings that are yours to send on a regular basis, and to ask them for help and advice as needed.

Energy Drain

The people you spend time with and the way you spend your time either adds to your personal power or depletes it. Pay attention to the effect the people around you have on your energy. We discussed the concept of psychic vampires in an earlier lesson. Many people who drain your energy aren't aware of it and don't do it on purpose, but the effect is the same for you. When you must be around these people, make a practice of doing extra shielding.

When you spend time doing things you enjoy, you increase your energy and therefore your personal power. If you don't allow yourself time for these things, you drain away your power.

Negative emotions and thoughts drain your power too. Spend some time each day being aware of what you think and feel. Consciously release all thoughts and emotions that do not serve you. We all have people and situations that irritate and anger or depress us, but dwelling on them only hurts us. Bless these things when you are aware of them, and then release them. Consider this energetic housecleaning and be consistent with it.

Another area that drains your energy is anything in your life that you feel you

have to explain or justify. Live your life as close to your values and ideals as you can. If you feel you have done something that betrays these, make whatever amends you can and go on. Explore these areas that you feel defensive about and see why this is so. Then make whatever changes will help you. Never explain, justify, or defend your beliefs or actions. No matter what you do, you will never please someone else all of the time. Release this expectation, if you have it, and watch your personal power increase.

• • • •

Visualization Exercise

This week you will sharpen your visualization skills. You will do this by using a picture as a starting point for a guided visualization. This can be a picture you own or a picture from a catalog, magazine, or the Internet. It can be a picture of a real place or an imaginary one. Be sure the scene in the picture is a pleasant one. Since you now know that all visualizations are real experiences, be careful not to let in negativity by a poor choice of picture.

Study the picture until you are familiar with it. Choose a point of entry, then ground/release, shield, and enter your stillness. Enter the picture at the point you have chosen and walk beyond it, being aware of landmarks that will allow you to return to your entry point easily. If you forget the landmarks, you can return to normal consciousness simply by choosing to—in fact, program that instruction into your visualization. But by remembering the landmarks and returning by them, you build greater control of the experience.

Experience this in as much sensory detail as possible. Be aware of any other beings you see or encounter. When you are through, return by the landmarks to your point of entry, step back through it, and ground/release, then write your experience. Do this no more than two times a week, as it can drain your energy if done too often.

An important part of dream work is taking action on guidance received in your dreams. In a dream where the guidance is clear, this is easy to do. In a dream with no clear guidance, you can honor a dream by enacting some part of it. An example of this is if you dream of wearing a certain color or eating a certain food, you can do that in waking life. This keeps the door open between your dreaming self and your waking self. Whatever message a dream seems to contain for you, it needs to be honored with action. In your dream journal, make a place in your interpretation for the action you will take on the dream.

Balancing Your
Fifth Chakra

This week you will balance your fifth chakra, the throat chakra. Aquamarine, sodalite, apatite, celestite, blue lace agate, and azurite are blue stones to balance this chakra. Aquamarine purifies, relieves stress, and aids in psychic awareness and self-expression. Sodalite is good for honesty in communication; apatite brings harmony and inner peace, aids intuition, and aids in meditation. Celestite is a strong stone that raises your spiritual vibration, aids communication, brings healing and compassion, calms, and helps in astral travel. Blue lace agate gives peace and calmness and aids creativity and spirituality. Azurite aligns all of the chakras, helps increase psychic awareness, and is good for meditation.

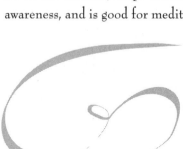

Lesson 22: Numerology

In this lesson, we will begin our discussion on numerology as it relates to you as an individual, and we will continue this topic in the next lesson. The focus we want to present is numerology as a guidepost to your strengths, weaknesses, and your innermost desires, which you may not consciously be aware of. We do create our own reality, but often what our conscious mind wants is in conflict with our deepest selves. We are influenced more than we realize by society, our peers, and our family's perceptions and expectations of us. Numerology is a mirror for us of our true selves. A chart can show us qualities and abilities that we lack and those we can improve by being aware and working with them.

Numerology works with your birth date and the numerical value of your name. In this week's lesson, we will work with your birth date. The numerical value of your birth date shows your destiny number—in other words, what your purpose is in this lifetime, what you need to learn and accomplish. To find this number, write out your birth date in a straight line, using the following example. Total the numbers, reducing them to a single digit. For August (the eighth month) 28, 1974, you would write:

8+2+8+1+9+7+4=39, (3 + 9) which reduces to 12, (1+ 2) resulting in the number three. Three is the destiny number for this person.

If your intermediate result is a double-digit number such as 11, 22, 33, etc., do not reduce any further. These numbers are master numbers and have meanings of their own.

Here is an example of a birth date that ends in a master number: August 29, 1945.

8+2+9+1+9+4+5=38, (3 + 8)=11. Eleven is the destiny number for this person.

Now let's look at the positive and negative energies of the numbers.

One

Positive: One is independent and very creative, with strong physical and creative drives. If an introvert, one is often a loner, with a strong need for solitude and personal space. If an extrovert, one is very sociable and a natural leader.

Negative: One can be selfish, obstinate, and overbearing.

Two

Positive: Two is the number of the peacemaker. Twos need balance in their life and harmony in their surroundings. Twos are sensitive and caring individuals. They enjoy working with others and need to share their feelings with others. They are very psychic and often artistic.

Negative: When twos express in the negative, they are overly dependent and too easily influenced by others. It is easy for twos to look on the negative side of a situation and become depressed.

Three

Positive: Three is the number of the positive extrovert. These people are friendly, outgoing, and a pleasure to be around. Three is a number of luck, prosperity, and good fortune.

Negative: Threes can be lazy and take their good fortune for granted. Things come easily to them, and they don't work to develop their abilities.

Four

Positive: Four is the number of the practical person with common sense who is a builder and deals with the mundane world. Careful and methodical, they do their work well and function efficiently in the real world. They were born knowing that two plus two make four. Four is the number of stability and structure.

Negative: Four needs to learn the lesson of taking one step at a time and building carefully. They struggle to understand the practical, real world.

Five

Positive: Five is the number of the person who enjoys change and living on the edge. They seek to thoroughly understand a person or a situation. Unfortunately, they can lose interest in the person or situation when they achieve this understanding. Their lesson in life can be to accept the change they crave or to put down roots and release the need for change.

Negative: Five can be scattered, take on too many projects at once, and not pay attention to details. A five expressing in the negative can be dishonest in pursuit of their goals.

Six

Positive: The energy of six tends to focus on family, home, and security. Sixes need balance, harmony, and peaceful, secure, predictable surroundings. Their destiny is to learn the lessons of home and family.

Negative: Sixes can become self-centered and only able to see their own point of view. Six is an intense and driven number. These people can

be obsessive/compulsive when under stress. They may appear callous and uncaring to other people, all the while driving themselves to be and do more and judging themselves harshly when they feel they can't.

Seven

Positive: Seven is the number of the seeker after spirituality and truth. Sevens may explore many paths and occasional strange byways in their pursuit of this understanding. They are driven by a need to know and understand everything that enters their awareness. These people are original, idealistic, and definitely follow a different drummer.

Negative: Sevens crave freedom and independence but are not always willing to grant that freedom to others. They can be opinionated and resent any attempt at control by others.

Eight

Positive: Eight is the number of money and power. Eights may be born knowing how to acquire money and handle power, or their destiny may be to learn this lesson. Eight is ambitious, determined, and willing to work hard to accomplish their goals.

Negative: Eights can be bossy, domineering, and vindictive. They may run roughshod over other people to achieve their goals, or they may run from money and power and resent others who have it. They may gossip and be backbiting.

Nine

Positive: Nine represents a love of humanity and an active practice of spirituality. Nine is optimistic, helpful, positive, giving, and sees the good in everyone.

Negative: Nine can be so focused on others that it neglects its own welfare. Placing all their focus on the spiritual, they can be innocent babies in the everyday world. They can be impractical and unaware of the realities of daily life.

Double Digits

Eleven is a number of strong psychic and magical talents. Elevens can be spiritual teachers who are driven by high ideals and perfectionism. Elevens are artistic and expressive. Having this as a destiny number may indicate fame.

Twenty-two is a number of manifestation and the ability to work one's will in the physical world. Twenty-two is extremely energetic and creative, constantly restructuring and improving things.

Thirty-three is a number of living one's ideals to the fullest, of putting the welfare of others before one's own. Thirty-threes are dedicated and capable of self-sacrifice.

Forty-four is a number of one who teaches by example. It is the number of teachers and spiritual leaders.

Fifty-five is a number of one who seeks the answers to all things. The pursuit of knowledge and understanding is their driving force.

Sixty-six is a number of rebirth, regeneration, and transcendence. This is one who seeks to ascend the material world and merge with the divine.

Seventy-seven is a number of spiritual knowledge and wisdom, the quest for spiritual growth.

Eighty-eight is a number of success, achievement, excellence, and accomplishment. Harmony is created by living one's higher purpose.

Ninety-nine is the number of Samadhi, the attainment of perfection and oneness with the divine.

All double numbers can be expressed in three different ways: either one at a time, or all three in different areas of one's life. For example, the number eleven can be expressed as such or reduced to two and expressed that way, or it can be lived as a double one, which intensifies the one vibration and doubles the effect. One may be a well-known teacher of metaphysics, thus expressing the eleven vibration, while expressing the energy of two in their relationships and the independent and artistic double one by also being an artist, whether a professional artist or doing art as a hobby.

Author Dan Millman wrote an excellent book on the destiny number and the ways it can express in your life. If you want to truly understand yourself and your purposes for this lifetime, it is recommended. It is *The Life You Were Born to Live: A Guide to Finding Your Life Purpose.*

Next week we will cover the energies of the numbers associated with your name and the insights we can get from them.

• • • •

Connecting with Earth Energy

A way to strengthen your connection with earth energy is to take time each day to send energy and blessings to each direction, including the above, the below, and the center, which is also yourself. You can use any imagery that you want for these directions.

The Native American associations are winged ones for the east, trees, and plants; two-legged for the south; all that swims for the west; and the stone people for the north. For below, the image of Mother Earth (the physical earth) and Grandmother Earth (the energetic Spirit of Earth). For above, the sky, stars, and planets; the center is yourself, where all of these energies meet.

• • • •

Guided Visualization

This week, you will use a picture for a guided visualization. Choose a picture of an actual place you haven't seen and know nothing about. Enter and explore it, as you did for the picture you used last week. Pay attention to all details, telling yourself you will remember all that you see and experience. Return and write down your experience, as you did before.

Next, find out all you can about the place you visited. Find other pictures of it, if possible. Check to see how many of the details of your visualization are accurate. After you have done this a few times, pick a picture of a place, such as a sacred site like Stonehenge or a well-known castle, that is centuries old, and use it for your visualization. It is possible that you can visit it at a time in its past. As before, do this no more than twice a week.

• • • •

Balancing Your Sixth Chakra

This week, you will balance your sixth chakra, your third eye. Lapis lazuli, sugilite, selenite, and moonstone are among the stones to balance the sixth chakra.

Lapis lazuli protects against psychic attacks and increases intuition, inner power, and creativity. It expands awareness and mental power. It activates and energizes the throat and brow chakras, and helps in working with dreams. It increases awareness and spirituality.

Sugilite increases psychic ability and spirituality. It protects against psychic attack.

Selenite is a stone of very high energy. It helps to open the sixth and seventh chakras.

Moonstone opens the psychic centers, and aids trance, psychometry, astral balance, and spirituality. It is an excellent stone to use for inner work and growth. It banishes negativity from the chakras and helps to open the emotions. It brings confidence, happiness, and good fortune.

Lesson 23:
Numerical Value of Letters

This week, we will work with the numerical value of letters. The numerical value of all the letters in your name is your expression, or base number. This number is the essence of who you truly are and what you came into this life already knowing. Below is a chart showing the numerical value of each letter:

1	2	3	4	5	6	7	8	9
A	B	C	D	E	F	G	H	I
J	K	L	M	N	O	P	Q	R
S	T	U	V	W	X	Y	Z	

To find your expression, or base number, write out your name as it appears on your birth certificate. Using John Henry Smith as an example, add the numbers together across the line, reducing the result until you get a single number, unless you get a master number.

John Henry Smith
1685 85597 14928

Added together as a single line, 1+6+8+5+8+5+5+9+7+1+4+9+2+8=78=15=6.

The base, or expression, number is six.

Now we will find the numerical value of the vowels and consonants of the name. The numerical value of the vowels shows the soul urge, or the heart's desire. It is the secret, innermost longing. It is what the soul wants to accomplish regardless of what the conscious mind chooses. Some numerologists believe that the soul number shows the wisdom learned in other lives, the growth of the soul through time.

The numerical value of the consonants in the name is the personality number. This is how you appear to others. This number can show you talents you may possess without being aware of them.

You will notice in the name John Henry Smith the letter y is counted as a vowel. This is because each syllable of a word has to contain a vowel. Y and W can be used as vowels in this way.

6 5 7 9 =27=9
John Henry Smith
1 85 85 9 14 28=51=6

For John Henry Smith, the expression/base number is six.

The soul, or heart's desire, number is nine.

The personality number is six.

The expression/base number of six, expressed in the positive, shows a person to whom home and family are important. This is a person who drives himself to achieve, to whom status and recognition by others is important.

Expressed in the negative, he may be so focused on his own interests and feelings

that he is unaware of the feelings and interests of others.

The soul number, or heart's desire, is nine, which expressed in the positive shows a person who lives their spiritual understanding and is optimistic, helpful, positive, giving, and sees the good in everyone. This person loves humanity.

Expressed negatively, this person can be impractical and unaware of the realities of daily life. There is a danger that they will neglect their own needs while attending to the needs of others.

The personality number is six, the same as the base, or expression, number. This reinforces the energy of both numbers and also shows that the way others see him is the way he truly is.

Now we will explore the numerical values of the name in a different way. Pythagoras developed the numerical square to show which numbers, and therefore their qualities, were strongest, weakest, or missing entirely, in the numbers of the name.

Any number on the chart without a circle is a "missing" number (see charts, opposite page). The qualities of that number are not part of our experience. We can work to overcome this and consciously develop these qualities, but we will have to put effort into it. Below is a list of the numbers the way they express as "missing" numbers:

When one is a missing number, the person lacks confidence and may not have a strong sense of self. They react rather than taking action.

When two is a missing number, it is hard to experience and express emotions. It can be difficult for this person to understand how other people feel. They can feel a lack of connection to other people.

When three is a missing number, communication and self-expression can be a problem.

When four is a missing number, the person can have trouble coping with the practicalities of the everyday world. It may be difficult for them to manage money or to understand that to get to point E you must go from A to B to C to D first.

When five is a missing number, the person has a hard time dealing with change. They may lack a zest for life and merely exist, wondering why life is so dull.

When six is a missing number, the person may have no sense of family connection. It is possible that family has been their source of greatest emotional pain and may be part of their karmic lesson.

When seven is a missing number, the person may have no spiritual understanding or desire for knowledge. This can be a nose-to-the-grindstone person.

When eight is a missing number, the person isn't comfortable with money, success, or power. There isn't a drive to succeed. They may have low energy and stamina.

When nine is a missing number, the person lacks compassion. They probably don't live whatever spiritual ideals they have, preferring instead to live on the surface of whatever spiritually is commonly accepted.

Below is the number square with the numbers of John Henry Smith's name entered onto it. Each time the numerical value of a number occurs in the name, the number is circled. John Henry Smith lacks the number 3 in his name. This shows that communication and self-expression may be difficult for him. The numbers with the most circles are 5 and 8, showing that he is adaptable, comfortable with change, and adventurous (5), and has a strong drive for money, power, and success (8). The other numbers have at least one circle, so while they are not as strong, the qualities of these numbers are available to him.

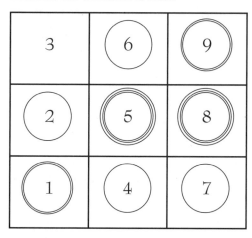

Many people use only their first and last names. This changes the qualities they have access to in their lives. You will notice in the chart below that by leaving out his middle name, John Henry Smith loses the energy of the number 7, which is now a latent quality he isn't using.

John Smith
1685 14928

3	6	9
2	5	8
1	4	7

When women marry and take their husband's name, they may gain or lose desirable qualities by the name change. A woman should use the number chart before marriage to decide which name is most beneficial for her to use.

The lines created by the numbers on the above chart, such as the vertical line created by 1, 2, and 3, also have meaning. All horizontal, vertical, and diagonal lines have specific meanings. There is not enough room in this lesson to go into these meanings, but it is recommended you get a

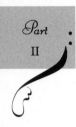

numerology book that discusses this (not all of them do), and see how they apply to your name.

If you go by a nickname, you change the numerical value of your name as it expresses in your life. This, too, can be positive or negative. Once you know how to find these values, you should see what value this name usage adds to or detracts from your life. If you don't like these values, change the form of the name you use, or change the spelling of it, and work with it until you are happy.

The values of your birth name will always be available to you as latent energies, whatever name or form of your name you may choose to use.

This is a complex subject that has only been touched on in this lesson. If numerology interests you, further research is recommended. When you find one or two books that you really like, work with them.

. . . .

Bonding with Elements

Beginning in this lesson, you will learn to bond with the elements. To bond with the earth, find a private place outside, if possible, or you can do this exercise inside if necessary. Allow yourself about an hour and fifteen minutes for this exercise. You will need something to cover your head with; this can be a shawl, scarf, or afghan. Lie facedown on the earth or on the floor. (If you are lying on the floor, be aware of

the earth, however far below you it may be. You still connect to the actual earth.) Stay there for fifteen minutes, which you will estimate. At the end of the fifteen minutes, sit up, and cover your face and head with the shawl. Sit there for five minutes, then lie facedown for an additional fifteen minutes. Sit up and cover your face and head again. Do this a total of four times.

This will change your experience of the physical world.

. . . .

Telepathy

Telepathy is a skill you probably already practice without being aware of it. You have experienced thinking of something or starting to say something when someone you are close to, such as a family member or friend, says exactly what you were thinking or starting to say. Telepathy is easy with the people we live with and love. The bonds of love and relationship have already made a path between our minds, and the doors are open.

You can learn to do this consciously by working with someone you are close to. There is an exercise you can do to practice this. One of you should pick a category, such as fruit, flowers, jewelry, cats, dogs, etc., and choose a specific one. Then the other person tries to "feel" the specific thing being thought of. Allow two answers—the first one is usually the conscious mind trying to answer, and the second choice has a better chance of being correct. Then the other person picks a category and a specific choice within that category, and the first person tries to "feel" the correct answer. This is easier if you make a game of it, and keep it light and fun. The purpose of this exercise is not to be right all of the time, but to learn how an answer *feels* to you when it is correct.

You will find that this exercise is easier for you with one or two specific people. Work with them, and try to send each other messages. Keep them simple at first, such as a number, name, or object. Then gradually increase the complexity of the messages. You may be surprised at how well you can communicate with someone in this way.

Each of you should practice sending and then receiving a message. You may find that you are better at one skill or the other, but you should continue to practice both, and develop your abilities to your fullest potential.

• • • •

Visualization

You can visualize a web of light to use to travel in consciousness to another person. When you first practice this, do it with the person you practice telepathy with. Get the permission of the person you are working with to do this, and give them permission to travel to you. Pick a day to do this;

it isn't necessary to pick a specific time. Start by grounding, then enter your stillness (or you can do this from your Hall of Consciousness if you prefer). Visualize a web composed of light stretching out in all directions, with yourself at the center. Hold the image of the person you want to travel to in your mind while you look at the web. One strand of the web will "pull" you to follow it. Walk along it, still holding the image of the person in your mind.

When you get there, carefully observe all details, telling yourself that you will easily remember them. Then follow the strand of the web back to the center, and return to normal consciousness. As always, write down this experience while it is still fresh in your mind. Write down the time you return so you can compare it to what your friend was doing at the time.

It is possible that your friend will have a feeling of your presence while you are there, or that you will feel their presence when they travel to you. With practice, you will become proficient at this.

• • • •

Advanced Dream Work

Now we begin some advanced dream work. Pick a dream, perhaps one that has stayed with you but isn't really clear. Go to your Hall of Consciousness, and create a door that will take you back into your dream. You are conscious in this experience, so you

can ask questions of the people or symbols and get answers. You can experience parts of the dream that you don't remember. Explore this concept. Do it at least three times this week, and be sure to write down your results immediately after you return from the Hall of Consciousness.

• • • •

Balancing Your Seventh Chakra

Now we will balance the seventh chakra, the crown chakra. Stones for this purpose are clear quartz, white howlite, moonstone, and amethyst.

Clear quartz amplifies energy, both physical, mental, and electric. It brings the energy of the stars to the spiritual self.

Howlite increases subtlety, tact, and creativity.

Moonstone opens the psychic centers and aids trance, psychometry, astral balance, and spirituality. It is an excellent stone to use for inner work and growth. It banishes negativity from the chakras and helps to open the emotions. It brings confidence, happiness, and good fortune.

Amethyst balances the emotional, physical, and intellectual bodies and stabilizes kundalini energy. It clears the aura of negativity and helps to keep you grounded, calm, and contented. It relieves stress, raises spiritual vibrations, and is a valuable aid in meditation.

Lesson 24:
The Nature of Reality

The wider society tends to think of everything in linear terms. In Wicca, we think of things in cyclical terms. What does this mean to our understanding of reality? Many people, even very spiritual people, think of spirit as being "above" and "over" and of the material world as being "below" and "under." To this is added the idea that spirit is superior and the material world inferior. Because of this, some religions have gone so far as to look upon the world itself as evil and physical life as a trial to be endured and eventually escaped. This is not a Wiccan view.

Wiccans look at creation more as successive emanations from Spirit. The following chart illustrates this. The circle at the very center is Spirit: the All, the Void,

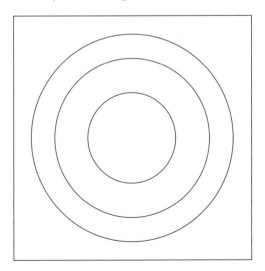

Goddess Before Creation. This is the very heart of all existence. Radiating out from this is the world of spirit: Goddess and God, the polar forces of yin and yang, the many personal gods, the monads and the many souls. The outer circle is the physical world as we know it, including our physical bodies. Everything in the physical world radiates out from the center into physical manifestation as we know it.

Rather than being a "creation" apart from Goddess, the physical world flows outward from her being. The difference in these two ideas may not at first seem so important, but when we are aware that we, along with everything else, flow into being from the heart of the Goddess, we remember that everything is valued and sacred.

This lesson is the last lesson of the second part of *Living the Wiccan Life*; this is the halfway point of the lessons. In the second half of the course, many things will be different, because we have used the first half to build up the basics and now will move on to deeper things.

· · · ·

Connecting with Goddess

We are all one with the Goddess, who is the Nuos (Greek for "the World Soul"), the universe soul. All things are connected through her. We often identify the Goddess with Earth, which is thought of as her body, but of course this is only one part

of her all-encompassing whole. The following visualization draws strength and healing from Earth, renewing our eternal connection to it and through Earth to the Goddess.

Find a comfortable position. Begin by clearing and releasing as always. Now, send down a tendril of energy, a beam of light passing down your legs and out through your feet to descend through the floor and down into Earth. Imagine that beam of light going down into the soil, deeper and deeper…down into and through the bedrock…down through Earth's crust to the very molten core of the planet. Here is the molten magma that forms Earth's center, the glowing, golden heart of Earth. Feel the heat of the magma, feel the strength, the passion, the stability of the Earth Mother. Begin to draw a bit of that glowing, golden energy upward into your beam of light. See the golden energy traveling up the beam, rising through Earth's crust, through the bedrock, up through the soil, and ultimately up through the floor and into you through your feet. Allow the golden energy to move up into your body. Let the golden energy spread through your legs, up into your hips and abdomen, into your chest and arms, and into your head. Let the energy fill you completely. Feel the strength and power of Earth's core as the energy fills you and moves through you, burning away toxins, impurities, and

blockages. Let the heat fill your body; feel it in your bones.

Now, pull your beam of energy back up from Earth's core, up through the ground and back into your body. Hold on to as much of the golden energy as you need, then release the excess, and let the image fade.

. . . .

Spirit Guides

We all have spirit guides, even though we do not all know it. We are born with some, and others come and go throughout our lives. Usually there are from five to seven guides at any given time. Most people have no conscious knowledge of their guides, but their guides are there and help them nonetheless. Some people call guides "guardian angels." Before we enter physical life, we make agreements with one or more people to be with us as guides. In between lives, we may choose to be a guide for someone else.

What do guides do? A guide reminds us of our purposes for coming into this life. A guide isn't infallible, but they can see at least a little more than we can. If we have clear goals, our guide/s can give us guidance about opportunities available to us. They can help us manifest the things we want in our lives. They are a source of comfort and help in our lives.

Are the ancestors guides? Yes, but they are not the only guides. Some guides will be ancestors—especially in certain families—but many others will not. Guides are sometimes people we have known in this life, but often they are spirits we have known in other lifetimes. In any case, the guide does not represent the conscious self of the person but rather the Higher Self, or soul. This is why sometimes a person who was not all that great in life (or even downright crummy) can be a really wonderful guide as a spirit.

Guides help us whether we are aware of them or not, but obviously the stronger our conscious connection to them and the more intentional our interactions with them, the more help they can be. This is why it is important to build a relationship with our guides.

To build a relationship with your guides, set aside a regular time to commune with them, perhaps once or twice a week, or whatever you feel comfortable with. It is good to light one or more candles and to speak to the guides, stating your purpose: that is, that you are there to commune with them and build a closer relationship with them. You might want to make a token offering to them of a small glass of water or other beverage, or a piece of candy or other small food item. This is simply to show respect—the guides do not need physical sustenance as such. The offerings can be later consumed by yourself or, if the offering is nonconsumable in nature, you should bury it outside.

Now put yourself into a comfortable position, ground, and release, then still your mind as you have learned to do. Images will come into your mind, but do not grab on to them—just let them move through. However, you should make note of these images, and write them down on a piece of paper or in a special Spirit Journal during or after the session. These may be visual images, words, or they may simply be a "knowing." In any case, make note of them. When you first start doing this, the images you get may have no special meaning, but soon enough they will begin to form coherent messages. Do realize that this may take a few tries to achieve, however. Once a connection is made, you will realize you recognize your guide by the feeling of their energy when they come in. If asked, they will usually give you a name, and you will generally have a mental image of how they look. This name and image are for your convenience, to help build a feeling of connection with them. The totality of their being can't be confined to a name and an image.

When you finish, make it a point to thank the guides. Then ground and release any excess energy. You should never try to analyze the messages you get from your guides while you are receiving them—wait

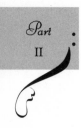

until afterwards. Suspend all judgment during the session, even if you appear to be getting nonsense. Judgment will tend to stop the process. You can analyze the information after—and you will sometimes be surprised to find meanings you did not catch at first.

Your guide/s can help you manifest the things you want, but *you* have to choose. They can't choose for you.

Rev. Don Lewis often tells the story of "The Miracle of the Jelly Roll." It goes something like this:

Back in the seventies when I was being trained by Lady Krystel, who is my cousin and went on to become the First Priestess of the Corellian Tradition, we worked quite intensely with the ancestors and the guides, as we do still today. One day they gave us a vision which we call the Miracle of the Jelly Roll. In the vision, my grandmother Mable, who is my principal guide, appeared riding a bicycle up and down the hills of San Francisco. Grandmother was wearing a very distinctive costume from a WWI-era photo of her, but oddly her face in this vision was not her own but rather the actress Jane Wyman's. It was later explained that this was to create greater distance in order to help get the message through, since it was to be acted out rather than explained.

Grandmother came to a sweet shop and, parking her bicycle, went in. She walked up to the counter and surveyed the many wonderful-looking desserts and pastries behind the glass. She said to the proprietor, "I would like a sweet, please!"

The proprietor replied, "Certainly! Which one would you like?"

Grandmother was puzzled. All the sweets looked so good. "I don't know," she said. "Which one *should* I have?"

Now the proprietor was puzzled. "You can have any one you want—you just have to choose."

"But I don't know which one is best!" Grandmother protested.

"They are all good," said the proprietor. "Which one do you *want*?" At length, Grandmother realized that the proprietor would not tell her which one to take and selected the jelly roll, which she then thoroughly enjoyed. For our part, we realized that the message was that it is the role of the guides to guide and to advise, but not to make our choices for us.

• • • •

To work with your guides, continue to sit for them two times a week. After they adjust your energy, talk over any problems or concerns with them, and be open to any guidance from them. Sometimes you will get an answer immediately, but other times the answer may come to you later. The more you do this, the stronger the connection will be. Don't just blindly do what they say if it doesn't feel right to you. Guides can advise you, but you should always keep the responsibility for making your own decisions. A guide is an advisor, not the decider.

In addition to the spirit guides you are born with, others come to you at times in your life when you are in need of their special skills, and they leave after the need has been met. As a rule, these guides come and go without your having consciously had much to do with it. However, it is also possible to recruit guides.

You may ask how on earth one would *recruit* spirit guides? By asking them for their help, of course. It is quite possible to seek out guides who have special knowledge in the areas you need help in, such as financial, spiritual, artistic, etc.

To do this, you can send out a call to the universe asking for a guide or guides skilled in the area you need. Send this call through prayer. Or you can select individuals who are in spirit and who would have the knowledge you need, and ask them if they would be willing to give guidance and help. You would do this by talking to them just as you talk to your regular guides and express your desires. They may or may not be willing, and it can only be their choice, but they are often quite amenable.

Assuming the individual spirit or spirits are willing, you would set up a time to meet and talk with them just as you do your regular guides; usually once or twice a week is good. Imagine them being there with you just as if they were alive, and discuss your concerns with them and ask them for their advice. You may not receive any information at the time but receive answers later. Eventually, you may find that your visualization has a life of its own and that your advisors communicate with you directly.

You will receive helpful information straight from the source as you continue to do this.

It is possible to add living people who are experts in your field to your board. They probably won't be aware of this, although they may dream of being there. Be sure not to cross the line of manipulation and taking advantage of them. Invite them at the level of their Higher Selves to be sure their contribution is voluntary.

• • • •

Manifesting

We will now return to our discussion of manifesting. A good way to manifest something you want is first to choose what you want. Be clear about it. Every day, as you think of this desire, daydream about it, seeing yourself having and enjoying it. Do not work hard at this. Keep it light and casual. It is almost like pretending

you have it. Make this fun and easy. Then think about something else, and say: "I now ask for, accept, receive, and give thanks for (whatever it is that I want); it is mine now. So mote it be." Do this once a day until it appears in your life.

Form follows energy, or put another way, manifestation follows attention (intention). Take some time each day to see/imagine yourself enjoying/having what you are manifesting, then let it go, knowing that it is yours now and is coming to you from the world of energy into the world of form.

This approach combines creating your reality with the essence of a spell. Do not be deceived by the casualness of this approach. It is very effective.

• • • •
Personal Cycles

Review your life for the past five or ten years, and see if you can discover your personal cycles. You will find that things happen to you or begin (or end) consistently at certain times of the year. Do you normally have more energy at certain times of year than at others? Have your personal relationships tended to start or end at a particular time of year? Some people will find that they have a history of completing projects at certain times of the year. Once you are aware of your cycles, you can plan your decisions to coincide with the best times to make them.

Part
III

Lesson 25:
Pathworking

In lessons 1–12, you focused on expanding your worldview to include the consciousness of all that is, to building a relationship with the Goddess and the God, and to developing your ritual skills, learning about spells, and beginning to work with your dreams. You were introduced to your Hall of Consciousness, therefore learning about altered consciousness. You learned to communicate with the dead and to build an ancestor altar.

In lessons 13–24, you developed your psychic abilities, learned the skills of protection, warding, and binding, studied divination, and learned more about dreams. You connected with the spirits of your place and your power animal and totems. You learned to increase your personal power and about the chakras and how to balance them. You experimented with time and used numerology to better understand yourself.

In lessons 25–49, you will learn to do specific pathworkings that will cleanse, heal, and transform you at your deepest levels. These pathworkings will expand and deepen your magical skills and prepare you for the self-dedication that will be offered in lesson 49, should you choose to do this.

. . . .

Working with Your Shadow

Shadow work is among the most important work you can do as a Wiccan. Shadow work is the practice of self-healing, which is necessary to resolve inner blockages and limitations. Shadow work is always good, but it is especially necessary before doing deeper magical working.

The shadow is that part of yourself you reject—aspects of yourself that you dislike or fear or that you repress. People usually make an effort to not express or even acknowledge the shadow parts of themselves, but these parts come out nonetheless. Sometimes the shadow manifests itself through our fears or phobias, other times through attractions or obsessions. Very often, the shadow manifests itself through "crossed wires"—that is, when we think we want one thing with our conscious

mind but want another contradictory thing with our subconscious mind.

People often think of the shadow as negative, but this is not really so. Rather, it is our unwillingness or inability to deal with these aspects of ourselves that can lead to negative outcomes. When worked with in a positive manner, the shadow can be a source of great energy and talents.

To find your shadow, you first need to look for it. Obviously enough, the things that bother us about ourselves are part of our shadow. Often the things that bother us about others can also be keys to our own shadow selves, for other people—or more precisely, our reactions to them—can often be mirrors for us.

For example, some people have a fear of success as part of their shadow. Sometimes such people will feel that they could never be truly successful either because of "the way things are in this world" or because they feel they lack the needed skill or talent. They may have a deep resentment of other people's success because they feel they cannot achieve their own. Or, conversely, they may consciously feel that they can be successful and unconsciously sabotage themselves because subconsciously they believe that they could not or should not have success. The origin of such a shadow may lie in having copied such attitudes from parents as a child or from having absorbed a belief that success was bad—perhaps thinking that for one to be successful, another must suffer. Of course, this is not usually a conscious awareness—again, this is part of why it is called a shadow. If such a person were to begin to become successful without having dealt with this shadow, they would likely feel anxious and uncomfortable without understanding why.

If you've ever wondered how someone can say they feel or think one way and act exactly the opposite, this is the reason.

By working with the shadow, it can be healed and released—reintegrated into the conscious person in a positive manner.

The shadow can be fear of money and power, a desire for control, strong sexual desires, anger, aggression, or many other things. It is a quality always verbally or mentally rejected by the person. It will either be totally repressed, as when the person who fears money and power has a subsistence job and barely makes ends meet, or it will be visibly expressed by them in a negative way they won't be aware of.

Sometimes, instead of expressing our shadow in our own lives, we will draw people around us who express it. For example, if you desire only peace but are surrounded by fighting, this may actually be your shadow being expressed through others.

How do you discover what your shadow is? The most obvious way is self-examination, either of your emotions or of your life

situations. What is blocking you? What do you fear or resent? These are likely aspects of your shadow. Ask your guides for help in this, and pay attention to your dreams.

Do not think that your shadow is only one thing. The shadow is a catch-all for rejected parts of the self and usually has many aspects that must be worked with one by one over a long period of time. Additionally, the more parts of your shadow you heal, the more able you will become to see still *more* parts that need healing. But fear not—the reward of such healing is great, as you will learn.

How do you heal the parts of your shadow? Perhaps the best method is soul retrieval, which we discussed in lesson 7. It is recommended you work with soul retrieval about once a week. The steps are repeated below for your convenience.

Begin by sitting in a comfortable position. Be certain you will not be disturbed. Clear and release all excess energy.

Breathe quietly for a few minutes.

Ask Deity (Goddess and God in union) to be there with you.

Tell Deity what you want to be healed, describing this in detail. You can do this out loud or in your mind.

Ask Deity to heal this issue. See/imagine the healing as a shower of golden light flowing through you. Take a few minutes to experience this. See/imagine the light entering from above you and flowing through every part of your body.

Ask Deity to help you to have the acceptance of the healing. Imagine this as a wave of warm energy moving through you. Say:

I accept, I accept, I accept.

Continue to say this until you have the feeling of acceptance.

Ask Deity to help you integrate this healing into your being. Imagine the integration as a wave of energy flowing into your heart. Say:

I integrate the healing, I integrate the healing, I integrate the healing.

As above, continue saying this until you have the feeling of integration.

Give Deity all of the burdens and pain associated with the issue that has been healed. See them as packages, stones, or as whatever image has this meaning for you. Hold your hands out in front of you as though you were holding these packages, and physically put them into Deity's hands.

See/imagine them consumed or absorbed by purple light as Deity takes them.

Forgive every person, place, and situation that is involved with this issue that has been healed, and release all attachment to these. Forgive yourself as well for anything you blame yourself for, then forgive Deity too. Say:

I forgive, I forgive, I forgive.

Ask Deity to help you reclaim the lost parts of your being that have been caught in the issue that has been healed. Imagine these returning to you as bits of colored light.

Now ask Deity to heal the lost parts of yourself that have been returned to you. Visualize the healing as a shower of golden light. Say:

I am healed, I am healed, I am healed.

Now ask Deity to help you have the acceptance of the healing of the lost parts of yourself. Imagine this as a wave of warm energy moving through you. Say:

I accept, I accept, I accept.

Ask Deity to help you integrate the healing of the lost parts of yourself into your being. Imagine the integration as a wave of energy pouring into your heart. Say:

I integrate, I integrate, I integrate.

Finally, give thanks to Deity for the healing you have received. Then ground and shield.

Do not do this more often than twice a week. This is simple to do but can have powerful effects. If you have someone who will read this while you do it, that can be helpful. You don't need to know exactly what you need healing for. If bringing money into your life is difficult or you have problems with relationships, for instance, ask to be healed of whatever is blocking you from the things you want.

Most issues can be healed with doing this once. Some issues may need two or more soul retrievals, as healing may happen a layer at a time.

• • • •

How to Bond with Water

This week, we are going to bond with water. In order to bond with water, go to a stream, river, or beach. If you do not live anywhere near any of these, select another source of moving water, such as a fountain. The water must be moving, like the current of a river, waves on the shore, or the trickle of a fountain, in order for this exercise to be efficacious.

Take a seat near the water. Make yourself comfortable. Sit and watch the water, listening to its sound; do this for about fifteen minutes or so. Now, turn away from the water, and close your eyes. Stay this way for about five minutes. Then turn back to the water and watch it again. Repeat this four times. Though it seems very simple, it is actually very transformative and will change your experience of water and your relationship with it.

Another way to bond with water is to imagine yourself submerged in moving water—a river, for example. Feel the water flowing all around you, enveloping you, caressing you. Allow yourself to become one with the water. The water flows through you now, as well as around you; you become part of the current. Your physical body dissolves, and you *are* water. Feel yourself flowing, carried by the current, shaped by the current. Experience fluidity. Experience what it is like to *be* water. Enjoy this for as long as you want, and make a habit of it. It is a good way to relax.

• • • •

Energy/Astral Body Exercise

Do the following exercise to become familiar with your energy/astral body and facilitate lucid dreaming and astral projection. The following exercise is intended to help you become familiar with your energetic body and facilitate lucid dreaming and astral travel. Do this exercise in bed when you have fully relaxed but before you fall asleep.

Become aware of your body. Check it for tension, pain, or discomfort from head to foot. If you find any, simply hold your consciousness there without trying to change it. Often it will dissipate. Then move on to another part of your body. Now keep your consciousness in your body and see if you can induce a rocking sensation, a side-to-side rocking movement that feels physical but is actually your energy body. This is a pleasant way to go to sleep.

Another technique: again before going to sleep, try to reshape your energy body. Begin by imagining your energetic body just as your physical body is. But then change it. Imagine the legs of your energy body being a foot longer than your physical legs. Imagine this as clearly as possible; make it as real as possible. Now make them shorter than your physical legs. Try to feel it as fully as you can. Now do this with your head. Imagine being a foot taller than you are, so your energetic head is a foot higher than your physical head. Now imagine being a foot shorter, so that your energetic head is within your physical chest. Imagine it as fully as possible. Alter other dimensions as well—play with it. In this way, you will gradually gain facility in shaping your energetic body to whatever form you choose for it.

• • • •

Exercise to Increase Your Energy

Pathworking requires a great deal of energy. In order to do the work of the pathworkings, you need to increase your own level of energy. The following exercise will help you to increase your basic energy.

Find a comfortable position. Begin by clearing and releasing all excess energy, as you know to do.

Imagine a sphere of white light about six inches above your head. This sphere of light is about four to five inches in diameter. This ball of light is a point of conscious connection to the energy of the universe. It is the light of Deity and is filled with divine love.

Now imagine a beam of white light coming down from that ball of light and entering your body through the top of your head. Let the energy come down into you, filling your body with clear, white light. Feel the love and peace of the divine energy—feel the strength and power within it. Allow this light to fill you, to suffuse your entire being. Let the light fill your body, and then let it begin to expand beyond your body, filling your aura as well. Let the light stream into your aura until it too is full of divine energy, and you are within a large ball of light.

By the nature of its spiritual purity, this light cleanses and heals you, filling you with a deep reserve of energy. Feel this energy surround your body and aura on all levels: soothing, healing, strengthening you. Now see your aura surrounded by a thin layer of deep blue light to seal in the energy.

Now let the image of the light fade, but know that the energy remains with you.

Take a moment to clear and release any excess energy, keeping only what you need.

・・・・

Visualizing the Entrance You Will Use in Pathworking

We are now going to visualize an entrance that we will use in all of our pathworkings.

Find your comfortable position. Clear and release excess energy. Fill your aura with divine energy, as discussed above. Now imagine yourself in a forest. You stand upon a small earthen path. All around you are trees and plants; above is the sky. Be aware of all these things. Feel them as fully as possible: What do they feel like? What do they look like? Is it day or night? Is it summer or winter? Is the forest thick with growth or is it scraggly? How does the forest make you feel? Take note of these details and remember them; when you have finished the exercise, you can go back and analyze them, because they are clues to your internal state.

Go forward on the path through the forest. As you walk on, be aware of the ground beneath your feet, the smell of the forest around you, the wind in the trees. Ahead of you is a hillside, and in this hillside is an opening. Take note of what the opening looks like—is it easily accessible or partly obscured by bushes or undergrowth? Is the opening large or small? Enter it. Inside is a cave.

What does the cave feel like? Is it large or small? Can you stand comfortably? Is there much light in the cave or is it dark? Ahead of you is a passageway that curves to the left, but you do not enter it now. Rather, take some time and explore the part of the cave you are in.

After five or ten minutes of exploration, turn and leave the cave. Follow the path back through the woods to your starting point, again being aware of everything around you.

Do this visualization once a day this week. Become as familiar with the cave as you can, so when you do a pathworking the cave is real and familiar to you.

・・・・

Daily Meditation

Do fifteen to twenty minutes of meditation daily. You should already be doing this, but if you have let this practice slide, begin again.

At this point in the course, we also will stop using the earth, air, fire, water, and Spirit format that we have followed so far, so that we may adopt a more holistic approach and examine more complex subjects in future lessons.

• • • •

Weekly Question

At this point in the course, we are going to include a weekly question or questions for you to consider. These questions are not tests but rather are questions for you to ponder and reflect upon. Think about the question, and write your answer to it in your Book of Shadows.

This week's question is: What does it mean to you to be a Wiccan? Consider this in the light of your practice and personal experience. The only right answer here is the one that comes from your heart.

Lesson 26:
Healing Your Shadow

This week, we are going to introduce you to more ways of working to heal your shadow. Remember that your shadow is the disowned part of yourself. The shadow cannot be dealt with by trying to banish it—that is more or less how it is created—but rather must be dealt with through healing.

The technique we will be discussing does not require you to know what your shadow is; we will be working with it intuitively. However, the technique is just as effective if you have, in fact, identified one or more specific aspects of your shadow.

• • • •

Journey to Heal the Shadow

Set your intent to work with healing your shadow and enter your Hall of Consciousness, as you have learned to do. Among the many doors in the hall, you will find one that is different. This is the door to the parts of your shadow that you can work on healing at this time. Go through this door. In the room beyond you will find disowned parts of yourself—parts of your shadow. These disowned parts will appear as people or archetypal figures. They are likely to

appear as people with serious injuries or deformities, or they may appear as "monsters" or in other symbolic forms. Sometimes these images can be quite frightening, but do not worry—these are merely wounded parts of yourself that have been repressed, becoming shadow.

Occasionally people will encounter these shadow aspects of themselves without understanding what they are, and this can be a very disconcerting experience. It is especially common in dreams. Here, however, we are fully aware of what we are doing, and we know that even if the image we see might be frightening, there is still nothing to be frightened of.

Make a prayer to Goddess and God to help you heal the shadows you see. Select one of the figures to work with. Call the energies of the universe into yourself, and from your heart send forth a beam of white light into this shadow aspect, and focus on healing. Fill the shadow creature with healing energy. At first, it may not seem to like this, but keep sending healing energy. At a certain point, the creature will begin to transform, changing form even as you continue to send it healing energy. From its original injured or monstrous condition, it will change into something beautiful. When this transformation is complete, you can stop sending it healing energy.

Even if there are several shadow aspects in the room, you may only wish to heal one,

as the process can be rather tiring sometimes. If, however, you feel up to it, heal as many shadow figures as you can. When you are finished, flood the room itself with white light and see it transform itself into a place of beauty.

In this way, you can work on healing aspects of your shadow one at a time, without necessarily having to know what they are. This technique of seeing the shadow aspects as people is called "personification" and can be very useful in magic.

You should return to this place on a regular basis and continue to heal any shadow figures you find, sending them love and affirming their worth.

This is obviously ongoing work. Because our shadows have been built up over a long period during our lives, we must expect it to take some time and effort to heal our shadow completely.

Not healing your shadow completely can result in a less fulfilling spiritual life, and those things not healed in this lifetime will carry over into your next one.

• • • •

How to Bond with Fire

We will now discuss bonding with the element of fire. To do this, you will need an actual fire to bond with. You can access fire in any of several ways: you could build a small bonfire outdoors, you could use a fireplace, or you could use a candle flame.

You will bond with the fire in the same way that you bonded with earth and water. Gaze at the fire/candle flame for an estimated fifteen minutes, observing it carefully, then turn away from it and cover your eyes for five minutes. Now turn back to the fire and observe it again. Do this a total of four times.

• • • •

Exercise to Experience the Astral Body

The following exercise should be added to help you experience your astral body, as we have previously practiced.

Before you begin this exercise, walk around your living room or your bedroom five or ten times, and notice everything in detail. Do this until you can mentally recall every detail of the room correctly. Then when you are lying down, visualize yourself walking around the room again, still seeing every detail clearly.

After you have practiced this for a number of times, you may find that you are out of your body, doing this in your astral body. The shock of this awareness may send you right back to your physical body, but practice will overcome this.

Weekly Question

How does the Wiccan path help you to express your True Self, your most deeply held beliefs?

Some might render this question as "Does the Wiccan path express your most deeply held beliefs?"—and at first glance, this might seem a proper way to put it. However, this is not the right way to look at it at all. In reality, it is not the path that expresses our beliefs but rather how we walk that path. Merely standing still on a given path expresses nothing at all. We can express our deepest beliefs and purposes no matter what religious path we walk—the path only helps us to do this. So our question asks us to consider how we interact with the Wiccan path and how this aids us in expressing our deepest, truest self.

Lesson 27:
Increasing Your
Magical Energy

There are many ways we can increase our magical energy, and we have examined a few of these already. Every spell, ritual, and exercise also helps to increase magical energy, much in the same way that exercising a physical muscle increases its strength. However, in the end, your magical energies come from within and are only as clear and effective as you are yourself. The issues and patterns, fears and unresolved emotional pain you carry affect you on every level. These things control the way you perceive the people and events in your life; they color every decision you make. This is the reason to do soul retrieval on a regular basis for the remainder of these lessons.

Any time you experience powerful psychic and spiritual energy, it expands and brings to light all parts of yourself, positive and negative. This is especially true in Wicca. You may have noticed that many spiritual people in the Wiccan field seem to change after an initiation. Ideally this change is expressed in positive ways. However, if the person has not worked with their shadow, initiation or other powerful spiritual experiences may tend to bring it to the forefront. A person who was posi-

tive, tolerant, and balanced in their relationships may seem to become controlling and power hungry or express some other form of negative behavior. This is because these issues have been unresolved within them. This is why it is so important to work with healing the shadow.

Below is the first pathworking you will do. It is the journey to the Great Mother.

• • • •

Pathworking to the
Great Mother

Read these instructions, take a ritual bath, ground/release, shield, and enter your stillness.

Now begin your journey to the cave. Use all of your senses—feel the path beneath your feet, smell the scents of the woods, feel the warmth of the sunlight as you go. Notice the trees, plants, animals, and birds. Be alert to all of the sounds that you hear.

At the entrance to the cave, stop and enter your stillness again. Then enter the cave. Use all of your senses inside of the cave. Feel the vibrant energy of expectancy within the cave. This is a special visit, and all of the energies of the cave are aware of this.

Opening to one side will be a passage leading deeper into the earth. Enter this passage and proceed forward. Notice the size and shape of the passage, and how it makes you feel. This reflects your personal connection to Goddess. Continue forward, moving still deeper into the earth. You are moving toward the very center of being. At length, you emerge into a room. As with the passage, take notice of the size, shape, and details of this room. How does it make you feel?

In this place, you are at the center of existence, of all that is. Feel the strength and power of the energy here. Feel the love of the Great Mother flowing out in all directions, flowing into existence as everything that is. Feel yourself as part of this flow—experience yourself as one with the energy of the Mother Goddess and as one with everything that is.

In this room is the Mother Goddess herself. Try not to have any preconceived notions as to the way in which she will present herself to you. Let her take whatever form is best for this specific interaction. However, do pay attention to the form she takes and how it makes you feel.

The Great Mother turns her attention to you. You feel as if she knows you completely and loves you unconditionally. You see yourself as the Mother sees you—perfect, whole, and Love incarnate. You realize that she has always been with you: that you are never alone and have never truly been alone.

Now she speaks to you, telling you of her love for you, and gives you a personal message just for you. Allow that message

to come through in whatever way is best for you, and again have no preconceptions about it. You are forever changed by this time spent with the Great Mother. You will never feel alone again. You now truly *know* that you are held always at the center and heart of the Great Mother.

Now thank the Great Mother for her message, and go back up the passage into the cave. Sit on the floor of the cave and absorb and integrate the experience you just had. Think about the personal message she gave you, and carry it in your heart. When you are ready, leave the cave and return by the path through the woods, being aware of everything, as you were on your journey to the cave.

When you return to normal consciousness, stretch and come back fully into your body. Ground and release.

As always, record your experience in your Book of Shadows.

• • • •

Changing the Past

We have all done things in the past that we wish we could change. It is possible to affect the past to a greater or lesser degree. To do this, pick an incident in your life where you wish you had acted differently, and decide now how you would change the situation if you could.

Set your intent and go to your Hall of Consciousness. Look for the door that

is different from the others and that will open onto this past incident. Go through the door and enter the situation as it was—but this time, instead of repeating what originally happened, behave as you wish you had instead. See the situation as clearly as possible as you do it, and put as much energy as you can into it. Be in the situation as much as you can with all of your senses and emotions. When you are finished, return to the present and let the situation go.

Will this change the situation in the present so that everyone involved remembers it as you now choose? It is possible but not likely. What can certainly happen is that all of the people involved in the situation will be affected in subtle and positive ways in the present, as though they are aware on some level of the changed incident. This will likely be a gradual process, but pay attention and you will notice changes.

• • • •

Exercise to Find a Lost Object

This is an exercise to learn to find a lost object or to locate something in a store you know is there but cannot find. Have someone hide an object from you in a room. Ground/release, shield, and enter your stillness. Slowly walk around the room in a relaxed yet focused way. Go around the

room two or three times, paying attention to the way you feel. Reach out with your inner senses and try to "feel" where the object is. You should feel pulled to a particular spot. Once you feel that pull, stand at that spot and consider where in that area the object may be. Give yourself time to feel where the pull is strongest, then check to see if the object is there.

It may take several tries to master this, but the effort is worth it. In this exercise, you are learning to pay attention to your inner knowing, for your inner self always knows the answer you are seeking.

• • • •

Exercises to Absorb the Sun's Energy

You interact with lunar energy at your monthly esbats. This energy strengthens your inner psychic abilities. The energy of the sun is equally important, as it strengthens you physically and increases your energy. Below are two ways to absorb this solar energy.

Stand or sit where the sunlight will reach you. Raise your hands, palms upward, to face the sun. Feel the sun's warmth on your palms. Let the energy penetrate your being. Stay in this position for as long as you are comfortable doing so. You should also be aware of the feeling of the sun on the rest of your body. Do this daily when weather permits.

This next visualization increases your energy and well-being. Ground/release, shield, and enter your stillness. Imagine that you are walking upward along a beam of sunlight toward the sun. Continue until you are standing directly in front of the sun itself. Feel the white-hot, deep, penetrating heat of the sun. Allow it to enfold you. Walk forward into the heart of the sun and stand there, feeling the sun's purifying, energizing, vibrant heat. Feel the happy, generous, joyful energy of the sun. Allow it to suffuse you, surrounding and filling you. Soak this up for as long as you like. Now walk back down the beam of sunlight into normal consciousness.

· · · ·

Qualities of Some Animals, Birds, and Insects

During these lessons, hopefully you have become more aware of your surroundings. The unexpected appearance of any animal may be treated as an omen—that is, their qualities may be taken as a message for you from Spirit. Below are listed qualities of some animals, birds, and insects. These are animals you may see during your day or they might be one of your power animals. They might also appear to you in your dreams.

Ant: The ant represents industriousness, hard work, preparation, and sensible planning.

Part
III

Bear: A dreamer and a healer, the bear is an animal who knows where to find the healing herbs it needs. It is a lunar symbol also, as it is connected to the subconscious and unconscious minds. Bear is also a spiritual power and strength.

Buffalo/Bison: A symbol of abundance, divine providence, and protection, the bison represents connection to Deity. This symbol is most closely associated with the Plains Indians. The buffalo was a mainstay of their diet, and what couldn't be eaten was used in some other way; no part was wasted.

Butterfly: Butterfly represents cycles, transformation, and the soul. They can appear as a communication from a loved one who has died. Their lives express the strength hidden in gentleness.

Cat: The cat is a symbol of feminine and psychic energy. It is independent and possessive, and enjoys hunting for its own sake. A cat wants to know everything that is going on in its territory. Cats don't share power, they rule. They are usually very affectionate with the people they choose to share their lives with, although they will choose when to express that affection.

Crow: The crow represents sacred law and the power of working together as a team. Crows are aggressive opportunists and can be destructive to smaller birds. They are attracted to bright, shiny objects, whether they have value or not. They are watchful and prepared, always keeping a lookout wherever they are.

Deer: A deer represents gentleness, innocence, and unconditional love.

Dog: Dogs represent faithfulness, protection, companionship, and the proper use of wild, untamed energy. Long domesticated by man, this is a relationship they have consented to. They are affectionate, have a bottomless capacity for love, and are territorial.

Fox: A fox represents craftiness, trickery, a sense of humor, and a strong instinct for survival.

Hawk: Hawk is the messenger from Spirit. When it appears in your life, you should be open to omens, synchronicity, and dreams. Something important is coming to you or needs to be known. It is an excellent hunter and easily able to provide for itself.

Kestrel: This small falcon represents speed, communication, and taking advantage of opportunities. It can be a totem and a teacher for writers.

Mouse: A mouse represents attention to detail, innocence, and trust. Mice are cautious and family oriented. They are adaptable and survive well in the city or the country. They are alert to and take advantage of any opportunity. They can also be symbolic of thriftiness.

Owl: Owl represents magic, mystery, and hidden knowledge. It is a nocturnal animal and is symbolic of the Crone Goddess. It is also associated with the goddess Athena/Minerva as guide and goddess of wisdom. Its appearance may indicate that you need to pay close attention to something in your life, possibly your health or a situation going on around you.

Snake: Snake is a symbol of magical energy, personal power, and healing. Snake represents the flow of the universe, the Tao. It can also represent earth energy.

Spider: Spider represents creating your own reality by what you weave into existence. It is also a symbol of written language and, therefore, communication. Its appearance may warn you not to be trapped in webs someone else has woven.

• • • •
Weekly Question

There are many facets to Wicca—spells, ritual, healing, teaching, herbalism, the Wiccan garden, oils and incense, working with your spirits of place to heal the earth. Which of these do you most enjoy doing? Which of these do you think you might choose to focus your Wiccan practice on?

Part
III

Lesson 28:
Free Will

This week we will discuss free will. Many religions give lip service to the idea of free will, but in Wicca it is a fundamental concept. In Wicca, we believe that we not only have free will in the situations where our circumstances are obviously under our own conscious control, but also—by virtue of the powers of the Higher Self, magic, and the nature of reality—we believe that the soul has free will in situations where the conscious person has no apparent control. We believe that we absolutely create our own reality and that we absolutely have free will within certain self-imposed limitations.

Before we enter a life, we decide what lessons we will set up for ourselves to learn. We consider our past lives, our personal goals based on our unique soul pattern, and the judgments we have made about our growth and actions in our past lives. We make agreements with others in our soul, or spiritual, family, agreeing to certain meetings and possible relationships. We choose our birth family and the conditions we are born into so that we can best fulfill our purposes for coming into this life. This is absolute free will at the soul level.

Some people are born into extreme poverty or abusive family situations, or with poor health, or possibly mentally handicapped. You may wonder why someone would choose such a life. If it gives an opportunity to learn the chosen lessons or to fill a need for the experience, then it would be chosen by the soul.

Some traditions teach that those choices are made because of a debt owed from a past life. We would say that the soul chooses what it will experience not from a debt owed but because of a desire to learn and grow.

Often a soul will choose to work with a single specific concept as its primary lesson, at least for a time. This might be a concept such as romantic love, compassion, creativity, mercy, justice, or any of many other things. A soul who chooses justice, for example, must experience all sides of justice, the spirit of justice, and justice experienced as the letter of the law. This soul will choose lifetimes as a judge, an officer of the law, or perhaps a politician. The soul will also choose lifetimes as a criminal or a self-righteous ruler without mercy, thus experiencing all sides of the concept of justice. The soul has a right to choose what it will experience, regardless of whether that life seems positive or negative to someone else.

Does this mean that you can do whatever you want without concern for someone else? No, not at all. Remember the Wiccan Rede—"Do as you will but harm none." All that we do comes back to us through karma until we learn the lessons implicit in the experience. Therefore, if you murder in this life, you will likely be murdered yourself, whether in this life or another life.

However, it does mean that you should not be judgmental about other people's lives, because you do not know the underlying soul lessons they are learning or how they got to be where they are. Deplore bad actions by all means, but do not assume that a bad action means a bad soul—it does not.

Just as the circumstances of our birth are set up by our soul, so too our soul sets up the circumstances of our life. As a rule, we have no conscious knowledge of this, and it is to gain such conscious participation in this process that we study and practice magic, which is nothing more or less than doing consciously what we constantly do unconsciously from the higher levels of our being.

The universe is set up so that your thoughts, expectations, and emotions create your experience. This does not mean we can simply choose to be beautiful, rich, and famous, and automatically become those things—the way magic works in the movies. No, it takes work. This is because while our thoughts and emotions can be focused toward magically achieving goals like these, that magic can be blocked internally by negative expectations and limiting belief systems. This, again, is why it is so important to work through our shadow issues.

The major rule of manifestation is that you don't necessarily get what you want,

but you always get what you expect and believe you are able to get.

The situation and family experience you were born into have given you certain beliefs, often ones you are not aware of. This gives you the opportunity to learn the lessons you chose to learn and to overcome the conditions of your childhood. Your hidden beliefs and your shadow contribute to the challenge you need to master. These give you the opportunity to learn to consciously create the reality you want.

One of the primary lessons of life in this plane, regardless of the other lessons you chose to learn, is how to create consciously in the physical world.

Our soul sees the physical world as an opportunity to joyfully learn, grow, and experience.

· · · ·

Your Higher Self

In lesson 30, you will do a pathworking to your Higher Self. Your Higher Self is that portion of your self that is consciously aware of your connection to Deity. It remembers all that you have done and been, and what you came into this life to be. It often communicates with you in your dreams, giving you guidance and commenting on the actions you are taking in your life. When you wake up in the morning feeling down, depressed, or some other negative emotion, your Higher Self may be

telling you that you aren't living up to your goals and ideals. Unexpected inspiration, understanding, and/or impulses may also come from your Higher Self.

Your Higher Self is a resource for you, always available to guide you in the direction of your life purpose. The Higher Self is always positive and incapable of doing harm. It works always for your best interests and the best interests of everyone else in any situation you are involved in.

• • • •

Symbols

Symbols are an important part of magical practice. Symbols evoke an emotional reaction from us and connect us directly to our Higher Selves, bypassing the possible interference of the conscious mind, which wants to question and reason. Choosing symbols that represent Spirit, the Goddess and the God, protection, prosperity, etc., and then building an emotional connection to them allows them to be used immediately when what they represent is needed.

The pentagram is the symbol of the Wiccan religion to many people. The five points are the four elements—earth, air, fire, and water—which represent the body, mind, will, and emotions under the control of Spirit (the top point). The pentagram is often used as a symbol of protection. You can ward a room by drawing a pentagram in each of the four directions or at each door and window.

Draw a pentagram on a piece of paper and sleep with it on the nightstand next to the bed with the purpose of protection. Do this for a week, and see how this makes you feel. You will find it actually makes a difference in how you feel.

The moon is a common symbol for the Goddess, and the sun is used to represent the God. You can make this more personal by working with the symbols of the aspects of Deity that you work with. There are traditional symbols for many personal deities, such as a mirror or menat (an Egyptian religious amulet) for Hathor, an owl for Athena, or the Mjollnir (Thor's Hammer) for Thor. But you can also create an original symbol that represents Deity for you.

For prosperity, use the symbol $ or perhaps a bag of coins. The best symbol is whatever best represents a particular deity, object, or quality for you.

This week, work with the symbols of your choice. It is important that the symbols you choose evoke an emotional response from you. This can be a natural response or come from sustained contemplation on what the symbol is meant to represent. Have these symbols where you can easily see them, and each time that you do, think about what the symbol represents. Soon you won't have to think about it—the symbol will immediately connect you to the meaning it represents.

. . . .

Using Color for Healing

You have worked with color to add energy to a spell and to clear and balance the chakras. Now we will discuss healing with color. Color can have a real effect on your energy and on how you feel. Below are listed some of the basic uses of color for this:

Black is grounding. When you feel spacey or need to be especially focused, wear black. Ritual robes are traditionally black because this color helps people to stay grounded while dealing with higher energies. Black represents the psychic realm and mystery; wearing black increases your connection to these things.

Blue is a healing color. Surround yourself with it for general healing, and breathe it into your body. Blue is also for anything dealing with the throat. Too much exposure to the color blue can tend to be depressing, so don't immerse yourself in it all of the time.

Indigo is good for psychic opening and development. It is also said to be good for communication in general and for the eyes, ears, and nose.

Light blue is relaxing.

Turquoise is said to be beneficial in lessening emotional or physical tension.

Clear yellow is a sunny, positive color and also helps to induce sunny, positive feelings. It is a good color to help improve your mood and outlook, assists with mental clarity and focus, helps with cleansing and purification, and combats stress.

Lemon yellow is good for purification and for releasing.

Dark or muddy yellows have a negative effect.

Pink is a color that promotes relaxation and calmness.

Red is energizing and invigorating. However, too much red can tend to overstimulate and may leave one feeling drained as a result.

Green is a healing color and stimulates growth.

Violet promotes spiritual growth and opening, and is said to help with stress, depression, and issues of cleansing or releasing.

Bonding with Air

We will now discuss bonding with the element of air. This is a little different from bonding with the other elements, as air can be more difficult to perceive. Here we will be working with air in its form as wind, and so you will have to choose a day when the wind is blowing.

Sit outside on a windy day. Watch the wind and listen to it. Notice its effect on the things around you—how the wind blows through the trees and bushes, ripples through grass, and so on. Listen to the wind's distinctive sound, with its many variations. Watch and listen to the wind for about fifteen minutes, then close your eyes, as we have done before when bonding with the elements, for about five minutes, but this time cover your ears also, so that you don't hear the wind.

Now listen to the wind again, and watch the effects as you just did, repeating this cycle until you have done this four times.

• • • •

Weekly Question

What difference has working with this course made in your life?

Lesson 29:
Reincarnation

Reincarnation is the concept that the soul lives many lives, experiencing and learning from each, then deciding (usually from the life just ended) which experiences and lessons it wants to learn in the next one.

It is possible to carry issues and relationships from life to life if they have not been resolved, and these issues can affect the present life without any obvious cause for their effects.

There are many famous and somewhat clichéd examples of this sort of thing: the person whose fear of water is based on having drowned in a past life, the person whose fear of heights is based on having fallen to their death in a previous life, the person attracted to some far-off country because they lived there in a previous life, etc. There are many ways in which issues, patterns, and relationships can be carried over from past lives in this manner, both positive and negative. It can even be done intentionally, although we will not go into that just now.

Relationships are an area where past-life influences tend to be especially prevalent. An especially strong reaction to someone or an unusually strong attraction is almost always carried over from a past life. This

is called an "attachment." Such an attachment may arise regardless of whether the interaction in the previous life was positive or negative in character, because it is based in depth of emotion.

This sort of attachment has given rise to the idea that each person has a special "soul mate" with whom they may expect an intense attachment. Although the term "soul mate" may be loosely used, there are in fact many such people to whom our soul has such an attachment, and the relationships we have with them are not always easy or even pleasant—rather, they tend to be intense.

It is possible to find, love, and marry someone and be very happy—and you may even do this with a soul to which you have this sort of past-life attachment. However, such past-life relationships are often centered around the need to work out difficult lessons. So while the attachment may be strong, the relationship is often quite tempestuous.

Look for areas like this in your life, and work to resolve and release them as part of the cleansing work of these lessons. You can do soul retrieval for anything you are aware of, and ask that anything you are not aware of be healed also.

The only person you can control in any relationship is yourself. If you have issues with people in your life that you cannot change, do soul retrieval for yourself, for the situation, and to release your attachment to the situation. Once you can release

a person and genuinely wish the best for them, whether you are ever able to like the person or not, you are energetically freed.

A simple and effective prayer, especially for situations that you are emotionally involved in, is:

I ask for the best good and highest outcome for this situation and for everyone that is involved in it.

By taking your personal desires, hopes, and fears out of the prayer, you leave room for Spirit to act in the situation.

• • • •

How to Create Sacred Art

In lesson 21, we discussed how to make a mask, or shield, to express and increase our personal power. In this lesson, we will create sacred art. What is meant by sacred art in this sense is artwork that embodies and magically helps to create a given goal or intention. This works best for a specific goal you wish to accomplish, rather than a general quality you might wish to develop—though it can be used for that, too.

Begin by defining the purpose of this piece of sacred art. What is it that you wish to accomplish?

Now take some time and consider what objects, colors, and symbols express this goal for you. You will use these objects, colors, and symbols in creating your piece of sacred art.

You can do this as a mask, a shield, a wall hanging, a three-dimensional work of table art, or as a drawing or a painting. You can even use a poem to express this if you draw pictures or symbols to accompany it.

Write your ideas down, and do a rough sketch of your art. Ask your dreams for guidance, and stay open to what your inner self tells you. When you are ready, you will create your piece of sacred art and, if you choose to, you may dedicate it in ritual. You will then keep the finished work of art in a place where it can disseminate the energy with which it has been charged and where you can easily see it.

As you make your piece of sacred art, make it a point to focus strongly upon your goal—the goal that the artwork is meant to express and help manifest. In this way, the work will not only reflect that goal in its visual appearance but will also have the intent imprinted energetically during its creation. Stay open to inner guidance while you are working on the piece, and be willing to allow it to deviate from your initial plan, as this may be necessary for it to fully fulfill its purpose magically.

For this form of sacred art, you are limited only by your need and your imagination. There is no wrong way to do this. By making your intention physical in an art form, you have created a physical spell that will pull your intention more quickly into the world.

The Moon's
Zodiacal Position

In this section, we will discuss the importance of the position of the moon in the zodiac. The sign in which the moon is placed on any given day affects the energies of that day at an inner level (whereas the position of the sun in the zodiac has a more external influence). The astrological position of the moon particularly affects the emotions and imagination, as well as psychic receptivity. The energies of the astrological sign the moon is in affects you. It is helpful to note the moon's position each day of the month. You can find this information in a good almanac such as *We'moon Almanac* or an astrological calendar such as *Llewellyn's Astrological Calendar* or *Llewellyn's Witches' Calendar*.

The sign the moon is in changes every two to two-and-a-half days. It progresses in order through the signs of the zodiac. Below are listed the basic energies of the moon signs. If your sun, moon, or ascendant is the same as the sign the moon is in, these energies will affect you more strongly.

Moon in Aries: This energy is impulsive, dynamic, and acquisitive. Ideals and energy are high, and ideas for career and prosperity may abound. Be careful of impatience, anger, and a tendency to control others.

Moon in Taurus: Enjoyment and sensual pleasure are highlighted when the moon is in Taurus. This can be a passive, laid-back energy. You may feel ultra-conservative and stubborn. Beware of a tendency to overindulge in food and drink.

Moon in Gemini: This is a light, changeable energy, which tends to make focus more difficult. The mind spins in many directions and is often superficial. It is a great time to get new ideas but a bad time to try to carry them out. Social life, short journeys, and a desire for novelty are highlighted.

Moon in Cancer: This energy makes for strong emotions that can swing from one extreme to the other. The family and home are highlighted, but it is easy to worry about loved ones, even when everything is going well. Psychic abilities are strong. Beware of the potential for being obsessive or manipulative.

Moon in Leo: This is a social, creative, generous, and extravagant energy. If your sun, moon, or ascendant is in Leo, you may be overly extravagant at this time and regret it later. Beware of a tendency to be overbearing and selfish.

Moon in Virgo: This energy emphasizes attention to detail and concern with controlling one's environment. There can be anxiety over responsibility and performance. Beware of insecurity and of being critical, nitpicking, and judgmental.

Moon in Libra: This is an energy that seeks balance and tranquility, which inversely tends to make one more aware of imbalance or strife. Relationships, making money, and increased communication are highlighted now. Beware of a tendency to be stingy, stubborn, and moody.

Moon in Scorpio: Desires and emotions are intense. There is a desire to push all boundaries. Psychic experiences, especially communication with the dead, are more likely at these times.

Moon in Sagittarius: This energy is physical, generous, competitive, and acquisitive. When expressed in the negative, there is a tendency to jealousy and possessiveness.

Moon in Capricorn: Ambition is strong now. The energy is not selfish so much as self-centered—one's own desires are paramount. It is easy to focus on one's goals now. Stubbornness can be an issue. Beware of steamrolling anyone in your way.

Moon in Aquarius: Intellectual curiosity and philosophy are emphasized. Emotions tend to be minimized and mentality maximized. If your sun, moon, or ascendant is in Aquarius, this energy may tend to cause you to focus on your inner ideas to the exclusion of people and things around you.

Moon in Pisces: This energy is compassionate and nonjudgmental but may also tend to be moody. Psychic abilities are highlighted at this time.

To learn how the signs of the moon affect you on a personal level, keep a daily journal of your feelings for two or three months, then check back and see what sign the moon was in on each day. Check through your dream journal, too, and see if there is a pattern that corresponds to the moon signs.

. . . .

Weekly Question

Which part of these lessons have you felt most deeply connected to?

Lesson 30:
Your Inner Senses

Your inner senses are used during lucid dreaming and astral travel. They correspond to your physical senses of sight, hearing, touch, taste, and smell. Below you will find exercises to develop the inner senses. With practice, you will gain proficiency in these areas. However, sight is not included here since we have been working with it continually throughout these lessons.

· · · ·

Your Inner Sense of Smell

We will begin by working with our inner sense of smell. Smell is certainly the sense we take most for granted; however, it can be more important than most people realize once they understand how much of our interaction with smell is unconscious. Developing your inner sense of smell can help you to attain this realization for the outer world of smell as well.

To develop your inner sense of smell, find a comfortable position; now relax. Become aware of everything you can smell. Take some time to become aware of the many different scents around you; remember that these are always there, but you are usually not conscious of them. Here you will become conscious.

You will undoubtedly find that there are many more individual scents present than you had any conscious idea of before you began this exercise. Savor them all. Some will be pleasant, some will not, but our goal is to experience them, not to judge them.

Now choose any one of these many smells and try to focus on it alone for a minute or two. Discern its individual character. What is it like? Does it remind you of anything else? Now that you are focusing on it, does it actually smell the way you would have thought it smelled before undertaking this exercise?

After a moment or two with the individual smell, turn your attention back to the totality of smells around you. Focus on the whole again for a few moments. Go back and forth between the individual smell and the full array of smells several times. Notice how many of these scents you have not been aware of before.

When you have finished this exercise, make it a point to be more aware of smell in your daily life. Go around your home smelling different scents—closets, bed sheets, cleaning supplies, ice cubes—each will have its own distinctive scent that you may never have been aware of before. This should prove quite an interesting experiment to do.

Do this same thing in other settings. Go to a park, and smell the different scents.

Go to a public building, like a library or a post office, and smell the scents there.

Do this exercise on a regular basis for a few weeks. Then see how many smells you can experience by thinking about different objects.

. . . . .

Your Inner Sense of Taste

To develop your inner sense of taste, gather several foods and place them in front of you. Now pick up one kind of food at a time and, from memory, imagine how that food tastes. Do this in great detail, and then actually taste the food you are holding. How close was your perception of the taste to the actual taste? Now do this with the remaining foods.

Now gather nonfood items you have washed, and place them in front of you. These can be a ceramic object, a piece of silverware, something plastic, etc. Make the selection as varied as possible. This time, taste the object by placing your tongue on it, and then reproduce the taste in memory. Do this until you have tasted everything you selected.

Mentally practice experiencing these tastes in your spare time.

. . . .

Your Inner Sense of Touch

Choose a room with a comfortable chair or do this exercise in your bedroom, lying down. Choose five or more objects of different textures. Feel each object so you know how it feels. Then sit in your comfortable chair or lie down.

Look at one object at a time and imagine running your hand over it. Feel the texture of it as though your physical hand were touching it. Then go on to another object. Do this until you have "felt" all of the objects.

Now imagine yourself touching something you did not touch first, such as the wall or the curtains. Imagine the way this feels. When you are done, check the actual texture against your perception of it.

Do this exercise a few minutes each day for about a month.

. . . .

Your Inner Sense of Hearing

Sit where you can hear sounds, both from inside your home and the sounds outside—birds, traffic, children playing, even sirens or a jackhammer, whatever is going on at the time. Enter your stillness.

Relax your focus and be aware of as many sounds as you can, letting them be what they are. Be a receiver; let the sounds come to you. Enjoy this for a few minutes, then focus on one sound only, such as the sound of a vehicle passing, and let your awareness follow it. Follow this sound until it is gone. Now relax your focus and be a gentle receiver once more, letting all of the sounds come to you.

Go back and forth between relaxed receiving and focusing on one sound at a time.

With practice, you will find yourself in a delicate balance with what is going on around you, almost as though your consciousness is floating and touching the sounds. Don't try to force this—let it happen.

When you have mastered this exercise, go to a busy place, such as a mall or a busy park or a movie theater. Practice the exercise in this busier setting.

• • • •

Magical Names

In this lesson, we are going to discuss magical names. Many Wiccans want to choose a special name that defines their magical self. This can be an empowering thing to do. In the Wiccan community, you will find those who are only known by a name other than their birth name. Two of the most notable examples are Starhawk and Silver RavenWolf. Conversely, there are other well-known Wiccans that use their given name, such as Margot Adler and Isaac Bonewits.

If you choose to take a magical name, careful consideration should be given. The obvious meaning of the name naturally must express your own inner nature, but

this is not the only way in which the name has meaning. We learned in the lessons on numerology that the numerical values of the letters in your name have a real effect on the energies of your life and the qualities that are available to you. Be sure to check out numerically any name you consider to be sure these energies are ones you want.

Magical names can be a very empowering practice, but sometimes they are often confused with pseudonyms. Magical names are adopted for spiritual purposes, not to use as a glorified nickname. When magical names are used as pseudonyms, they can create a bad impression in the wider society among people who do not understand the practice and only see them as "silly names." Using magical names as pseudonyms also creates a sense of anonymity, which sometimes allows people who should know better to behave badly in the knowledge that "no one knows who I really am." A magical name is supposed to help you to learn who you "really" are, not disguise who you really are.

Another reason people choose a magical name draws on the idea of anonymity and has to do with the potential reaction that the non-Wiccan public may have if they become aware of this religious affiliation. Like it or not, there is still a great deal of prejudice against those of us who practice this religion.

The first Wiccan group I became a member of, many of the members were introduced to me with a name other than their given name. For months, I never knew their real names. As a novice, I assumed this was just the way things were done—as if it were a requirement to have a magical name to be Wiccan. As I gained more experience, I realized this was a very individual choice, and there are as many reasons to take a magical name as there are people.

An alternative practice in the Correllian Tradition is to discover your personal symbol once you have become part of the High Priesthood. This symbol is then incorporated as part of ritual wear. One example of these symbols is the phoenix, which represents birth, death, and rebirth.

In this lesson, you will do a pathworking to your Higher Self. The effects of the pathworkings you do will continue to be felt for at least a week or two after you do the pathworking. Be sure to note these continuing effects in your Book of Shadows.

· · · ·

Higher Self Pathworking

Read over the pathworking, then take a ritual bath.

Ground/release, shield, and enter your stillness.

Begin your journey to the cave. Be aware of this journey with all of your senses. At the door to the cave, enter your stillness again. Enter the cave. Be aware of the cave with all of your senses. Be aware of the heightened, almost electrical energy in the cave.

Look for a passage leading off from the main cave. Enter this passage and follow it, paying attention to what the passage looks and feels like. The passage will take you deep into the earth, as when we journeyed to meet the Great Mother—however, it will take you to a different location within the earth this time.

At length, you will emerge into a room. Pay attention to what this room looks and feels like. Every detail is a symbol of the qualities of your higher self and the nature of your relationship with it.

A pillar of light forms in the center of the circle. It changes and flows from one color to another. This pillar of light calls you by name, and you walk to the center and merge with it.

You are surrounded and filled by pure light, pure being, pure love, and pure joy. This is your Higher Self, your inner self, your true nature and being. All of this light, love, and joy dances through you, and you realize that this is your essential nature, your truest being. In this merging, you experience more love than you have ever imagined possible.

Here you realize that you are Love and Perfection. There is nothing to do, be, or strive for. Enjoy this energy for as long as you like.

Your Higher Self has a personal message for you. Listen to it.

Your Higher Self now offers you a gift. Do not have any preconceived notions as to what this gift will be, but allow it to be whatever is needed. Accept this gift from your Higher Self, and place it into your heart.

Thank your Higher Self for the gift. Return to the passageway that leads back to the main cave.

Sit in the cave for a while and contemplate this journey. You can feel the gift still in your heart. Anytime you want to experience the love of your Higher Self, touch your heart gently, and the gift will sing to you.

When you are ready, leave the cave the way you came, using all of your senses for the journey back. When you return to normal consciousness, ground and release.

• • • •

Weekly Question

After you finish this course, do you want to continue your study of Wicca? Why?

Lesson 31:
Personal Sovereignty

In this lesson, we wish to discuss personal sovereignty. We spoke of this concept earlier, but now it is time to examine it more deeply. Sovereignty is personal integrity, truly being who you truly are. Sovereignty is acting from the wholeness of yourself, not just the parts you like best. When we act from our sovereignty, we are able to draw upon our entire being, not just our more attractive qualities.

We all have parts of ourselves that we like more than others. Most of us have aspects of ourselves that we would like to change if we could, and the good news is that we can. We have discussed ways of making such changes in previous lessons and will speak more of it in the future. However, it is important not to confuse changing aspects of ourselves that we do not like with merely hiding those things.

Often when we decide that we wish to be a good person, a spiritual person, we make a list in our mind of qualities we associate with such people and then claim these qualities for ourselves.

The problem with this is that it is one thing to say you are "honest," "compassionate," "courageous," or any other similar virtue and another thing to actually be it.

When we simply say that we are virtuous without actually becoming virtuous, we are deceiving ourselves. This often leads us to develop a very false image of ourselves based on what we *think* we should be rather than what we actually are.

Does this mean we should not try to be a "good person"? On the contrary! What it means is that it is not enough to say we believe something, we must make the effort to actually practice it.

It is more honest to be a self-respecting, competent pickpocket than to be a person who prides himself on honesty yet in reality lies frequently.

Instead, when we make that list of spiritual qualities, we must then proceed to actively develop those qualities in our lives—not just give them lip service. It is wrong to pretend that we are what we are not, but it is good to actively work toward becoming what we wish to be.

So what can we do about this? Let us examine our beliefs and our behaviors. Do we just talk the talk, or do we actually walk the walk?

Take one value at a time, such as honesty, compassion, courage, etc. Examine how you really feel about this value, and write down all of the feelings you can identify. Then go back through this list and examine the things you have written. Are your feelings about the chosen value the same as your ideas about it? If your thoughts and feelings are in sync, then you are on solid ground. If, however, there is a dichotomy between what you think and what you feel about any of these values, then you have a problem. If such a dichotomy arises, you must work to resolve it. First, ask yourself which of the conflicting points of view you wish to keep. Which point of view truly speaks to who you are today and who you wish to become? That is the one you want to maintain. Now, do releasing for the other point of view—as with a paper burning spell, for example.

In doing this exercise, you may be surprised at what you discover about yourself.

Date these writings, and compare them to the dreams you have afterward. This work is ongoing; you won't likely do all that needs to be done in a week's time. Be patient with yourself and be consistent.

By doing this exercise, you will become much clearer on who you really are, and you will greatly strengthen your sovereignty.

• • • •

The Importance of Boundaries

Setting boundaries is an extremely important part of being your True Self. When people do not set boundaries, they often end up spending much of their time placating others and trying to be who those

others want them to be rather than who they truly are.

We will now discuss a simple exercise that can be very helpful in developing healthy boundaries. Take some time to think about your life as it is. Do you have clear boundaries that separate what you want in your life from what you don't? Are these boundaries effective? Pay special attention to those things in your life that you do not want to be there, and also to those things that you do want to have in your life but which are not present.

Now consider your life as you would like it to be. Pay attention to the things that you desire to have in your life as well as the things you desire *not* to have in your life. We are now going to make a physical representation of the boundaries between what you do and do not want in your life, and use it to help manifest this state of being.

Now draw two circles. First make an inner circle, making sure to leave space to draw or write those things you choose to allow into your life. Next, make a larger circle surrounding the smaller one. The larger circle will contain the things you choose not to allow into your life.

Write the things you want in the inner circle and the things you don't want in the outer circle. Read it to yourself when you are finished. Charge this drawing in ritual

space, and place it on your altar where you will see it often.

This is magic on two levels. By taking time to think about this, you automatically begin to create these conditions in your life by focusing your intent upon them. By charging the diagram in ritual and placing it where it can be easily seen, you have empowered it as a physical spell.

• • • •

Releasing Spell

The spell below is to release someone from your life. This works best when the relationship has already ended but you still feel an emotional attraction or vulnerability to the person.

You will need:

- Two black candles
- Black thread
- Candleholders
- Scissors
- Anointing oil—one for releasing or banishing
- A lighter or matches

Put the candles in the candleholders and place them about two to two-and-a-half feet apart. One of the candles is to represent you, the other to represent the person you are releasing. Pick up the candle that represents you. Hold it as you think about the good things that were a part of the relationship. Give thanks for what was good.

Now think about your decision to release this person from your life. Think about the future you want for yourself now. Anoint this candle with the oil, and say:

I release myself from (name)
and go to my future free, happy,
and without limitation.

Pick up the other candle, and say a blessing for the person. Ask that his/her best good and highest happiness come into their life. Anoint this candle with oil while saying:

I release you to your future—a
future that does not include
me. May what is best for
you be yours now.

Set the candle back down.

Cut a length of black thread about a foot longer than the distance between the candles. Tie this to the candles, connecting them. Now light both candles. Hold the scissors in your hand, and cut the connecting thread while saying something like:

What was one is now two.
I am free, and so are you.
No more together shall we be;
you now are gone, and I am free.

Let both candles burn for a while. Let the candle that represents you burn down completely. Snuff the other candle, and bury it deeply somewhere. If the person you are releasing is not someone you were in a relationship with, adjust the spell accordingly.

Do not do this spell lightly. When you release a person from your life in this way, they are gone.

• • • •

Healing or Manifestation Energy

To raise energy for healing or manifestation, ground/release, shield, and enter your stillness.

Focus your attention on the energy center of your body (usually near the navel).

See/imagine a sphere of white light in your energy center. Know that this sphere of light draws its energy from universal energy.

Feel this energy sphere pulsate with energy and expand in size until you are surrounded by this divine white light. Do this until your body tingles with the energy.

Now focus on your hands. Feel the energy you have raised. Keep focusing on your hands until they pulsate and are hot.

Create an energy ball between your hands, and visualize a goal you want to manifest or something you want to be healed. See this as clearly as you can and concentrate upon it. Imagine the energy in your ball of light rushing into your pictured desire. Clap your hands, and release the energy.

• • • •

Dream Symbols: The Body

Parts of the body can figure as symbols in our dreams. Such symbols can represent any number of situations that have nothing whatsoever to do with the actual body part. Below is a list of common symbolic meanings of body parts, illustrating how they might appear in dreams.

Ankles: Like knees, ankles represent flexibility and willingness to bend and adapt, but in this case specifically in terms of your direction in life.

Arms: Arms in a dream often have to do with strength and ability to take action in the world. Strong arms can indicate confident, successful action. Weakness or injury to the arms can indicate a feeling of inability to take action.

Back: Like the shoulders, the back often represents our ability to deal with pressure. Back problems in a dream may indicate that we are carrying too much responsibility or are feeling overburdened. Often the back has specifically to do with financial pressures.

175

Breasts, Women's: In a dream, breasts usually represent nurturing and sustenance. They can represent abundance, divine providence, and wisdom.

Chin: The chin relates to willpower and stubbornness. Issues regarding the chin in a dream may indicate a need for greater determination, or conversely a need to be less rigid and more accepting, depending on the manner in which the chin is featured in the dream.

Eyes: Not surprisingly, the eyes can be a symbol of whether we are seeing situations clearly or not. Vision problems or blindness in a dream may indicate a need to pay closer attention to situations.

Feet: Feet in a dream indicate your life path—how you live; how you feel about your life; where you are going in life and where you wish to go. Sore or damaged feet in a dream may indicate dissatisfaction with the life path.

Hair: Hair represents thoughts and ideas. Unusual conditions of the hair in a dream often indicate one's state of mind. Trying to straighten messy hair, for example, can represent an attempt to clarify one's ideas. Getting a new hairstyle may

indicate that a new understanding is developing. Washing one's hair can indicate a need to release old ideas.

Hands: In a dream, the hands represent the ability to create. If you happen to work with your hands in a particular way—say you are a pianist, for example—then dreaming of hands may also represent that specific skill or profession.

Knees: Knees in a dream indicate flexibility and willingness to bend and adapt to situations.

Legs: Legs in a dream indicate our ability to move forward in life. Problems with the legs can suggest that we are feeling blocked or otherwise unable to progress.

Mouth and Lips: The mouth and lips represent self-expression and communication. Problems with the mouth or lips can indicate issues around communication—things you want to say but can't, for example, or things you have or might have said but shouldn't have. The inability to speak in a dream indicates an inability to express something important in one's life. Wearing an unattractive lipstick in a dream could indicate that you feel badly about something you have said or will say.

Neck: The neck represents flexibility and openness to new ideas. A stiff or broken neck in a dream can indicate that you are being too stubborn about something and need to become more accepting.

Nose: The nose is often taken to represent the ego. The nose is the part of the face that projects farthest forward, and it therefore represents our public image. Problems with the nose in a dream may indicate insecurity regarding how others see you, or perhaps a need to adjust how you present yourself.

Sexual Organs: In a dream, the sexual organs may represent creativity and self-expression. Problems with or injuries to the sexual organs in a dream may indicate that you feel unable to express yourself.

Shoulders: Shoulders in a dream often indicate our ability to bear pressure or responsibility. Sore or injured shoulders may suggest that we are having difficulty holding up under some strain in our daily lives.

Skin: The state of one's skin in a dream may relate to your emotions. Dirty or blemished skin may indicate emotional upset or embarrassment over some issue.

Teeth Missing: Missing teeth in a dream can mean that something you have said or may say might somehow damage you or your reputation.

Teeth That Fall Out: Losing teeth in a dream can symbolize an upcoming death around you.

Throat: The throat represents communication. A sore throat can indicate a need to say something you have been holding back. Garments that are too tight at the throat can indicate being too concerned with how others perceive you and a desire to express a specific image of yourself.

Toes: Toes tend to indicate balance. Injured or missing toes in a dream may indicate being off-balance in life or lacking tranquility. Brightly painted toenails may indicate a need to cultivate greater balance or inner peace.

These are but a few of the possibilities of what body parts can mean in a dream. Similar meanings also attach to those items of clothing that are associated with the various body parts. Hats (ideas or beliefs) and shoes (life-path issues) can be especially important dream symbols.

Although we have listed these meanings, it is important to remember that in dreams it is what a symbol means to *you* that is most important. So if you have different

associations for specific body parts, you will want to pay attention to those associations in interpreting dream symbology. Remember that while others can help you interpret your dreams to some extent, your dreams use your own internal symbolic language to communicate with you, and so your own personal associations must be paramount.

• • • •

Weekly Question

What areas of your Wiccan practice do you need to improve on?

Lesson 32:
Quartz Crystals

In this lesson, we will talk about some different kinds of quartz crystals and their properties.

Quartz crystal is considered to amplify energy and to add to the power of any working it is involved in. In addition, specific kinds of quartz crystal are said to have individual properties that are better for certain types of working.

Clear quartz crystals radiate energy outward and are considered "male" crystals. A container of clear crystals can energize a room. Cloudy crystals pull energy inward and are calming; these are "female" crystals. A cloudy quartz crystal placed near or under the bed helps promote restful sleep.

Quartz crystals can be held during meditation to induce altered states of consciousness. They amplify and strengthen one's energy when held, and they help to clear, align, and balance one's energy.

• • • •

Cleansing and Clearing Crystals

When choosing a new crystal to work with, you should always cleanse and clear it from all previously accumulated energies. The easiest way to do this is to hold it under cold running water with the intention that it will be cleansed. Visualize the water removing any stagnant and/or negative energy as you do this.

• • • •

Charging Crystals

Keep your crystal on your altar when not in use.

Crystals love sunlight, moonlight, and storms, especially storms with lightning. They respond very well to these types of energy. This is especially so when the crystal can actually be placed outside, but a crystal can be charged with sunlight and moonlight by placing it in a window.

You can use the energy exercise for healing or manifestation to charge your crystal also, as long as the intention of the energy is for charging. If you plan to use your crystal for a specific purpose, you will wish to attune it to this purpose when you charge it. Do this by declaring your intent and focusing on the intended use as you fill the crystal with energy.

You can also charge the crystal in ritual, as you did to charge your ritual tools.

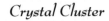

Types of
Quartz Crystals

Crystal Cluster

A crystal cluster is the occurrence of a number of crystal points together in a cluster. In this form, the energy of each crystal amplifies the energy of all the other crystals. This is ideal for creating energy in a room or a ritual space. For best results, it should be chosen for a particular purpose and used only for that purpose. Crystal clusters can meld and amplify the energy and intentions of a group, whether the group is family, spiritual, or business. It is important to cleanse and clear the crystal cluster at least once each month.

Double-Terminated Quartz Crystal

A double-terminated crystal is a crystal that is naturally pointed at each end.

These crystals can project energy out from each end or draw energy into the crystal from each end. These crystals are excellent for dreaming, especially lucid dreaming. They aid dream recall and dream re-entry.

These crystals have a higher energy than many single-terminated crystals.

Bridge Quartz Crystal

This is a crystal that has a smaller crystal partially embedded within it and projecting from it.

These crystals are a bridge between different levels of being, such as the physical and the spiritual worlds.

This kind of crystal is helpful in facilitating communication between people, beings, and the inner and outer selves.

If you work with a crystal of this type, it will tell you even more that it can do and the specific way it prefers to work out of the possibilities that it has.

Generator Crystal

A "generator" crystal has six crystal faces joined together at the terminated apex. These crystals generate energy, as their name implies. They also properly align energy in the body or in the room where they are used. Program this crystal to radiate your purpose or communication into the world.

. . . .

By using these different kinds of quartz crystal to help amplify the energies of your workings in the ways described, you can raise a great deal more energy and thus make your workings much more effective.

. . . .

Your Experiences
and Perceptions

Take some time now to think about your personal experience of these lessons. Using your personal experience of the lessons, write down the places where you agree with what you have been taught in the lessons, as well as any places where your experience leads you to differ. Continue this throughout the remaining lessons.

Your experience and perceptions are part of your personal power, your authority, and your sovereignty. Taking responsibility for what you think and believe is at the heart of living the Wiccan life. Your magic comes from you and through you, and it is strongest and most effective when it is based on your truest self.

• • • •

Weekly Question

How have you used what you have learned about Wicca so far in your daily life?

Lesson 33:
The Lost Jewel

One of the most ancient of all stories about magic is the tale of Khufu and the Magicians, which comes from the Westcar Papyrus. Khufu was the Fourth Dynasty Egyptian pharaoh who built the Great Pyramid at Giza. In the story, Khufu is regaled with stories of famous magicians before summoning a contemporary magician, Djedi, to his court. Among the tales Khufu is told is one involving his father, the pharaoh Snofru.

In the story, Snofru goes boating on a private lake with a number of ladies of the court, as well as his magician advisor Djadjamankh. During the trip, one of the ladies accidentally drops a precious jewel over the side of the boat. The lady is disconsolate, and the pharaoh tries everything to retrieve her jewel for her, but the water is too deep to reach down and get it and too murky to see where it is.

At length, Snofru turns to Djadjamankh and asks the old wizard to retrieve the jewel by magic. Using magic, Djadjamankh lifts up a single section of water, revealing the lake floor. The jewel is now plainly visible and easily retrieved.

We have all lost a jewel similar to that which the pharaoh's court lady lost. It is a jewel that we are all born with—our True Self. We lose it over time to false conceptions of the self, which cover and eventually hide it, even as the waters of the lake hid the court lady's jewel.

We do not have the pharaoh's magician to retrieve our jewel for us, but that is all right, because we can retrieve it ourselves. To do so, we must travel to the Otherworld, which is the place where the jewel originates, and speak to the Goddess of the Otherworld. It is she who gave us the jewel and she who can help us find it again.

• • • •

Journey to the Goddess of the Underworld

Read these instructions, take a ritual bath, ground/release, shield, and enter your stillness.

Now begin your journey to the cave. Use all of your senses—feel the path beneath your feet, smell the scents of the woods, feel the warmth of the sunlight as you go. Notice the trees, plants, animals, and birds. Be alert to all of the sounds that you hear.

Enter the cave. Feel the vibrant energy of expectancy in the cave. This is a special visit, and all of the energies of the cave are aware of this.

Opening off to one side, you will see a passageway. You step into the passageway. It slopes gently downward and curves to the left. Pay close attention to the details of the passageway and how it makes you feel.

You continue through the passageway for some time. The passage continues to slope downward, descending farther and farther into the earth as it goes.

The passageway makes a sudden sharp turn to the left. You find that your way is now blocked by a figure. This is the Guardian of the Gate, who stands guard between the worlds. Have no preconceived notions as to how the Guardian will appear, but let him take whatever form he chooses to best express himself to you. Do, however, take note of his appearance and remember it.

The Guardian asks who is traveling to the Otherworld.

You answer with your name.

The Guardian does not accept this. He says, "Names have no meaning here. Names are ephemeral. Who are you truly?"

You think for a moment and then answer by describing the roles you play in life—the labels you know yourself by. You might say something like, "I am a man/woman, mother/father, son/daughter, husband/wife, teacher/student," etc. Tell the Guardian all of the labels you use to describe yourself in the world.

The Guardian will not accept this. He says, "You cannot take those labels with you into the Otherworld. Leave them all here."

You find that you have all these labels in your hands. The Guardian holds out a jar, and you put all the ways you define yourself into the jar. You notice that you feel lighter without your labels—the names you have used to describe yourself for so long. It is a relief to release them.

The Guardian now steps aside and allows you to continue.

The passageway widens. All you can see in front of you is a pool of black water. Wade into the pool. The water is warm and soothing. Lie on your back, and float peacefully in the black water. Let the water carry you, and feel yourself becoming one with the water. The water seems to penetrate your very being, and you feel as if all of your memories are melting and leaving you.

A voice calls you—it is the voice of the Otherworld Goddess. Rise up out of the pool and go to her. She is off in the shadows and you cannot see her clearly, but you hear her voice calling.

Approach her. As you get closer, you will be able to see her more and more clearly. What does she look like? Have no preconceptions as to her appearance, but allow her to take whatever form best expresses your understanding of her. You may be surprised by the way in which she reveals herself.

"Why have you come to me?" the Goddess asks.

Explain to the Goddess that you have come in search of your missing jewel—your True Self. This is the self you truly are when all of your self-labels, perceptions, and roles are gone. This is the jewel you were born with but lost in growing up, as you saw yourself reflected in the eyes of others and in the mirrors of the labels you accepted.

The Goddess will now hold out the jewel to you. Again, have no preconceptions of what form it will take. It may be an exquisite diamond, a dancing flame, or a tiny, whirling engine. Whatever form the jewel takes, it reflects the nature of your truest self. Take it from the Goddess, and place it into your heart.

Feel the energy of the jewel within your heart as it radiates within you. Vow never to lose this jewel again.

Thank the Goddess for returning your jewel to you, and tell her of your love for her. She has a special message for you, and you should take time to listen carefully to this. The message may take the form of words, images, or simply a knowing that comes to you. Allow it to take whatever form it needs to. Tell yourself that you will remember this message when you have returned to normal consciousness.

Now return to the passageway by which you entered. Step into the passageway, and begin your journey back up to the cave.

As you work your way back up the passage, you will again encounter the Guardian of the Gate. The Guardian holds out to you the jar with your labels and self-definitions in it. The Guardian tells you to take back only the labels you now want in your life. Sift through the jar, considering carefully which labels you are willing to take back. Take the labels you wish, and place them into your heart.

When you are in the cave, sit and think about all you have experienced. Think about the ways your life may change now that you know your True Self. Be aware of your jewel that lives now in your heart.

When you are ready, leave the cave and return the way you came, using all of your senses. Ground and release.

Write all you have experienced in your Book of Shadows.

· · · ·

Aromatherapy

Aromatherapy in its simplest sense is the use of specific scents to create specific emotional, spiritual, or energetic effects. The scent may be used in any of several forms, including scented oil, scented candles, incense, or the direct use of herbs or flowers heated in water, either in a pan on the stove or in a potpourri pot.

Some purists claim that only the finest essential oils can or should be used for this sort of purpose. They are usually selling the finest essential oils when they make this claim. In fact, the finest essential oils can be very beneficial, but they are by no means the only thing that can be effectively used for aromatherapy. It is good to experiment with a wide range of scents and see which types work best for you.

The following scents are good for magical purposes:

Cornflower: psychic ability

Eyebright: clairvoyance

Heliotrope: clairvoyance and prophetic dreams

Honeysuckle: clairvoyance

Iris: wisdom

Marigold: dreams and clairvoyance

Nutmeg: clairvoyance

Rose: divination, clairvoyance, and psychic power

Thyme: psychic power

Willow: divination

The following scents are good for emotional purposes:

Basil: memory, concentration, and exhaustion

Bergamot: anger, anxiety, confidence, exhaustion and fatigue, fear,

happiness, peace, insecurity, loneliness, and stress

Black pepper: exhaustion, burnout, memory, and concentration

Frankincense: depression, fatigue, fear, and stress

Grapefruit: confidence, depression

Jasmine: anger, confidence, fatigue, fear, insecurity, and stress

Lavender: stress, anxiety, depression, and irritability

Rose: depression, anger, peace, and happiness

Rosemary: concentration, fatigue, and confidence

Sage: anxiety, depression, exhaustion, fear, and loneliness

Sandalwood: irritability, anxiety, grief, and stress

The following essential oils are toxic and should not be used: bitter almond, arnica, sweet birch, Spanish broom, melilotus, mugwort, mustard, onion, pennyroyal rue, calamus, camphor, sassafras, and wintergreen.

These are but a small sampling of scents and their uses. I recommend that you try a few of them, and if you want to know more, get some good books on aromatherapy and increase your knowledge.

· · · ·
Weekly Question

Do you believe you have lived as a Wiccan
in other lifetimes? Why?

Lesson 34:
The True Nature
of the World

The world has two parts—the physical world we live in and the energetic, spiritual world that creates and sustains our physical earth. This energetic, spiritual reality is the Otherworld, whose Goddess we visited in our last pathworking.

These two worlds are actually one reality, but most people are only aware of the physical expression, having little or no awareness of the spiritual. It is said that the Otherworld is the perfect pattern from which our physical world originated.

There are many beings who make their home in the Otherworld. Among these are animal totems, the beings we call faerie in their many forms, spirits of place, mythical beings such as unicorns and griffins, and all the plants and animals that are now extinct on earth.

Beginning with this lesson, you will develop the skills you need to travel to the Otherworld and experience its wonders. You need to strengthen your inner senses, beginning with your inner vision.

• • • •

Seeing Subtle Energy

In this section, we will practice seeing subtle energy—this is the spiritual energy that surrounds all things and from which all things are made. The term "subtle" is used to describe this energy, because it is not visible to the eye and can only be seen with the inner eye.

To do this exercise, you will need a plant—preferably a smallish potted plant that you like a lot. Place the plant in front of you, where you can gaze at it without straining your eyes. When you are learning this exercise, it is best that the light around the plant be dim. Sit and gaze at the entire plant—not a specific part of it—and let your eyes be relaxed. Your gaze should rest between the leaves and/or flowers, or just beyond them.

Be careful not to strain your eyes. You want to see the subtle energy of the plant, not the white-light/halo effect that happens when your eyes are strained.

At some point, you should begin to see a smoke-like mist rising and swirling around the plant. Continue to gaze softly, and it will increase. Do this exercise for only five or ten minutes at first. You can do it more than once a day, but not too long at a time.

Once you are able to do this, practice seeing this energy in full light. Then go outside and practice seeing this energy around plants, the leaves of trees, around flowers, etc. Eventually you will be able to see this energy in the air itself.

When you do this exercise, you are training your inner vision. This will increase your psychic skills and deepen the experience of the pathworkings you do.

Visualizing Clearly

In previous lessons, we have worked with exercises intended to improve your ability with visualization. Notably, we have worked with exercises in which you visualize being in a room you have just been in physically and whose features you have committed to memory. In this lesson, we will take this technique a little further.

Begin with the intention that each time you do this, it will be easier, and you will see and experience more.

Find a comfortable position in a place where you will not be disturbed. Ground/release, shield, and enter your stillness.

Select a location that you are familiar with—this can be a place you go to in the present or somewhere from your past, whether it still exists or not. It is not necessary to go to the place physically and familiarize yourself with its features as we did in the previous exercise—here we will be working with your memory of the place.

Enter your stillness. Imagine that you are in the place you have chosen. See this as clearly as you can. Walk around this place and experience it as intensely as possible with all of your senses. Spend at least ten minutes here, then return to normal consciousness. Record your experience in your Book of Shadows.

Understand that this, as is the case with all guided visualizations, is a real journey.

It is energetic in nature rather than physical, but it is real nonetheless.

As you do this exercise, keep your awareness open to the possibility that you may see or sense energy that is not a part of your memory of the place. Explore any energy you may sense as completely as possible in a respectful way.

You may be aware of energy without being able to actually see it. Check it out as much as possible, then return to normal consciousness.

Do this exercise once a day for the remainder of these lessons.

Vary the places you visit to keep the exercise fresh.

Weekly Question

Is your practice of Wicca grounded in your daily life? Are you a better husband/wife, friend, neighbor, parent, etc., because of your practice of Wicca? If not, why not?

Lesson 35:
Life, Death, and Rebirth

The Wiccan sees life and death not as opposites but as complements. They are points on a continually turning wheel—we live, we die, we are reborn. Because of this, we look on the idea of death without the fear found in some other religions.

To the Wiccan, death is not an ending but merely a passage into a different state of being. The "dead" are just as "alive" as we are, but they are in the Otherworld. We do not believe that death is the end of life, and we interact with the beloved dead in many ways—working with spirit guides being one example.

The dead are not judged "good" or "bad" in the Otherworld—these things are balanced by karma in this world, not the next. The Otherworld is a place of rest between lives.

Before we are born into the present life, we set up the basic framework of what our lives will be: the lessons we hope to learn, experiences we wish to have, other souls we wish to work with, etc. We set up what we anticipate to be the major events of our life or possible variations on these. However, because we have free will, we can and do make constant changes to these arrangements.

Also before birth, the soul sets up one or more possible endings for the life; those too can and frequently are changed as the life progresses.

All of the prearrangements—sometimes called our "contract"—are subject to constant revision. Although our contract is set up before birth, it is also rewritten in every moment that we live.

There are those who say that once you become a Wiccan, you will return to Wicca lifetime after lifetime—at least until you learn all it has to offer. We believe that this is why many people who are new to Wicca in this life say that it feels as if they are coming home or that its tenets are what they have always believed but not had a name for.

When we die, we return to the Otherworld and rest between lives. Here we evaluate the life just ended and the extent to which it did or did not fulfill its purposes. Here, too, we are reunited with the souls of others we have known. The soul may choose to advance itself in the Otherworld through studying with other souls or by working as a spirit guide. The possible experience of the soul is open-ended, without limitations. The tapestry of the soul's experience, spread across time and space, is breathtaking.

When the soul is ready for rebirth, it once again sets up goals and challenges for itself, makes agreements with other souls to fulfill them, and is reborn into this world again.

Dreamwalking

Dreamwalking is the art of deliberately communicating with someone in the dream state. We do this unconsciously all the time, but we can learn to do it consciously. This is very much the same technique as mindwalking, which we discussed in lesson 6's section on psychic communication. You can tell a dream in which this type of communication has occurred by its hyper-real feeling, very unlike most dreams.

Begin by deciding you want to connect with someone in your dreams, maybe someone you do not see often. As in mindwalking, see yourself talking to that person, saying what you want to say—only see it happening in a dream setting, either one you are familiar with or an astral setting you have created. Tell yourself you want to have this actual experience in your dream. This takes practice but is not hard to do.

If this practice interests you, a recommended book is *Psychic Dreamwalking: Explorations at the Edge of Self* by Michelle Belanger. She teaches how to do this consciously, including ways to enter the dreams of other people. As always, do this with permission, not by invading the privacy of someone else.

Art as a Spiritual Practice

Art is an important spiritual practice. Whether you are a professional artist or can barely draw a crooked line, art is a way of expressing your feelings, especially the feelings it is hard to find words for. By expressing these feelings externally in artwork, we grow more aware of and more in touch with our emotions and our inner nature. This can greatly increase our self-knowledge, which, as we have discussed, is vital in spiritual work.

Artistic expression, done on a regular basis, keeps the door open between our inner and outer selves; is a divine trait we share with Goddess and God (the ability to create); increases our psychic ability and our personal power; and is an expression of the element of fire, which is creativity, sexuality, spirituality, and psychic ability. By opening the door to one of these expressions, we are open to all of them.

There are many simple ways to express yourself in art. If all you can draw are stick figures and you want to make a picture, draw stick figures. If you are expressing a feeling, the energy will be there. Technical excellence is not the point of spiritual art.

You can use crayons, watercolors, markers, colored pencils, oils, or do collage. In lesson 15, we discussed making a treasure map by doing a timed collage. You can use this same technique without a specific intent, to see what you are feeling in the moment.

Sit with the materials of your choice, and take one feeling at a time, such as joy, indecision, sadness, etc., and practice drawing something that expresses that feeling. The drawing can be anything from a picture to a scribble, as long as it encapsulates the feeling you have chosen to express. This exercise can be challenging but rewarding.

Poetry, writing, pottery, and other forms of three-dimensional art are all valid ways to do spiritual art.

Work with this for two months, and see the difference it makes for you.

• • • •

Weekly Question

What is your preferred method to express yourself artistically? How does expressing yourself creatively enhance your life?

Part

III

Lesson 36:
Journey to the Otherworld

When you journey to the Otherworld, it is best to have a specific reason for going. The reason can range from connecting with a specific deity or energy to asking a specific question. Having a specific reason for your journey serves to focus your journey. You might think that being an Otherworld tourist would be fun, but the Otherworld is a big place, and without a specific goal you are likely to have an experience that has no relevance to you and may not even be comprehensible.

For this journey, our purpose is to explore the underlying cause of whatever is the most important issue in your life at this time. You do not need to know what the most important issue in your life at this time is. Sometimes there will be no doubt as to what that issue is, of course, but other times it may come as a surprise.

For example, you may think that the most important issue in your life is something happening at your job, only to be shown it is actually what is happening in your relationship—which you may not have seen while you were worrying about the job.

Other times the issue will be all too clear, but the causes may not be what you expect.

For example, you may think that a failing romance is the most important issue in your life at this time, only to learn that the underlying cause is actually how you feel about your parents' relationship during your childhood, and these feelings are what has caused your present-day romance to fail.

Or you may feel that prosperity is your most important issue, only to be shown that the underlying cause is actually a need for security, which may be either helping or hurting your goal of prosperity.

Sometimes, too, the causes of issues may be revealed to lie in past lives.

Read these instructions, take a ritual bath, ground/release, shield, and enter your stillness.

Now begin your journey to the cave. Use all of your senses—feel the path beneath your feet, smell the scents of the woods, feel the warmth of the sunlight as you go. Notice the trees, plants, animals, and birds. Be alert to all of the sounds that you hear.

Enter the cave. Feel the vibrant energy of expectancy in the cave. This is a special visit, and all of the energies of the cave are aware of this.

Look around the cave. You will see a passageway leading off from the main cave. Follow it. As you proceed down the passage, concentrate on your reason for making this journey—to explore the underlying causes of whatever issue is most important in your life at this time.

As you come to the end of the passage, you will emerge into a new place. It may be an indoor space or it may be an outdoor space. It may be a brilliant day or it may be darkling night. Pay close attention to all that you see in this new place, because every detail comments on the nature of the pattern you have come to study and your relationship with it.

Momentarily, a guide will approach you to lead you forward. This guide may take any form, and you should have no pre-conceptions as to the form the guide may appear in. As always, allow the form to take whatever shape is needed. The guide may appear as a person, an animal, or something more abstract, like a mist or a light.

Your guide will lead you to what you have come to see. You may ask questions, and you may ask to be shown specific things if you wish. The guide will comply.

This part of the journey will be different for each person. You will be shown what you need to see. The issue will be revealed to you, perhaps in words or perhaps in pictures, or played out for you like a movie. Then the causes will be shown. Have no preconceived ideas as to how these things will reveal themselves, as this will limit the experience and may interfere with your ability to receive the information. Rather, allow the experience to unfold in any way

that it needs to. Sometimes what you are shown may not appear to make sense at first—allow it to continue anyway; usually its relevance will become clear presently, though sometimes you may only see the relevance of certain things later, well after the pathworking has ended.

Allow the experience to continue as long as it needs to. When it has finished, thank the guide. Allow the guide to lead you back to your passageway, and return by the passageway to the cave.

When you are in the cave, sit and think about all you have experienced.

When you are ready, leave the cave, and return the way you came, using all of your senses.

You may make this journey many times. It is recommended to not do this more often than once a week. Remember that you need a definite purpose for this journey, and you should use the experience or the information you receive in some practical way in the physical world.

• • • •

Moon, Sun, and Stars

You interact with lunar energy at your monthly esbats. This energy strengthens your inner psychic abilities. The energy of the sun is equally important, as it strengthens you physically, increases your energy, and grounds you in daily life. Now you will learn to work with the energy of the stars.

When you interact with this energy, it begins to awaken ancient memories within you.

• • • •

Experiencing the Energy of the Stars

Ground/release, shield, and enter your stillness.

If you can do this exercise outside in total darkness on a moonless night, do so. If you cannot, stand in total darkness inside and visualize the stars glowing, brilliant, and casting a delicate light.

Visualize the light of the stars as it actually is—softly glowing, filled with a delicate energy, caressing your skin, permeating every portion of your body. Feel this energy as a glowing, conscious awareness that fills and explores all of you. Bathe in this light as long as you are comfortable.

Do this two to four times a month, every month. You may be surprised at the change in your energy and awareness.

• • • •

Weekly Question

What difference have these pathworkings made in your life so far?

Lesson 37:
Conscious Dying

The ability to be conscious during the transition to death will help alleviate any fears you may have about the process. During these lessons, you have had many experiences of other levels of being, including visiting with the dead. By now, you are aware that death is a doorway, not the end of being.

Death is not a symbol; it is a reality. Because of this, there are certain things about death that are common to all cultures, no matter what they formally "believe."

Before a person dies, they will often be visited by the spirits of their beloved dead. The person who is dying will be able to see and interact with the beloved ones, although other people present will usually neither see nor hear these spirits. This is a very real experience to the person and not a dream.

Often when a person is dying, their soul will leave their body and travel to the Otherworld to visit with their beloved ones. Usually this will happen when the person is sleeping, but it is not a dream. Sometimes it comes as a vision when they are awake.

During such a visit to the Otherworld, a dying person often experiences being with Deity—though they will perceive Deity in the manner that is best for them.

Usually the person experiences traveling through a tunnel to reach the Otherworld and emerging into a beautiful light. This is the light of Deity and is filled with strength and love. The person is normally greeted at the end of the tunnel by their loved ones and/or guides. Usually the person will perceive the Otherworld as being much like this one, with familiar landscapes and sometimes buildings.

The Otherworld is analogous to Plato's World of Ideas—it is the blueprint from which reality takes form. Everything that exists in the physical began as an idea here in the Otherworld. Here, thoughts are literally things. Because of this, the person will find that they can create whatever they desire for themselves. Unlike this world, where such creation requires time and sustained focus, in the Otherworld it is instantaneous.

Of course, it is also important in the Otherworld, as in this one, to be clear on what we want and what we believe. It is even more important, because in the Otherworld manifestation is much more immediate than here.

Traveling to the Otherworld before actual death makes the transition easier when we actually die. This is why so many people have these experiences as death is approaching—it eases the way. For those

Part
III

of us who practice magic and make many such journeys during our lifetimes, the transition can be very easy and should be free from all fear.

When we have actually died and gone to the Otherworld, we will review our life here on earth and assess our feelings about it. Did we do a good job with the life? Did we learn the lessons we had hoped to learn? Did we achieve the things we had planned? If things went differently during the life than we had anticipated before it began, did we benefit from these changes? The soul is not judged in the Otherworld—it assesses itself. The soul then applies what it has learned toward its next life.

• • • •

The Death Walk

Journeying to visit the land of the dead and becoming familiar with it is an aid to conscious dying. As you can see from our discussion above, the ability to visit the land of the dead is very important. While it aids conscious dying, it also allows us to have direct contact with our own beloved dead.

It is important, however, to remember that, as in all practices involving spirit communications—ranging from receiving the messages of our guides to guided visualizations and pathworkings—that anything you see or experience must pass through your conscious mind in order for you to understand it in this world. Some-

times, your conscious mind will warp the experience because it may not have any context in which to understand certain spiritual experiences, and also because it may tend to reject things that it cannot fit into established context. Therefore, you must never mistake such contact for being infallible, because the messenger can and sometimes does warp the message.

In this section, we are going to discuss the idea of the death walk, a term that is used to describe the symbolic path one follows to reach the land of the dead. The death walk can be used in meditation to visit the land of the dead, as described above, but its most important use is as we are, in fact, dying. When we feel that death has come for us, at the end of what is hopefully a very long and very happy life, assuming that we are conscious as this is happening, we can use the death walk to ease our transition by taking a more conscious part in it. In this way, our consciousness may enter the land of the dead before we have completely died.

Everyone has a death walk—a path they expect to follow into the Otherworld when they die—whether they have consciously built it, as we will do, or whether they have merely absorbed it from the ideas of ambient culture around them.

The ancient Egyptians, for example, used the path and challenges described in the Book of the Dead—the Pert Em

Heru—to establish the form of their death walk. This particular death walk involved passing through many challenges and successive gateways.

In many cultures, the Otherworld was entered by crossing a river—the River Styx for classical Pagans. Others entered the Otherworld through a cave and then proceeded down a passageway, as we have done in many of our exercises. Each of these death walks is equally valid and served their culture by establishing an accepted route to follow. It is also equally valid to create your own death walk, which can draw from any or none of these images.

Most important, however, is that whatever form your death walk takes, it should have meaning for you. Take your time with this, and consider carefully the form you wish to assign to the death walk.

Once you have chosen the form of your death walk, write it down. Read it once a week, and journey to the afterlife at least once a month to stay familiar with it. Share this with a friend, and make an agreement that, if possible, your friend will be with you when you die to read your death walk to you as you make the transition.

Throughout your lifetime, you may change the form of your death walk many times. But when you die, you will have a well-known path to follow, and you will go to a well-known place instead of an unknown destination.

Weekly Question

What are your present beliefs about dying and the afterlife? Why do you have these beliefs?

Part
III

Lesson 38:
Practical Spirituality

Walking a spiritual path does not protect anyone from pain, loss, and death. It does give you the tools you need to cope with life's challenging events. You grow in your spiritual path by being fully present in life, by accepting your life as it is in the moment, not as you wish it to be, and by sinking deeply into it.

When it is said that spiritual growth occurs by accepting your life as it is, that does not mean a passive acceptance of problems. This means facing the situations in your life and dealing with them by choosing how you will act and react in a situation.

Death happens to all of us. We know that death is only a doorway to the afterlife and not an ending, but we still experience grief when someone we love dies. The only way to move out of grief is to walk through it, to process it through your being. This is painful. You develop spiritual muscles by doing this. If you suppress grief, it doesn't leave.

Pain and loss happen for many reasons. Often, before we come into a life we choose unpleasant events we will experience. We do this to aid our soul's growth or to be there for someone else and to support them emotionally or otherwise through the experience. Sometimes the soul chooses something that our minds label as negative, but the soul chooses to experience it for its own purposes.

Why discuss this in a lesson on Wicca? Many people on a sincere spiritual path have an unconscious assumption that if they are spiritual, they are protected from these things. It can come as a rude awakening to discover that they are not. Life itself is the ultimate initiation, and we came here to experience it—the challenging parts of life as well as the pleasant parts.

. . . .

Creating Your Reality, Continued

We have discussed the nature of reality to some extent. Now we will revisit this topic. The physical reality we know around us is not as solid as it seems but rather is created and re-created in every moment. This creation occurs because energy shapes itself in reaction to the focus it is given. We focus energy through thought and feeling. What we believe, what we expect, what we habitually think about—these things create our reality.

Our desires can also help create our reality when we focus our energy on them. So can our fears—again, when we focus our energy on them. The true art of magic lies in learning how to focus energy to create reality, but it also lies in learning what to focus on and what *not* to focus on.

If it is this simple, why do we use spells? Because spells work with symbols, they bypass our thinking mind and work directly with our Higher Self. If we have limiting belief systems or blockages, we can sometimes bypass them in this manner. However, having done a spell, it is important that we accept it and believe that it can and will work. If you do a spell for a specific goal, but afterwards you go back to thinking you could never have the given goal come to pass, or focus on the idea of the goal not being in your life, you are apt to cancel the effects of the spell.

Are spells necessary? They are a large part of present-day Wicca, but do we really need them? Well, necessary is a big word. Nothing is ever "necessary" beyond your personal, internal connection to Deity. But spells can be helpful.

We create our own reality, every day of our life, either consciously (by being clear and focusing on the life we want) or unconsciously (by default). Implicit in this is that we are clear within ourselves and have identified any blockages to our desires and healed and released them.

The more clear you are about what you want, the more you are able to believe that you are able to have what you want, and the more you focus your thoughts on what you

do want, the more quickly you will manifest it.

In working through these lessons, we have done much to achieve inner clarity. We have worked extensively to clear energetic blockages, to release limiting thought patterns, and to heal our shadow.

We are now ready to practice conscious manifestation. To do this:

Choose something you want in your life, ask the universe/Spirit to give it to you, accept it, see yourself receiving it, feel yourself experiencing the pleasure of having it, and give thanks that this is yours now.

Now, you might say: If this is mine now, then why don't I have it?

When we say that it is "ours now," we mean that we have restructured the energetic pattern in order to bring this into our life. Energetically, it is a reality in our life now. If we continue to focus on what we have asked for, what we do want now, it will appear in our life presently. However, this requires us to have clarity and focus in our habitual thoughts as we continue to focus on what we want, day by day.

Every time you remember it this week, pay attention to what you are thinking, especially about what you have asked for. Almost certainly, you will find yourself thinking about not having it or thinking about reasons why you cannot have it. This is an excellent practice for re-training your

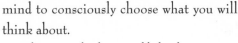

mind to consciously choose what you will think about.

When you find yourself thinking negatively about what you have asked for, say to yourself: "I cancel this negative thought," then replace it with a thought of having what you want. Immediately after, feel the pleasure of having what you want, and give thanks that it is yours.

To recap:

- Cancel the negative;
- Restate the positive;
- Feel the pleasure of having what you want; and
- Give thanks that it is yours.

As you work consistently at being aware of your thoughts and immediately correcting the negative, you will find it is easier to focus on what you want and to manifest it into your life.

• • • •

Weekly Question

How do you think you can best apply what we have just discussed?

Lesson 39:
Group or Solitary?

These lessons were created with the solitary Wiccan in mind. However, these lessons can be just as helpful for Wiccans who work in a group. When several Wiccans work together to learn and grow and worship, the group may be known as a study group, coven, or more formally as a temple.

Each of these alternatives—solitary or group working—has its advantages and disadvantages. Each is an equally valid choice. However, for many people there really is no choice, as there are often no groups available in their area. In this case, the person is obliged to be solitary by circumstances, and the vast majority of Wiccans around the world fall into this category.

Solitary work has the great advantage of being completely self-directed and totally tailored to one's own needs and desires. The solitary practitioner can progress at their own pace and not have to worry about other people's deadlines. The disadvantages of solitary practice include the fact that when study and practice are completely self-directed, it can be easy to become lazy and ignore the harder lessons that might be demanded in a group. The greatest dis-

advantage to solitary practice, of course, is the sense of isolation from other Wiccans and the lack of interaction with and feedback from others.

Group work also has both advantages and disadvantages. The greatest advantage is that being in a group can give a stronger sense of connection and community. Also, when studying with others, you have the benefit of their experiences and feedback to help with your own growth. Usually a group will not let its members avoid specific lessons simply because they are more difficult, and procrastination is harder when someone else is setting the deadline. The disadvantages to group work include the aforementioned fact that groups can be hard to find and are not present at all in many places. In addition, there are many, many Wiccan traditions, and finding a group in a tradition you wish to belong to is even harder than just finding a group in the first place. Wiccan traditions range from the extremely open and easygoing to the extremely rigid and hidebound; which tradition a group belongs to makes a huge difference in how they practice.

Many people who are in a position to do so will combine the best of both approaches by following a very active solitary path while at the same time belonging to one or more groups. This again, however, presupposes that one has access to one or more groups at all.

The advent of the Internet has changed this equation considerably. Online schools like Witchschool.com have made it much easier to find people of a like mind to study and work with via email, instant message, and chat. People who were formerly geographically isolated solitaries are now often part of online groups far larger and more diverse than any local group. Because the Internet community is global in nature, it is unnecessary to accept the luck of the draw in seeking or choosing a group—the whole world of choices is quite literally available.

All of these are equally valid choices. You really need to ask yourself which is right for you, and this should be your only criteria.

You may encounter people who will try to tell you that only group work is legitimate or that only their tradition is legitimate; some go as far to forbid you to associate with any group if you wish to belong to theirs. Such people love to criticize people who think differently from themselves as being "fluffy." What does "fluffy" mean? Anything that differs from their own opinion, of course. You should be extremely cautious of people like this. In considering what they have to say about the superiority of their views, you might ask yourself a number of things: one, do they, in fact, appear to be in any way superior? If they say that they are highly superior but cannot tell you how or why because it is "secret," this should be a huge red flag to you that there is something wrong in what they are saying.

Another important question to ask yourself in this and all other situations is: "What are these things, and who do they serve?" That is, is the person trying to help and guide you, or are they just trying to help themselves? If someone is attacking the legitimacy of another path, it may be nothing more than an attempt to proselytize you into their own tradition. Wiccans often claim that we never proselytize, but the truth is that certain Wiccan traditions constantly proselytize by attacking other traditions and seeking to convert their members—the very definition of proselytizing.

No one tradition is superior to any other, and anyone who says otherwise should be treated with extreme caution.

If you are invited to join an existing coven, use your common sense. Do not think because they may have been a coven for years and you are a beginner that they are wiser than you are. Take time to get to know them, and be alert for ego games. Always trust your gut instinct. If anyone tells you or suggests you do something you are not comfortable doing, do not do it. You should always be the final authority in deciding what is or is not best for you, because it is you, after all, who must live with the results of the decisions.

Changing Your Experience of Time

In this lesson, we are going to discuss our experience of time. Though time appears to be a very rigid structure, completely objective in nature, our experience of time is actually very subjective. Time as we think we know it is an illusion—and one which we move beyond in magical working.

Time is the way in which the soul structures experiences in order to be able to understand and analyze them to best effect. However, this structure is nowhere near as solid and binding as it appears. This exercise is intended to begin developing an understanding of the true nature of time.

Many of our habits are based on schedules imposed from outside. Because we accept these schedules, we sometimes come to think of them as being "natural." An example of this is the person who eats at the same time each day and becomes hungry because it is "time to eat," not necessarily because they are in need of food.

To change your experience of time, take a day when you are not on a schedule, when you do not need to be aware of the time. Cover all clocks or turn them to the wall. Turn off all electronic devices. Eat when you are hungry, sleep when you are tired. Let your body dictate when you do what. You will find that the very speed at which time seems to move changes when you do

this. Time may seem to move more quickly or more slowly, but it will definitely move differently in the absence of external measurement. Not only this, but at the end of the day, you are also likely to find that you feel far more relaxed than usual.

This exercise will show you how much more elastic time can be when you are not watching it—how much more subjective your experience of time really is than you may have thought it was. In this, as in many other things, the limitations we feel hold us back often come more from ourselves than from the external factors we may be attributing them to. Take your life back as much as you can. You will enjoy it more.

The Witches' Bottle

The Witches' bottle is a protective spell that can be used for yourself, your home, your workplace, etc. This is an ancient type of spell with a long history. There are many variations on the Witches' bottle, but here we will give a fairly common one.

To make your Witches' bottle, you will need the following:

- A small glass jar, such as a baby food jar or something of similar size, with a lid
- A number of sharp objects— razor blades, needles, straight pins, nails, tacks, etc.

- Holy water (salt and water that has been cleansed, blessed, and charged)
- Super Glue
- A black ribbon

This spell should be done during the waning, or dark, moon. You can do it as part of your esbat ceremony or as a ceremony unto itself.

Make sure that you have all of the items you will need for the spell gathered beforehand and placed upon your altar.

Begin your ritual as you normally would: casting your circle and invoking quarters, Goddess and God, etc. When you come to the working part of the ritual, take a few moments to state your intent—creating a Witches' bottle for protection—and to concentrate on the idea of this.

Take up the empty jar. Imagine the jar filled with a clear, white light. Say something like:

> *Behold, I bless this jar that*
> *it may be the vehicle of*
> *protection for me and mine.*

Add the sharp objects to the jar. Imagine the various sharp objects glowing brightly, as if they were white-hot. Say something like:

> *May any who would harm me*
> *or mine be stopped by this spell.*

> *May it be a barrier against all*
> *harm, intentional or unintentional.*

Now add the holy water. Imagine the water glowing brightly with light. Say something like:

> *I infuse this spell with power,*
> *and through it I work my will*
> *that I and mine be protected*
> *now and henceforth.*

Place the Super Glue around the inner rim of the lid, and place the lid on the jar, closing it tightly. Tie the black ribbon securely around the rim of the jar.

Imagine this bottle trapping any and all negativity that may be directed to you, consciously or unconsciously.

Now say something like:

> *By all the power of three times*
> *three, as I do will, so mote it be!*

You have now completed your Witches' bottle and may continue with your ritual as you normally would.

After the ritual, you will need to find a place for the Witches' bottle. The ideal location is buried in the earth just outside your front door. If this is a possibility for you, it is the best place to put your Witches' bottle. However, many people today live in apartments, and their front doors open onto hallways, not yards. In this case, you should keep your Witches' bottle just inside your front door, inside a container that represents earth—perhaps a larger bottle, vase, or decorative box. The larger container should always be kept closed and never opened. The same considerations would apply if you are protecting a place of business.

If you later leave this residence, do not take the Witches' bottle with you to your new home, but rather make a new one. If you buried your Witches' bottle, then when you move, you should leave it buried. If you kept your Witches' bottle in a container, then when you move, you should take the container—unopened—to someplace where you can bury it. Bury the bottle there, and release it.

• • • •

Weekly Question

Would you prefer to work as a solitary, or do you want to be part of a group?

Lesson 40:
Dedication, Initiation,
and the Three Degrees

In the Wiccan religion, the term "dedication" refers to the ceremony by which one declares their commitment to the religion. This ceremony is also sometimes called a Wiccaning. These lessons are designed to prepare you for that commitment, if you should choose it. Of course, this choice is yours alone.

Wicca is not an exclusive religion. It is quite possible to be a Wiccan while simultaneously following one or more other disciplines as well, provided that these do not conflict with essential Wiccan teachings. Thus it is not uncommon to find Wiccans who are also Buddhists, Santerians, or even Christians—because the particular way that they practice these other religions is such that they do not conflict with their Wiccan beliefs. Nor are these things compartmentalized—a Wiccan Buddhist integrates their Buddhism into their Wicca rather than keeping it as a separate practice. The nature of Wicca, being experiential and highly personal, is such that it can integrate all manner of beliefs according to the individual Wiccan's need.

Many Wiccan traditions have an organized priesthood, usually structured in three degrees—though some traditions have more degrees and others have fewer. Entry into the priesthood is through a program of study leading to initiation. Not all members of the Wiccan religion become priesthood, nor does every Wiccan desire to be priesthood—although every individual can be thought of as priesthood for themselves.

An initiation is more than just a ceremony. It makes actual energetic changes in a person, opening them spiritually and psychically to deeper levels of their being. Every dedication or initiation is an ending of sorts and a rebirth into a new way of being.

A Wiccan self-dedication is a conscious choice to walk the Wiccan path, to honor the Lady and the Lord, to honor yourself and all of life. It is committing to be fully conscious in your life, to act from your inner sovereignty, from the essence of who and what you are, and to live your ideals and beliefs. It is expressing your True Will in the world. Your True Will is that portion of the Lady and the Lord that is expressed as you. It is what you came into this lifetime to learn, to do, and to be. To be a Wiccan is to practice integrity and wholeness, where who and what you are inside of yourself is who and what you are in the world.

When you dedicate yourself as a Wiccan, you put yourself in the service of life;

you choose to leave this world a better place than you found it. You choose to continue to learn and to grow, to celebrate the esbats that heal and empower you, and to celebrate the sabbats that heal the earth. It is to be consciously connected to active relationship with all beings in the sacred web of life. Being a Wiccan is a life-long path where the learning, the joy, the responsibility, and being responsive never end.

Dedication makes you a member of the religion. It does not make you a member of the formal priesthood—although, again, every person can be informally considered a priest or priestess in their own life. You can live the Wiccan life at this level for the rest of your life if you choose to. Choosing to continue your studies in the degree levels does not make you a better Wiccan. However, it does deepen your experience, skills, and responsibilities.

In the Correllian Tradition to which I belong, the studies for the First Degree broaden your understanding and increase your psychic abilities through a structured program of psychic exercises. The First Degree is the entry level of the Correllian priesthood. The first degree initiation can have a profound impact on your life. Although initiations cannot be discussed in detail, it is permissible to say that the symbolic rebirth that is part of this initiation will affect you even more deeply than

the self-dedication included with these lessons.

The Correllian Second Degree again leads to deeper knowledge and broader psychic and magical skill. At this level, one usually specializes their practice, choosing to focus on one or more specific skills. The Second Degree priesthood are the principle body of working priesthood in the tradition. The Second Degree initiation deals with overcoming limitation, and if an initiate still has unresolved issues, the initiation will cause these to be brought to the surface to be dealt with and healed.

The Correllian Third Degree deals with deeper understanding of the nature of existence and the ongoing process of creation. The Third Degree are the High Priesthood of the tradition. The Third Degree initiation brings home the full nature of cosmic oneness.

Any of these initiations should be undertaken with care and with a genuine desire for growth and opening, because the initiation will have a profound energetic effect on you, and growth and opening will proceed from this.

· · · ·

Gaia

In lesson 24, you were introduced to the concept of the World Soul, or Nuos. Gaia is the embodiment of the Nuos. At one level, Gaia is the spirit of the living earth.

At another level, Gaia is the spirit of the living universe.

In this lesson, we will be interacting with Gaia as the spirit of the earth. Wiccans believe that the earth and everything on it are an integrated whole—a single being made up of many individual beings. Consequently, though we are individuated, we are not truly separate. And just as the earth and everything on her make up a single system when viewed from that level, so do the earth and all other planets and stars form part of the single system of the universe. Ultimately, all that exists is one system, one being.

In lesson 1, it was stated that all water is one water. The water in our bodies is the same water that was or will be clouds, lakes, rivers, oceans, rain, and snow. The same water cycles through everything, present, past, and future. The minerals in our bodies come from plants that we eat which have been grown in the earth. We breathe in oxygen given off by plants and trees, who then use the carbon dioxide that we exhale. We are literally, physically, part of Gaia. There is no separation.

Why repeat this? Because it is important that this awareness, this basic relationship, be part of your experience, not simply mental knowledge. The following exercise will help you to experience this connection.

. . . .

Living Energy of Gaia

Ground/release, shield, and enter your stillness. Place some tobacco or cornmeal on your altar as an offering to Gaia.

Set your intent to experience the living energy of Gaia. Journey to your personal Hall of Consciousness. Seek out the door that is different from all the others. This door will take you to the heart of Gaia.

Go through the door, and enter the presence of Gaia. Have no preconceptions about how you will experience her, but allow her to take the form that is best for this. Open yourself to her, and feel the strength and love that is at the heart of her energy.

Ask Gaia what you can do to help heal her, to better ensure that she and all beings that are part of the web of life may endure and thrive. The goddess will give you an answer that is specific to your circumstances, skills, and willingness. If what she tells you is more than you feel you can do, be honest about this and say so—but it is unlikely that she will ask more than you can do.

Ask the goddess if she has any other messages for you, and if she does, take time to receive these. She may also offer you a symbolic gift of some sort, and if she does so, you should accept the gift and place it into your heart.

When the goddess has said all she has to say, you should give thanks to her. Then return through the doorway to your Hall of Consciousness.

Take time each day to send energy and blessings to Gaia. Offer tobacco or cornmeal to her. Perhaps place on your altar a picture or image that represents Gaia to you. The Venus of Willendorf is widely used as an image of Gaia, but it is only one of many possibilities. Spend time in normal consciousness being aware of her energy, as once you have experienced it, you can connect with it anytime or anywhere.

. . . .

Introduction to Astrology

Beginning in this lesson and continuing in the next two lessons, we will be giving a brief overview of astrology. Astrology is an excellent tool for self-knowledge. It identifies your talents, strengths, weaknesses, and the challenges you face in your life. It can make relationships easier to navigate as you learn how different astrological signs feel, think, act, and react.

Some people object to astrology because they think it limits your expression and choices in life. This is a common misconception. Actually, astrology is not a limitation, because it does not show what must be but rather what potentials are pres-

ent. What you do with those potentials is entirely under your own power. A yearly chart will tell you what areas of your life are highlighted during the upcoming period and where opportunities and challenges lie. What you do with this knowledge is up to you. You always have the final choice.

In this lesson, we will discuss the idea of the sun sign. The sun sign is the astrological sign that the sun was in at the time of a person's birth. This is the most familiar aspect of astrology, and almost everyone is familiar with the sun sign–based horoscope columns featured in many newspapers and magazines. However, the sun sign is only one part of what is actually a much more complex art. A full astrological chart includes many features, of which the sun sign is only one—however, it is perhaps the best place to begin an examination of the art of astrology.

The sun sign shows a person's basic personality. Once you are familiar with sun signs, you will know a great deal about a perfect stranger simply by knowing what his or her sun sign is. However, it is important to remember that the sun sign does not show everything and might be regarded as a general framework within which there are many other details.

There are many other influences in an astrological chart. These include the sign the moon is in, the ascendant sign, and the relationships between the other planets as they

are placed in the chart. Because of this, people with the same sun sign can be very different, but they will still share basic traits.

Each sun sign can express itself in positive or negative ways or have a mixture of the two. There are twelve sun signs. In this lesson, we will discuss the first four sun signs. They are:

Aries

Born March 21 through April 20. (If you are born on the first or last day before a sign changes, you need a professional chart done for accuracy. The sun changes zodiac signs on different days some years, and the time zone where you are born also can make a difference.) A fire sign ruled by the planet Mars. The symbol of Aries is the Ram.

Positive: Aries people are independent, dreamers, and romantics. They are excellent at starting new projects and developing new ideas. They are happiest when self-employed or in a position of authority. Status is important to them. They are energetic and ambitious. They can be patient to a fault, but they can also have a quick temper. Aries are natural flirts and like lots of attention.

Negative: Aries can get lost in their dreams and lose touch with reality. They can become bitter because they haven't accomplished their dreams or feel under someone else's thumb at work. Their desire for attention can lead them to extreme behavior and attitudes. They can run roughshod over the feelings of others and never know it. They can be controlling.

Taurus

April 21 through May 21. An earth sign ruled by the planet Venus. The symbol of Taurus is the Bull.

Positive: Taurus loves beauty and experiences the world through the senses. They want money, security, and pleasure. They are some of the hardest workers in the zodiac. They have incredible stamina. Taurus has great determination but can also be very stubborn. Although Taurus can be very generous and caring, they can also be rather self-centered in their outlook and do not always understand that other people see things in other ways.

Negative: Taurus expressed in the negative can be controlling and manipulative. They can use their generosity in an unspoken attempt to earn or buy the love they feel they lack. They can be lazy and look to others to support them. They can have an explosive temper and be mentally and emotionally cruel.

Gemini

May 22 through June 21. An air sign ruled by Mercury. The symbol of Gemini is the Twins.

Positive: Gemini are quick-witted, bright, entertaining, and fun. They tend to be artistic, and excel in communications of all sorts. They are charming and persuasive. They are also highly changeable and can seem to manifest different personalities in different circumstances, shaping their apparent personality to their various social or professional roles.

Negative: Expressed in the negative, Gemini can be controlling and dominating. They can be very possessive. They can also be given to unnecessary anxiety, worrying over imagined or exaggerated problems. They can also be scattered and fickle, often leaving projects or situations unfinished.

Cancer

June 22 through July 23. A water sign ruled by the moon. The symbol of Cancer is the Crab or occasionally the Scarab.

Positive: Cancers experience the world through their feelings. They are very psychic, feel things deeply, and get their feelings hurt easily. They also have great organizational ability. Having a home and family is important to them, and they focus most of their energy on these. This can be a danger, as Cancers sometimes need more emotional interaction than their family can supply, in which case they can become smothering.

Negative: Cancers can be overprotective of their loved ones, trying to shut out the world to keep them from harm. They can smother their loved ones and drain them emotionally to fulfill their own needs. They may lie and manipulate and can be vindictive when they are thwarted.

• • • •

Weekly Question

Has your experience of the energy of Gaia changed your experience of daily life?

Lesson 41:
The Web of Life

The web of life is a metaphor for the interconnection of all things. It is said that any action taken affects the farthest star. Rev. Donald Lewis-Highcorrell, First Priest and Chancellor of the Correllian Tradition, says that all existence is one being experiencing itself. All things are a single, integrated whole. If this is true, then the farthest star is also part of who we are, and our actions affect it at a spiritual level even as it affects us.

At our highest level of awareness, we are simultaneously the farthest star and the whole Milky Way galaxy, the sand on the beach and the fence post in the yard, as well as anything else you can think of. It is all one. We are all one.

We narrow our conscious focus to a limited range, such as the individual person we know ourselves as, in order to experience that specific aspect of existence fully, which causes us to forget that we are also one with the whole of existence. Remembering that oneness and reconnecting with that level of our being is a major goal of magic and the heart of what it is to be Wiccan. We worship the Goddess and the God, but at the same time we are the Goddess and the God experiencing life in all of its diversity.

In Hinduism, there is a story telling how the mother of Krishna, an avatar of the Hindu god Vishnu, looked into her little son's mouth and was amazed to see the entire universe within it. But to the Wiccan, this is the true nature of being. If you want to find the universe, look inside yourself. It is said that if what you seek you find not within yourself, you will never find it.

When we truly know that we are connected to and part of everything, we don't have to work to remember the morals of Wicca—they are right in front of us. Whatever we do to others, all beings in the sacred web of life, we truly do to ourselves. Learning Wicca is ultimately about remembering who and what we truly are.

• • • •

Experience Being Something Else

In this section, we are going to find out what it is like to be something other than our normal conscious self. Select something whose existence you would like to experience. This can be a plant, tree, animal, a piece of furniture, a vase, etc.

Ground/release, shield, and enter your stillness.

Imagine what it is like to be the thing you have selected. Imagine this as clearly as you can. Try to merge your awareness with the thing you have chosen. You may feel this as an energetic connection or you may not. Relax and have fun with it. It may take a few times of doing the exercise to succeed.

Try having a conversation with the object while you are also being it. This will be rather like an internal dialog you might have with your inner self. Learn what it is like to be aware of two experiences at once: being yourself, being the object, and having a dialog with the object at the same time. You will find that your consciousness can be expanded considerably more than you might think. Experience this.

When you are through, thank the object and return to normal consciousness. Ground and release.

Try this exercise with various different objects. You will find that there are both similarities and differences between the many different things whose nature you can experience in this way. Remember to dialog with whatever you are connecting with.

• • • •

Astrology, Continued

In this lesson, we will discuss the sun signs Leo, Virgo, Libra, and Scorpio.

Leo

July 24 through August 23. A fire sign ruled by the sun. The symbol of Leo is the Lion.

Positive: Leos can be joyful, dramatic, entertaining, creative, and brimming with energy. Leos are loyal and generous. Leos can be very affectionate and enthusiastic. They are natural actors and enjoy being the center of attention. Leos are proud and can be self-centered.

Negative: Expressed in the negative, Leo can be profligate and spendthrift. They can become arrogant and demanding. They can also tend to exaggerate, even to the point of dishonesty. If they don't get their way, they can become vindictive, often in subtle or well-disguised ways.

Virgo

August 24 through September 23. An earth sign ruled by Mercury. The symbol of Virgo is the Virgin.

Positive: Virgo is a hard worker, painstaking and thorough. Virgo often shuns the limelight, preferring to work in the background. They are perfectionists and can be obsessive in this regard. They need to feel absolutely certain about what they think they know—even when what they are absolutely certain about is wrong. They can be very literal, and because of this their sense of humor can seem out of sync to others.

Negative: A Virgo expressed in the negative can be a nitpicking, critical nag. Because of their perfectionism, Virgos do nothing halfway, including negatives—and this can manifest as obsession or addiction. For the same reason, Virgo can sometimes become emotionally paralyzed and unable to act at all because of their fear of not being perfect.

Libra

September 24 through October 23. An air sign ruled by Venus. The symbol of Libra is the Scales.

Positive: Libras are friendly, social people. They tend to be talkative. They are ambitious, hard working, and have a knack for making money. Libras, or people with a Libra moon or ascendant, are attractive to others regardless of their physical features. Libras crave peace and harmony but are by no means always good at achieving this in their lives.

Negative: Libras expressed in the negative can be moody, stingy, and indecisive. They hate to make decisions and often leave this to other people, whom they may then criticize if things turn out badly. They can be possessive of their loved ones, and in their desire for tranquility can become reclusive.

Scorpio

October 24 through November 22. A water sign ruled by Pluto. The symbol of Scorpio is the Scorpion.

Positive: Deeply emotional, Scorpios are great friends, natural leaders as well as natural healers. Scorpios tend to be very empathic and often psychic. Scorpios do not like to do anything halfway. They enjoy living on the edge and pushing boundaries. Scorpios, like Leos, need to be the center of attention. They are loyal and trustworthy, and also possessive. As a rule, they have a strong sense of self and are not influenced by either praise or criticism from others.

Negative: Scorpios expressed in the negative are vindictive, self-pitying, and jealous. Feelings of inferiority can be a major issue, and they can easily feel slighted and often consider themselves to be martyred and put upon.

. . . .

Weekly Question

How has your relationship to all beings in your sacred place changed as a result of these lessons?

Lesson 42:
The Beloved Dead

In lesson 37, we discussed the nature of death and rebirth, as well as the idea of the death walk—the way we consciously picture traveling to the land of the dead. In this lesson, we will be doing a pathworking to visit a departed loved one. We will not be using the death walk to do this (though it could be used this way) but rather will be using our cave.

As the subject of this exercise, you should select someone whom you have known in life but who is now dead. It is best to start with someone whom you liked but were not extremely close to, as choosing someone you were extremely close to for a first experience could be emotionally overwhelming. The exception to this is if you have a departed loved one to whom you were extremely close and with whom you have already been working as a guide or otherwise communicating with.

It is very important to remember that anything you experience in this way will be interpreted by your conscious mind. Because of this, it is extremely important not to have preconceptions about the experience, as your mind may tend to impose these upon what you see and distort the information. This does not invalidate the experience but rather means that you must not look upon it as being infallible. People who do this sort of work as a specialty work hard to develop a complete detachment, but even they occasionally experience distortion.

If you do not have a person in spirit who meets the criteria of this exercise—someone whom you liked but were not extremely close to—you might select a historical figure. However, in this instance, the danger of preconceptions can be especially strong, and so you might wish to choose someone of whom you know little.

Part
III

• • • •

Pathworking to the Beloved Dead

Read over the pathworking, and then take a ritual bath.

Ground and center. Begin your journey to the cave. Be conscious of all your senses during this journey. Enter the cave. Feel the heightened, almost electrical energy in the cave.

State your intention of journeying into the Otherworld to meet with the spirit of the person you have chosen.

Now look for a passage leading off from the central area of the cave, and follow this passage. Pay attention to what the passage is like and how it makes you feel.

At length, you will emerge into the Otherworld. Pay attention to the area you emerge into. What is it like? Is it beautiful? How is the weather? Are there buildings? Or are you perhaps already inside somewhere?

Is this a place you have known in this life? Or is it a place you have never seen before?

Your person should be somewhere nearby, as the passage will have brought you to where they are. If you do not see them, call for them. They should appear presently. Treat them just as you would if you were meeting them in this world. Be friendly and respectful.

Talk to your person naturally, and allow them to answer naturally. Have no preconceived ideas of what they will say or how they will say it—allow the experience to unfold as it will.

Talk to the person just as if you had dropped in for a mundane visit rather than crossed dimensions. Feel free to ask them anything you wish—though understand that they are under no obligation to answer. Usually, however, they will be happy to tell you most things you would want to know.

You might think they would also have a lot to ask you, but usually this is not the case. That is because this world is not hidden from them, and they probably already know anything they would wish to ask. However, if they do ask you anything, you should answer politely.

The first time you do this, the conversation you have with the person you have chosen is likely to be fairly superficial. This is because we have specifically advised you to select someone for your first experience with whom you have a fairly distant connection. Later, you can use this technique to visit other spirits with whom you have a closer connection.

When you have finished your conversation, thank the spirit for taking the time to speak with you. You might also wish to burn a candle in their honor after you return to normal consciousness.

Now go back through the passageway to the main cave. Sit in the cave, and think about all you have just experienced.

When you are ready, leave the cave and return the way you came, using all of your senses for the journey back. Return to normal consciousness, ground, and center.

. . . .

Astrology, Continued

In this lesson, we will discuss the sun signs of Sagittarius, Capricorn, Aquarius, and Pisces.

Sagittarius

November 23 through December 21. A fire sign ruled by Jupiter. The symbol of Sagittarius is the Archer, often depicted as a Centaur.

Positive: Sagittarians are sincere, loyal, and genuinely interested in other people. They make excellent friends and can often see the larger issues of life with great clarity. They are often philosophers but also enjoy variety and adventure in life. Sagittarians are extremely honest and can be quite blunt. Sagittarians also sometimes assume an undue sense of responsibility for the welfare of others.

Negative: Sagittarians expressed in the negative can be emotionally distant, controlling, and critical.

Capricorn

December 22 through January 20. An earth sign ruled by Saturn. The symbol of Capricorn is the Goat, sometimes depicted as a goat with a fish's tail.

Positive: Capricorns are ambitious, hard working, and stubborn. They are practical and competent. They strive hard to achieve success in their jobs or careers. Security is very important to them. They are tenacious and will push on until they eventually achieve their goals. Capricorns tend to be old when they are young and then to be young and light-hearted when they are old. They can be selfish and self-centered without being aware of it, because they are so focused on what they want.

Negative: Capricorns expressed in the negative are relentless and dominating. They can appear arrogant and even cruel. They can be very possessive and jealous, and may be given to hoarding possessions. These negative tendencies, when present, almost always arise from feelings of inferiority or insecurity.

Aquarius

January 21 through February 19. An air sign ruled by Uranus. The symbol of Aquarius is the Water Bearer.

Positive: Aquarians are idealistic and innovative, with original ideas that sometimes only they can understand—not because they are wrong, but because they are ahead of their time. Their minds are always working, and they have a knack for inventing and a yearning for deeper understanding of the way things work. Aquarians are deeply honest and have very high standards for themselves and others. They can be very competitive and focused.

Negative: Aquarians expressed in the negative can be rigid and close-minded. They can be emotionally distant, focusing only on abstractions and ideals. They can be unforgiving and may tend to hold long grudges on occasion.

Pisces

February 20 through March 20. A water sign ruled by Neptune. The symbol of Pisces is the Fish.

> **Positive:** Pisces are deeply emotional, empathetic, and imaginative. Despite this, they can also be very practical and are often very good at reading people. Pisces are naturally very psychic. They are creative, artistic, and make great mystics, ministers, and psychologists. Physically, they may be beautiful or plain but tend to have great personal magnetism.

> **Negative:** Pisces expressed in the negative can be impractical and unfocused. They may tend toward addictive behaviors and can be given to dishonesty, often choosing the path of least resistance.

• • • •

Weekly Question

What difference have these pathworkings made in your practice of Wicca?

Lesson 43:
Dreams of Past Lives

It is very common to have dreams that deal with our past lives. This often occurs when a situation in our present life is connected to that past life or if we are repeating the same issue in this lifetime.

In a past-life dream, it is not unusual to be wearing period clothing and have the setting look remarkably accurate for the time. However, it is also not unusual for there to be anachronisms and inaccuracies in these period details. This is because we access our memories of past lives through our present conscious mind, which sometimes has difficulty interpreting such details. Sometimes this kind of distortion of small details will happen even in memories from this life. Such anachronisms should not be allowed to detract from the experience, whose greater significance is spiritual and emotional rather than historical in nature.

In some cases, the dream may not be about a specific issue you are dealing with in your present life but can be triggered by an event that somehow touches on a past life. For example, you may meet someone that you have known in a past life and experience a feeling of immediate connection with them, which will then trigger a past-life dream. Or you may visit a location either where you lived in a past life or that reminds you of a place you lived in a past life, again triggering a past-life dream.

Such dreams can be very fascinating in themselves, but remember that they come to us because they somehow relate to the present, not because we are meant to relive the past.

Go through your dream journal, and see if any of your dreams may have been past-life dreams. Then ask that you be given dreams of any past lives that relate to your life now, and stay alert for them.

• • • •

Connecting with the Earth's Energy

This exercise is a variation of other exercises to connect with the energy of your place. It is valid on its own and slightly different from other exercises.

You can do this exercise sitting in a comfortable chair or when you are in bed before sleep.

Ground/release, shield, and enter your stillness. Be aware of the earth beneath the building you are in and the area surrounding the building. "Feel" the energy of this ground, and imagine it as a golden light that rises up to surround and fill you.

Connect with this energy from the earth. Try to feel its consciousness. What does it feel like? What are its dreams and goals? Feel the healing, the strengthening of this energy. Rest in it for as long as you wish.

Release, ground, and center when you are finished.

This exercise is similar to the grounding you do where you draw up the golden light of the earth, but it is different in that you are experiencing the energy of the earth in your specific place and in a more highly personal manner.

. . . .

Connecting with Your Inner Band of Guides

We have previously spoken about spirit guides. Now we shall return to this subject in greater depth. The term "inner band" is of Spiritualist origin and refers to the principal spirit guides around a person. These guides are conceived of as fulfilling certain specific roles. However, this classification must be understood to be rather generalized, because each person's actual experience will be individual. For example, though the inner band is normally thought of as being six in number, and is discussed as such below, some people will have more guides than this in their inner band, and other people may seem to have fewer.

Similarly, which of the inner band of guides is most prominent will vary from person to person and may also change over time. People with specific talents or interests may have a guide in their inner band who specifically deals with that subject, even though that guide is not normally included in the list of archetypical inner band guides.

The six archetypical inner band guides whom most people have include:

The Joy Guide: This guide is there to help promote joy in your life and keep you connected to the things that bring you happiness. It is not uncommon for the joy guide to manifest as a young person or a child, and they often exhibit a raucous sense of humor.

The Protector Guide: This guide is there to protect you on all levels, especially the physical and psychic levels. When you get a feeling of danger, it is likely this guide is sending it to you. You can also ask the protector guide for specific protection in situations where you feel threatened or endangered.

The Teacher Guide: This guide works with you on two primary levels. The first is to help you find your personal spiritual path. The second is to help you find information you want and make you aware of opportunities you might otherwise miss.

The Healer Guide: This guide is a healer and works with your energy bodies to keep you balanced and healthy.

The Master Teacher: This guide is specifically devoted to your spiritual growth and will help you with matters of inner development and life lessons. The master teacher is not often concerned with your daily life because your spiritual life is their primary concern.

The Doorkeeper Guide: This guide works with you when you are doing message work and controls who is allowed to step into your energy. Often this guide will convey messages from those on the other side to the loved ones waiting for the message. This guide ensures that communications you receive are positive and protects you from unwanted entities.

You have other guides in your life, considered to be part of your outer band. These guides may be with you for a day or for years. They come to you in response to your interests and needs.

Connect with your guides at a time when you won't be disturbed. Someone else can be there with you if they respect what you are doing and will not distract you.

Have a pen and notebook. Ground/release, shield, and center.

Still your mind, and open yourself to the guides. Ask your guides to speak to you, and listen for their messages. Allow these to simply float into and through your mind. Do not "grab onto" the messages and think about or analyze them. Just take note of them. Write the messages down either as you receive them or immediately afterwards. Remember that these messages can take the form of words, pictures, or simply knowing.

Ask about the different guides who compose your inner band. They may or may not tell you a great deal at first—allow it to unfold and take its time, if that is needed. Have no preconceived ideas about the individual guides, but allow them to reveal themselves. Soon you will begin to have a clear picture of each.

For now, each morning, as you think about the coming day, ask the guides to be with you during the day and give you any information you need as you need it. Ask your protector guide to protect you on all levels—physical, mental, and psychic—and to warn you of any dangers.

Remember that the information that comes from your guides comes to you through your conscious mind, and this can sometimes warp the message—especially at first. It may take time to develop clarity and accuracy. Because this is so,

you must never mistake psychic information for being infallible. You are allowed to question the information you get, and you should keep track of the accuracy of it. By all means, take the level of accuracy demonstrated over time into account when receiving new messages. This is not mistrusting your guides, it is developing a clear channel.

Always keep your own authority and make your own decisions about your life. Your guides are there to help you and advise you, and they will tell you what they think you should do—but this is by no means what you *must* do. That is always up to you. The responsibility for your life is still yours.

You can ask your guides for information that you need, such as advice on your diet. If you ask for their help, you should follow their advice if you think it is a good idea, or explain to them why you do not wish to follow the advice. If you simply ask questions and ignore their advice, the connection with them will close down. Treat them with the courtesy and respect you would of any human friend.

Weekly Question

What is your intention, your goal, in your practice of Wicca?

Lesson 44:
Healing Properties
of Stones

In the discussions of the magical properties of gemstones, we have already mentioned some of the qualities attributed to various stones. Now we shall return to this theme in greater detail. It is important to remember that each person may have a different reaction to a particular stone, so be aware of the way your body reacts.

As we have previously discussed in these lessons, the easiest way to use stones is to simply carry them with you. This will keep their energy around you and allow you to benefit from its effects. Start with one or more stones that either appeal to you or that you choose for their healing qualities. Once you have a collection of stones—if you really like stones, *they* will collect *you*—you can stand in front of them each day and ask which stones want to be carried with you that day. Listen to your intuition here—the stones may be aware of a need that you are not aware of.

Stones need attention. They like to be noticed and held. Cleanse them under cold running water from time to time to keep their energy clear. Do not let them sit in water—it can drain the stone of its prop-

erties. Expose them to sunlight and moonlight. They love storms. If possible, set them out in the rain. It recharges them.

As you work with the stones, they will begin to communicate to you how they want to be cared for and tell you uses that are not listed.

Approach this use of stones with an attitude of curiosity and with an open mind. Most of all, enjoy the stones.

Amber: Increases mental clarity and focus, and strengthens one's personal power.

Amethyst: Promotes psychic opening and spiritual growth.

Apache Tear: Helps to resolve emotional traumas and overcome sadness.

Bloodstone: Promotes creativity and self-expression. It is a good stone for helping develop or refine artistic or literary skill. It is also said to aid the healing process.

Carnelian: Promotes personal power and clarity of focus.

Citrine: Promotes inner balance and tranquility.

Garnet: Promotes personal power as well as aids communication and creativity.

Lapis Lazuli: Promotes psychic opening and the development of clairvoyance.

Magnetite (Lodestone): Considered a very lucky stone and one that increases personal power and magical ability.

Moonstone: Promotes psychic and magical abilities, as well as self-confidence. The stone is also considered to be protective in nature, with an ability to dissipate negativity.

Mother of Pearl: Promotes peace, tranquility, and all positive emotions. It is also said to promote psychic opening and spiritual abilities.

Sodalite: Promotes psychic opening and spiritual abilities.

Tiger Iron: (a combination of tiger's-eye, hematite, and red jasper) Promotes personal power and communication.

Tiger's-Eye: Promotes communication, persuasiveness, and commercial success. It is also considered a protective stone, especially when traveling.

Topaz: Helps with gout, tissue regeneration, the endocrine system, and reverses aging.

Turquoise: Brings spiritual growth and development, as well as protection from negativity. It is also generally considered a good-luck stone.

Daily Meditation

For the remainder of these lessons, you should talk to the Lady and the Lord about whether or not dedication is right for you, and ask them any questions you may have about it. Ask them if there is anything you need to know or do.

Weekly Question

What difference has connecting with your inner band of guides made in your life?

Lesson 45:
Predecication Work

We have been discussing self-dedication in a general sense in previous lessons. Now we will begin to approach the idea more specifically. If you have decided to do the self-dedication, there are some things you can do to help prepare for it. Even if you have not decided to do the self-dedication, these things may be of help to you, as they are designed to help remove blockages and free the self for greater growth.

In addition to the daily time discussing this with the Lady and the Lord at your altar, and the time spent in solitude and silence, the next step toward self-dedication may be taken during your dark moon esbat celebration. A simple releasing, outlined below, may be added to the ordinary esbat ritual to help prepare yourself for dedication.

For this, you will need a black candle, a piece of paper, and a fire-proof burning dish in which to burn the paper. You will also need something to write with. Some people may prefer to use exotic items like parchment paper or even real vellum, and a special ritual ink like dragon's blood, but this is not really necessary. Using special paper and ink is good, of course, but any paper and ink that you feel is appropriate will be fine.

Before the ritual, take some time to think of how you feel about the idea of self-dedication. Is there anything that you feel holds you back from this—anything that will interfere with your growth after the dedication? If so, take a few minutes to focus on these ideas. Also consider that there may be many things that might hold you back of which you are not consciously aware. Think about this for a few minutes. Then write down on your paper a statement along the lines of "I release anything that holds me back from self-dedication and spiritual growth." If you prefer, you might draw a design that represents this idea instead of or in addition to writing it down.

Now begin your esbat as usual.

When you come to the working portion of the ritual, you will want to do your releasing. You might start by saying something like:

Divine Mother Goddess, divine
Father God, I come before you
this night to prepare myself for
dedication. I sincerely desire to walk
the path of Wicca. I ask you to help
me this night as I release everything
that blocks or holds me back from
the fullest expression of this goal.

*Help me, I pray, to release those
limitations that I see, but also
help me to release those that I
do not see, that I may progress
unhindered upon your holy road.*

Now take the black candle you have prepared for this purpose. Hold the candle, and think of everything you feel limits or blocks you. Feel these things, and know that you are about to release them. Now light the candle.

Take the paper that you prepared before the ceremony. Light it from the black candle, and place it in the burning dish. As it burns, imagine the flames radiating bright white light out in all directions. As the paper burns, say something like:

*As this paper burns, so are
all these things released from
me and from my life.*

The paper will soon burn away. Afterwards, sit and watch the black candle burn for a time. Think about how you feel now that these things are being released.

When you are ready, continue with the ritual; let the black candle burn until the ritual is finished.

Keep the candle on your altar and gradually burn it each day until it is gone.

Be open for any insights that may come to you. Be alert to your dreams also.

Add this experience to your Book of Shadows.

You will do more preparation at the new moon esbat, and you will do your self-dedication at the full moon esbat.

· · · ·

Weekly Question

What are your feelings about dedicating yourself to the Wiccan path?

Lesson 46: Preparatory Dedication Ritual

In our last lesson, we presented you with a releasing ritual to help prepare you for self-dedication. The releasing was to be done during your dark moon esbat ritual. In this lesson, we now give you the next step toward self-dedication, to be done during your new moon esbat. As with the releasing, this should be the only work done during the working portion of this ritual.

Begin the esbat as usual. When you invoke the Goddess, ask her specifically to aid you in preparing for dedication. Your invocation might be something like this:

All-radiant Maiden Goddess,
mistress of the waxing moon, of
growth and creativity, I call on you
and ask you to be here this night
and aid me as I prepare myself
for dedication to the path of the
old gods. Bless me, O Goddess,
on this path that I shall walk!
I do say hail and welcome.

Continue with the ritual, and when you come to the working portion, you shall invoke the Goddess's blessing directly.

When you come to the working portion of the ritual, take a few minutes first to think about the ways the self-dedication will change you and what you plan to do with your skills and abilities as you practice Wicca. Now ask for the blessing of the quarters to energize and fuel your purposes and intentions for becoming a Wiccan.

Turn to the east, and think for a moment about all those things you have learned in these lessons and all that is yet to be learned. Embrace this path as a path of learning. Address the quarter, saying something like:

Holy power of the east, bless me
with your powers of intelligence
and inspiration so that I may
see all that is before me clearly
and truly, and that I may learn
all I need with an open mind as
I move forward on my path.

Take a moment, and receive the blessings of the east. You might imagine the blessings coming into you like a wave of light and filling your being, or in any other way that they wish to come to you. Have no preconceived notions of how this will be, but allow the blessing to take whatever form it chooses.

Turn to the south, and think for a moment about all of the things you have done in these lessons and all that is yet to be done. Embrace this path as a path of action. Address the quarter, saying something like:

*Holy power of the south, bless me
with your powers of passion and
creativity so that I may do all that
is before me with strength and
integrity, and that I may manifest
all I desire with an open hand
as I move forward on my path.*

Take a moment, and receive the blessings of the south. Again, allow the blessing
to take whatever form it chooses.

Turn to the west, and think for a
moment of all the spiritual connections
you have made during these lessons and all
that are yet to be made. Embrace this path
as a path of love. Address the quarter, saying something like:

*Holy power of the west, bless
me with your powers of empathy
and compassion that I may treat
all that is before me fairly and
kindly, and that I may love all
things with an open heart as I
move forward on my path.*

Take a moment, and receive the blessings of the west. Allow the blessing to
come to you in whatever form it chooses.

Now turn to the north, and think for a
moment of all inner understandings you
have gained during these lessons and all
that are yet to be gained. Embrace this

path as a path of wholeness. Address the
quarter, saying something like:

*Holy power of the north, bless me
with your powers of understanding
and integration so that I may know
all that is before me deeply and
fully, and so that I may commune
with all things with an open spirit
as I move forward on my path.*

Take a moment, and receive the blessings of the north. Again, allow the blessing
to take whatever form it chooses.

Take a moment, and consider all of the
blessings you have asked for and received.
Now address the Maiden Goddess of the
new moon. You might say something like:

*O Maiden Goddess, patroness
of new beginnings and of growth,
guide me, I pray, as I prepare
for my dedication. As I take
this new path, I pray that you
shall strengthen and inspire me,
leading me on in truth and honor.
O Goddess, I pray that you will
bless me so that I may be open
to the glories of the universe
and the beauties of Spirit!*

Now receive the blessing of the Goddess. Again, have no preconceived ideas of

what form it will take, but let the blessing assume whatever form is best.

Sit with these energies for a while, and reflect upon them.

Now give thanks to the Goddess and the quarters for their blessings, and continue your esbat as usual.

· · · ·

The Attributes of Metals

Metals, like stones and crystals, have energies that can be helpful. Below are some attributes of metals:

Copper: Copper is widely used in the creation of magical artifacts. This is both because copper was the earliest metal widely used by humankind and also because it is very conductive to psychic energy as well as physical energy. The unique qualities of copper are considered to be related to growth, expansion, and increase, as well as creativity and self-expression.

Gold: Gold is considered to be a metal of manifestation. Because gold does not tarnish, it is considered to represent permanence and achievement of goals. Gold is said to attract wealth, stability, and happiness. It is the metal for success in the physical world. Gold is also

connected to ideas of purification and balance.

Iron: Iron balances the mind and the emotions. It is said to promote inner strength, determination, and stability. Iron is considered very protective and was often used in old protection spells. It is also said to promote just outcomes to situations.

Silver: Silver is connected to ideas of psychic and spiritual opening and growth. It promotes creativity, emotional health, and inner balance. It is considered a protective metal.

Tin: Helps to clear the mind, aids reasoning, and releases depression and fear.

· · · ·

Weekly Question

What results have you had from working with stones and crystals? Which are your favorites? Why?

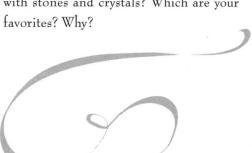

Lesson 47:
The Sabbats

In this lesson, we will discuss the sabbats in greater detail, focusing on some of the history and practices.

• • • •

Samhain

Samhain is a lunar sabbat, celebrated on November 1, although the festival is considered to start at sunset on October 31. This festival is related to the secular celebration of Halloween, which includes many of the same themes regarding death, spirits, and magic.

Samhain is the Wiccan liturgical New Year. Just as it is the birth of the new year, it is also the death of the old year, and it is this theme of death and rebirth that is the focus of this sabbat. At this time, we reflect on our own physical mortality and the nature of change and transformation in the cycle of life and death.

Samhain is sacred to the Crone Goddess, who is the patron of magic and the spirit world. She is the goddess of the dead, of wisdom, and of the ultimate spiritual origin of all things. The Crone is often pictured as a very old, powerful woman. This image is the origin of the Halloween Witch. The Crone is also the possessor of the cauldron of rebirth, through which

souls enter and leave this life—which is why the Halloween Witch is so strongly associated with cauldrons.

A common Samhain practice is to prepare an ancestor feast. This is a dinner in honor of the spirits of the beloved dead, and often features the favorite foods of specific ancestors. A special plate of this food is prepared for the ancestors and ceremonially offered to them during the meal. As always with offerings, this is done as a gesture of respect and not because the spirit "needs" the food. It is a symbolic act. Sometimes an empty chair or place setting will be reserved for the spirits, and sometimes the meal is served in complete silence, in which case it is termed a Silent Supper. There is an ancient custom of having a light in the window or on the doorstep to guide wandering spirits who are abroad at Samhaintide, and some Wiccans bury apples outside as food for these wandering spirits.

Because the Crone Goddess is the patron of magic and divination, Samhain is considered an especially favorable time for these acts. There are many forms of divination that are traditional at Samhain which are intended to forecast possible events for the coming year. The specific type of divinatory method can be specific to different geographical areas and vary between Wiccan groups.

Ancestor altars are also a special feature of many people's Samhain celebrations. Of course, many people keep an ancestor altar throughout the year, but at Samhain even people who don't normally maintain an ancestor altar often create one.

• • • •

Yule

Yule is an old Norse word meaning "wheel." Yule occurs in December on the winter solstice, the shortest day and the longest night of the year. Because of this, Yule is considered to be the rebirth of the sun. Yule celebrates the increasing daylight as the sun turns in its apparent journey away from the earth to move back again toward the earth. The lighting of candles and the burning of the Yule log are done to encourage the sun in its return toward the earth.

Yule celebrations will be very familiar to most people, as they are similar or identical to many aspects of the secular celebration of Christmas, whose roots are in the older celebration of Yule. The Yule tree (representing the survival of life after death), wreaths and decorations of holly and ivy, the giving of gifts in celebration of the rebirth of the sun—these are all common aspects of the Yule sabbat. The sabbat is sacred to the God in his archetype as Sorcerer and Lord of the Old Year, whose character and representations are very similar to Santa Claus or to Dickens' Spirit of Christmas Present.

A ritual to call back the sun and to honor the energy of Yule is to light candles at midnight to call the sun back home. Some Wicca practitioners stay up all night until dawn to witness the visible sign of the sun's return. If you can't stay up all night, you can set the alarm for shortly before dawn to see the return of the sun.

The most recognized celebrations of Yule are the ones we associate with Christmas: the sense of anticipation, the wonder, the gift giving, the beauty of the lights and decorations, the feasting with family and friends. All of these things honor the rebirth of the sun/son and the renewal of life on this holiday.

Some Wiccans only celebrate Yule and some celebrate both Yule and Christmas; they are essentially celebrations of the same holiday. This allows you to honor the form of the holiday that is sacred to you and also to be a part of the celebration of family and friends who don't walk your path.

• • • •

Imbolc

Imbolc is also known as Candlemas and celebrated on February 2. It is the festival of the Maiden Goddess, particularly Brigid in the Celtic traditions. Imbolc is associated with the dawn and the inner

fire, and it is the midpoint between winter and spring.

For Wiccans, Imbolc is the Festival of Light, where we are celebrating the return of the sun. Days have begun to lengthen. Typically, many candles are used during the ritual to symbolize the sun's return.

There are many different practices that are done at this time of the year. One is to make a crown consisting of candles, similar to those associated with Lucia Day in Europe. The crown consists of several lit candles surrounded by evergreen foliage. Another practice is to plant seeds in a small flowerpot and then, once the weather is warm enough, the resulting plant can be transferred to an area outside.

Of course, Imbolc would not be complete without talking about Groundhog Day. You can choose to enact your own Groundhog Day if you have a hamster or guinea pig, or you could simply go outside and see if you see your shadow.

• • • •

Ostara

Ostara was named for the Norse goddess of spring, Eostre. It is celebrated in March on the Spring Equinox. Many of our present-day customs at this time of the year come from what we know of how other cultures celebrated long ago. Eostre's sacred symbols included flowers, a white rabbit, and eggs. The flowers represent nature renew-

ing itself, eggs are the representation of rebirth, and the rabbit symbolizes fertility. These symbols are carried over to our secular celebrations with the presence of the Easter bunny and the tradition of dying eggs.

The idea of wearing new clothes at this time of the year also came from this older culture. It was even considered bad luck to wear your spring festival clothes before Ostara. You no doubt have heard the statement of not wearing white before spring or after fall—this is a custom that may have its roots in Ostara also.

One of the most obvious connections to Ostara is the Christian celebration of Easter. Many of the myths from several cultures involve deities going to the Underworld and returning to the earth—hence, the Christian resurrection concept.

The lamb was also a sacred animal to the virgin goddesses of Europe and was carried over into spring religious ceremonies of the Jewish Passover and Easter. Jesus is even called the sacrificial lamb.

• • • •

Beltane

Beltane is celebrated on May 1 and is on the opposite side of the Wheel of the Year from Samhain. It is considered the Great Festival of Life. It is not agreed upon where Beltane actually gets its name. Some believe it is named for the Irish death god

Beltene, while others believe it comes from the Welsh god Beli. Another possibility is it came from the Celtic god of fire, Belanos. But by far the most agreed upon, at least by today's Pagans, is that it came from the word *balefire*.

During Beltane, we celebrate the marriage of the God and Goddess, sometimes symbolized by a May King and May Queen. Although the Great Rite can be enacted during any ritual, it plays a special importance during Beltane to symbolize the return of spring and the replenishment of the earth.

One of the most popular customs during Beltane is erecting a Maypole. The Maypole is a very old tradition. In older cultural practices, the Maypole was made from the community Yule tree. Ribbons of white and red were attached to its higher branches—white representing the virgin goddess and red representing the god. The Maypole itself was a phallic symbol.

• • • •

Midsummer

Midsummer is also known as Litha and occurs in June on the Summer Solstice. It is speculated that the word *Litha* comes from the Saxon and translates as "light." Midsummer marks the time of the year when the sun is at its strongest and is the longest day of the year.

There were many and differing customs to celebrate Midsummer, depending on the culture. Some of the rituals of our ancestors focused on nurturing the seeds that were planted earlier in the year to ensure a bountiful harvest. Many cultures lit bonfires, symbolizing the victory of the sun over the darkness, lighting them at dusk and keeping them burning until dawn. Raising a Midsummer tree was common in Wales, England, and Sweden. It was decorated with ribbons, flowers, and sometimes pictures, then gilded feathers would adorn the top.

There has been an assumption in our modern culture that the month of June was chosen as the most popular to have a wedding because it usually marked the end of the school year. However, for many ancient societies, there was no formal schooling such as we have today, and it is speculated those who did have formal education systems probably didn't use the same calendar year to conduct their classes. In actuality, it was considered bad form to have a wedding in May since that is the celebration of the marriage between the God and Goddess.

Other wedding customs we have today are also rooted in Pagan customs, such as the shared wedding cake and throwing rice. The wedding ring represents the ritual circle, and crossing the threshold is symbolic of bringing fertility and prosperity into the union.

Lammas

Lammas is also called Lughnasadh and occurs on August 1. The word *Lughnasadh* comes from the Irish sun god, Lugh. He was also considered the god of the harvest, hence many of today's practices are credited to the Irish. The word *Lammas*, on the other hand, comes from the Anglo-Saxon meaning "loaf-mas" and is the more commonly used name.

Many cultures celebrated grain and corn festivals in early August. Native Americans honored the Corn Grandmother; the Romans honored Ceres, their grain goddess. In Egypt, the birth of Isis was celebrated.

Lammas is the first of three harvest festivals throughout the Pagan liturgical year and is also known the festival of the first fruits. It is the midpoint between summer and fall. One of the common practices was to make bread from the newly harvested grains, which was then consumed during the ritual celebration.

Mabon

Mabon occurs in September at the Autumn Equinox. It is the second harvest festival and named for the Welsh god. On this day, there is a balance between night and day. Mabon is also referred to as the Witches' Thanksgiving, and it is commonly believed that the first American Thanksgiving was actually held closer to this time

(it was not moved to November until the mid-1800s).

The use of wine is very prominent during the Mabon celebrations due to the harvesting of grapes. This was most prevalent in Greece, where the Festival of Dionysus was celebrated this time of the year. Apples are also a typical harvest item, and the use of foods and drinks that are made with apples are also present.

There is an abundance of differing cultural myths that surround Mabon, but the most notable one comes from the Celts. Mabon, the son of Modron, is stolen from her three days after his birth. During his absence, Modron grieves for him, and the light disappears from the earth at the Autumn Equinox. He is then returned to her at the Winter Solstice and the days begin to lengthen.

Lesson 48:
Review

This lesson does not contain any new information. Rather, we will discuss the best ways to apply what we have already learned in these many lessons.

Wicca, as we have made clear, is a very open system that allows for a great deal of individuality. How you apply what you have learned is largely up to you, as long as you remain within Wiccan moral teachings, as exemplified by the Wiccan Rede.

How you express your faith, too, is largely up to you. You are not required to belong to a group or temple, though you may if you wish. You are not required to pursue priestly degrees, though you may if you wish. Your faith is in your heart and is between you and Goddess.

In these lessons, we have discussed forms of ritual, but we have also discussed the importance of creating your own ritual— of allowing sacred expressions to take the form that is best at the time, rather than conforming to some preconceived idea. When we allow our spirituality to take the form that is needed at the moment, we allow Spirit to flow freely through us.

This is true not only in regard to ritual and to meditations, but also to the meanings we ascribe to things. You must allow things to take the meaning that they need for you. If you feel strongly that the proper meaning of a given thing for you is different from the meaning ascribed to it by us or by any other source, you should listen to the meaning that has come to you.

This is not to say that you should disregard other people's meanings and understandings, especially in group situations where agreed-upon interpretations may be of greater importance. Rather, we are saying that you must be open to the voice of Spirit within you, and listen to what it tells you, even when it differs from expectation.

We have talked at great length about dreams in these lessons. Dreams can be a very important way of keeping in touch with your inner self and of receiving information from Deity. Dreams provide you with feedback in all areas of your life and can be used as a springboard for astral projection. There is no limit to what you can do in dreams.

As you continue to walk the Wiccan path, be mindful of the concept of relationship, and remember that everything is aware and conscious of itself as itself. The dandelions in your lawn are as valid an expression of the Goddess experiencing herself in the physical world as you and I are. All of life is sacred, and you are connected to all of life in a dance of relationship that is born of beauty, love, and mystery.

As the Arch Priestess Krystel High-Correll has said, "One way to define a Wiccan is as a metaphysical scientist. Metaphysics is the study of the fundamental nature of all reality. Wiccans seek to understand how everything works and how it can work more effectively. The desire of the Goddess to experience physical reality is surely born of a desire to know and to understand. Fortunately, there is always more to know, and so the journey continues indefinitely. The Goddess continues to create and re-create herself endlessly, and the dance of life spirals ever outward."

Finally, it should be emphasized that these lessons were not written for any specific tradition. The lessons naturally reflect the views of the various people who have been involved in their evolution, but they do this in a personal manner. They are not the "official teaching" of any group, though they will be compatible with the views of most traditions.

I hope that you have enjoyed these lessons and that they have been helpful to you in your personal development. The next lesson will be our final lesson, and it will deal exclusively with self-dedication, which is more formally termed self-wiccaning.

Lesson 49: Summary

With this lesson, we finish forty-eight weeks of examining the Wiccan path and living the Wiccan life. If you have been doing the work laid out in these lessons, then you should now have developed a personal relationship with Goddess and with God, have a personal altar and working tools, know how to do ritual and how to enact effective spells, and be conscious of your connection to all things.

You have learned how to celebrate the esbats and sabbats, have developed your psychic ability, understand the nature of spiritual energy and how to use it, and have worked with the energy centers of your body and of the earth. You have learned how to use your Hall of Consciousness as a multidimensional doorway leading to a wide variety of places. You have learned how to communicate with the dead, whether awake, in your Hall of Consciousness, or in dreams.

You have developed a relationship with your sacred place and the beings within it. You have experimented with time and know how to visualize and how to do pathworkings. You have explored various forms of divination and understand the importance of your dreams. You understand that we

each create our own reality, and you have worked to do that consciously.

Most importantly, you have developed your Self. You have worked to heal your shadow, found your True Will, and act always from your sovereignty, the core of your being. You know yourself as the sacred expression of the Goddess and the God in the physical world. Now you are able to take these skills into the world in the service of life.

Because of the work you have done in these lessons, you are a Wiccan now. The self-dedication will not make you more of a Wiccan. It does announce to the Goddess and the God, and the universe, that living as a Wiccan is the life path you consciously choose, and it is a sacred commitment. It will change your life in ways that you can not now imagine.

You may decide to continue your studies and work within a degree system, or you may not. If you do choose to work within a degree system, we recommend the Correllian system, whose courses are available at Witchschool.com and whose textbooks are available from Llewellyn. But remember always that the Lady and the Lord are your ultimate teachers, no matter who else you study with. Stay close to them always.

Part
III

Self-Dedication

Although a dedication is not considered to be an initiation as such, in its own way this self-dedication can be considered a form of initiation in that it does mark a new beginning and in that it will have an actual energetic effect on you. Simply because you are conducting the ceremony yourself does not in any way lessen its value or its effect.

There are Wiccans who say that only another Wiccan can initiate or make a Wiccan. This is nonsense. Only the Goddess and the God can make a Wiccan, and you don't need an intermediary to connect with the Lady and the Lord. You are an expression of the Lady and the Lord in physical form.

Wiccans are born, not made. If this is the path of heart for you, you were born a Wiccan, and probably have been Wiccan in many, if not all, of your past lives. You are Wiccan because of who you are, not because of what you do or what someone else calls you.

Do this dedication at your full moon esbat.

• • • •

Self-Wiccaning Ritual

You will do your self-dedication, or more formally self-wiccaning, during your normal full moon esbat. Do the self-dedication

as the working section of the ritual, and make it the only work you do in this ritual. In addition to the regular supplies you would need for an esbat, there are a few special things you should have for the self-dedication. These include:

- Your written statement saying why you want to dedicate yourself as a Wiccan
- A "Wiccaning candle," preferably purple
- An anointing oil suitable to a blessing, such as a sandalwood

Read this ritual over, take your ritual bath, ground/release, shield, and enter your stillness.

Cast your circle at your working/ritual altar as usual. Invoke the elements and the ancient ones of the directions, and invoke the Goddess and the God to be present with you tonight and bless you as you dedicate yourself. Do this in words that reflect how you feel about this step you are taking.

Now you have come to the working portion of your ritual. Begin by silently asking yourself some questions. Do you understand the step that you are taking tonight? Are you doing it for good reasons? Are you prepared for the spiritual deepening this will bring into your life? You should reflect upon these questions seriously and answer them honestly.

Now take up your written statement of why you are making this dedication. Read it aloud to Goddess and to God. If there is anything that you would like to add to your statement, now is the time to do it.

Now take up your Wiccaning candle. Use the anointing oil to dress the candle. As you dress the candle, continue to reflect upon the meaning of the ritual and how you feel about the step you are taking.

When you have finished dressing the candle, hold it before you. Now light the Wiccaning candle.

You can either hold the candle or place it upon the altar. Gaze upon the candle's flame. See how it dances. See the intensity of its energy, its brightly shining light. Remember when you bonded with fire? This is different, for this candle flame is not just the flame itself—it represents something more.

The flame you are looking at is only a reflection of another greater flame—an eternal flame that burns within each of us; a flame that burns at the center of the universe and in our own hearts: the flame of Spirit. The flame of Goddess. This is what gives us all life. This is the origin of all being. The divine spark of life, the eternal flame, the single soul of all that is.

Through this eternal flame, you are eternally connected to the Goddess. You can never be cut off from her. You can never be

lost from her. Through the eternal flame you may always call upon the Goddess, for it connects you to her from within. Through the eternal flame you will always have access to her love, her strength, and her miraculous powers. This flame never burns out. If you deny your True Self, turn from Spirit, or become blocked through pain or anger, the flame may burn a little lower, but it can never go out.

This eternal flame has always burned within you, though you may never have realized it. Now you know it is there, and this night you acknowledge and honor it. You might say something like:

*It is not the flame of this candle
that lights my path but the greater
flame it represents—the eternal
flame that burns within all things.
That flame I honor, and I pray
that it may light my path always.*

Reflect upon the eternal flame within you—your own personal connection to Deity. Visualize that flame within you, and imagine it growing stronger and brighter. Feel its strength and beauty. Feel the love of Deity within the flame.

Now you must make an oath. The oath is to Deity and to your own Higher Self. You may use whatever words you wish. It might be something like this:

*I dedicate myself to the Wiccan
faith and to the Goddess and the
God. May they guide me and
strengthen me. I dedicate myself
to my Higher Self and my true
life's purposes. I shall be true to
myself and to my own highest
good. I shall honor the divine in all
people and in all life. I shall walk
in the ways of the Goddess, my
mother, and the God, my father. I
shall do my best to live up to my
own highest ideals always and to
express these ideals in my everyday
life. I so swear, so mote it be!*

If you held the candle, now place it back upon the altar. If possible, you should allow the Wiccaning candle to burn until it is completely gone.

Now take up the anointing oil to perform the ritual of self-blessing.

Begin by blessing your feet. Place a bit of oil upon your fingers. Touch the top of each foot, and imagine a ball of bright white light around your feet. Say something like:

*Blessed be my feet, that I may
walk in the path of Spirit.*

Now take a bit more oil onto your fingertips to anoint your knees. It is not necessary to touch the knees directly (as essential oil may sometimes stain clothing)—place your fingers a few inches before the knees, and imagine a ball of white light around them. Say something like:

*Blessed be my knees, that
I may kneel at the altar
of the ancient ones.*

Now take a bit of oil and bless your pelvic region. Again, you may hold the fingers a few inches before the pubic area, and imagine a ball of white light there. Say something like:

*Blessed be my loins, that
I may form my life in
creativity, joy, and love.*

Now take a bit more oil with which to anoint your heart chakra—the center of your chest. Place your fingers a few inches before the heart chakra, and imagine a ball of white light around it. Say something like:

*Blessed be my heart, which is
formed in beauty, that I may
give love and receive it.*

Now anoint your lips—again, you do not need to touch the lips directly (essential oil on the lips may burn), but place your fingers just before your lips and imagine a ball of white light conducting the blessing energy. Say something like:

Blessed be my lips, which
shall speak the words of
power in times to come.

Now anoint your third eye—the center of your forehead. Again, you may place your fingers just before this area and imagine a ball of clear white light. Say something like:

Blessed be my third eye, that
I may see all things clearly.

And finally, take a bit of oil and anoint the very top of your head. Imagine a ball of white light here as well. Say something like:

Blessed be my crown, that
I may receive always the
messages of Goddess.

Now imagine a column of white light coming down upon you from above, through the top of your head and into your body—a beautiful, clear white light. Let the light fill you, pouring into every part of you. Be one with the light, and let it move through you.

Let the light suffuse you for a few moments. Then release it—let it run down through your feet, retaining only what you need.

Now turn to your chalice.

Take up the chalice, and bless it. Imagine a ball of clear white light around the chalice, radiating out in all directions like a sun. Declare the cup blessed in the name of Goddess and God. You might say something like:

Behold, in the name of the Goddess
and the God, may this cup be
blessed. May it be a token of the
bond of love between myself and
them, and between myself and
all of creation—so mote it be.

Now take a sip from the chalice. If there are more than one of you, each person should take a sip.

Now sit in front of the altar again. The Lady and the Lord may have something to say to you. Listen for this. Also listen for anything your guides may wish to say to you.

Take the circle down in the normal way. Welcome to the Wiccan path.

Andrews, Ted. *Animal-Speak*. Llewellyn, 2002.

Belanger, Michelle. *Psychic Dreamwalking: Explorations at the Edge of Self*. Weiser Books, 2006.

Cunningham, Scott. *Cunningham's Encyclopedia of Magical Herbs*. Llewellyn, 2000.

Dugan, Ellen. *Elements of Witchcraft*. Llewellyn, 2003.

Franklin, Anna. *Midsummer*. Llewellyn, 2002.

K, Amber, and Azrael Arynn K. *Candlemas*. Llewellyn, 2001.

Lewis-Highcorrell, Rev. Donald. *Witch School Ritual, Theory & Practice*. Llewellyn, 2008.

Madden, Kristin. *Mabon*. Llewellyn, 2002.

McCoy, Edain. *Sabbats*. Llewellyn, 2002.

Millman, Dan. *The Life You Were Born to Live: A Guide to Finding Your Life Purpose*. H. J. Kramer, 1995.

RavenWolf, Silver. *Halloween*. Llewellyn, 1999.

Bibliography

Index

GET MORE AT LLEWELLYN.COM

Visit us online to browse hundreds of our books and decks, plus sign up to receive our e-newsletters and exclusive online offers.

- Free tarot readings • Spell-a-Day • Moon phases
- Recipes, spells and tips • Blogs • Encyclopedia
- Author interviews, articles and upcoming events

GET SOCIAL WITH LLEWELLYN

Find us on

www.Facebook.com/LlewellynBooks

Follow us on

www.Twitter.com/Llewellynbooks

GET BOOKS AT LLEWELLYN

LLEWELLYN ORDERING INFORMATION

Order online: Visit our website at www.llewellyn.com to select your books and place an order on our secure server.

Order by phone:
- Call toll-free within the U.S. at 1-877-NEW-WRLD (1-877-639-9753)
- Call toll free within Canada at 1-866-NEW-WRLD (1-866-639-9753)
- We accept VISA, MasterCard, and American Express

Order by mail:
Send the full price of your order (MN residents add 6.875% sales tax) in U.S. funds, plus postage and handling to: Llewellyn Worldwide, 2143 Wooddale Drive Woodbury, MN 55125

POSTAGE AND HANDLING:

STANDARD: (U.S., Mexico & Canada)
(Please allow 2 business days)
$25.00 and under, add $4.00.
$25.01 and over, FREE SHIPPING

INTERNATIONAL ORDERS (airmail only):
$16.00 for one book, plus $3.00 for each additional book.

Visit us online for more shipping options. Prices subject to change.

FREE CATALOG!

To order, call
1-877-
NEW-WRLDS
ext. 8236
or visit our
website

To Write to the Author

If you wish to contact the author or would like more information about this book, please write to the author in care of Llewellyn Worldwide and we will forward your request. Both the author and the publisher appreciate hearing from you and learning of your enjoyment of this book and how it has helped you. Llewellyn Worldwide cannot guarantee that every letter written to the author can be answered, but all will be forwarded. Please write to:

Debbe Tompkins
℅ Llewellyn Worldwide
2143 Wooddale Drive
Woodbury, MN 55125-2989

Please enclose a self-addressed stamped envelope for reply,
or $1.00 to cover costs. If outside U.S.A., enclose
international postal reply coupon.

Many of Llewellyn's authors have websites with additional information and resources. For more information, please visit our website:

http://www.llewellyn.com